PERSPECTIVES ON FIRST PETER

Barbara Rossing

PERSPECTIVES ON FIRST PETER

NABPR Special Studies Series, Number 9

edited by
Charles H. Talbert

MERCER UNIVERSITY PRESS, Macon, Georgia 31207

ISBN 0-86554-198-1

The paper used in this publication meets the minimum requirements
of American National Standard for Information Sciences—
Premanence of Paper for Printed Library Materials, ANSI Z39.48-1984.

Library of Congress Cataloging-in-Publication Data
Perspectives on First Peter
   (NABPR special studies series ; no. 9)
   Includes bibliographies.
   1. Bible. N.T. Peter, 1st—Criticism, interpretation, etc.
I. Talbert, Charles H. II. Series.
BS2795.3.P46   1986   227'.9206   86-8772
ISBN 0-86554-198-1 (alk. paper)

TABLE OF CONTENTS

With gratitude dedicated to the memory of

John Edward Steely, 1922–1986

*who fed the flock of God,
not by constraint, but willingly,
and of a ready mind (1 Peter 5:2).*

INTRODUCTION

After years of neglect, chronicled by John H. Elliott's "The Rehabilitation of an Exegetical Step-Child: 1 Peter in Recent Research,"[1] 1 Peter is once again a focus of exegetical and theological concern. To facilitate our work on 1 Peter, Dennis Sylva has put together a bibliography of books and articles from the nineteenth and twentieth centuries.[2] The recent revival of scholarly concern about 1 Peter has found expression in the work of two Americans, John Elliott[3] and David Balch.[4] At the annual meeting of the Society of Biblical Literature in 1982, these two men entered into dialogue with one another about their differing positions. Whereas Elliott sees 1 Peter mainly as a call to social cohesion within the Christian communities to which the letter is addressed, Balch's emphasis is on 1 Peter's advocacy of social adaptability as a style of life for the Christian communities. Although this was one of the best exchanges those present had heard at an annual meeting, these two presentations were not published. In this volume, however, updated versions of their responses to one another constitute the heart of the book. In spite of their differences, their agreements are striking. (1) Both assume the unity of 1 Peter. (2) Both find assistance in the insights of the behavioral sciences. (3) Both view 1 Peter as parenesis. In this regard, both are influenced by Eduard Lohse's "Parenesis and Kerygma in 1 Peter,"[5] offered here in an English translation by John Steely. Lohse's article is a turning point and helps explain why neither Elliott and Balch nor those they have influenced give any support to the old theory of a baptismal liturgy's being incorporated in the letter.

The influence of Elliott and Balch may be seen in the three final articles in this volume. David W. Kendall's piece is a digest of a doctoral dissertation

---

[1]Originally published in *JBL* 95 (1976): 243-54, and used by permission.

[2]Originally published in *JETS* 25 (1982): 75-89, and used by permission.

[3]John H. Elliott, *A Home for the Homeless: A Sociological Exegesis of 1 Peter, Its Situation and Strategy* (Philadelphia: Fortress Press, 1981).

[4]David Balch, *Let Wives Be Submissive: The Domestic Code in 1 Peter* (Chico CA: Scholars Press, 1981).

[5]Originally published in *ZNW* 45 (1954): 68-89, and used by permission.

done under Paul Achtemeier at Union Theological Seminary in Virginia. It celebrates the unity of 1 Peter, one of the main points of agreement between Elliott and Balch. Earl Richard's article on the Christology of 1 Peter breaks new ground in this area but does so out of the general orientation already established by Elliott and Balch. Charles Talbert's attempt to delineate the plan of 1 Peter not only builds on the work of W. J. Dalton[6] but also tries to incorporate the distinctives of Elliott and Balch in a larger whole, itself indebted to the behavioral sciences. Looked at in this way, this volume offers readers a sense of the direction of North American research on 1 Peter over the past fifty years or so.

It is the hope of the authors, the translator, the editor, and the NABPR that this volume will be useful for those teaching and studying 1 Peter. If it can serve, alongside a commentary, to facilitate the renewed investigation of this early Christian writing, our aim will be realized.

Special thanks must go to the Department of Religion, Wake Forest University, for the subsidy from its Robinson Fund that has made publication possible.

Charles H. Talbert
Department of Religion
Wake Forest University

---

[6]W. J. Dalton, *Christ's Proclamation to the Spirits* (Rome: Pontifical Biblical Institute, 1965), Part 2, ch. 2.

CHAPTER 1

THE REHABILITATION OF
AN EXEGETICAL STEP-CHILD:
1 PETER
IN RECENT RESEARCH*

JOHN H. ELLIOTT
UNIVERSITY OF SAN FRANCISCO
SAN FRANCISCO, CALIFORNIA 94117

INTRODUCTION

To judge from appearance, 1 Peter suffers second-class status in the estimation of modern NT exegetes. Along with other relatively neglected documents such as the remaining Catholic Epistles, Hebrews, and the Johannine
Apocalypse, it is generally treated as one of the step-children of the NT canon.
For those abreast of the literature exact statistics undoubtedly are superflu-
ous. New Testament introductions and theologies accord 1 Peter compara-
tively brief attention. This is matched by the relative paucity of monographs
and articles, and even these then fail to appear in reviews of current research.[1]
Furthermore, the inattention shown the document in working seminars of such

*Reprinted, by permission, from *Journal of Biblical Literature* 95:2 (1976): 243-54.

[1]Cf., e.g., the 110-page review of NT research in *Verkündigung und Forschung* 15 (1970).

societies as the SBL and the SNTS perhaps is to be seen in connection with the lack of interest in 1 Peter in the classroom. All this is striking, if silent, testimony of a disconcerting pattern of benign neglect. The reasons for this state of affairs are diverse, complex and far less evident than the results. Among the influencing forces would have to be included the historical decisions regarding the date of the document and the antiquity of its tradition, conclusions concerning its dependence upon or independence of Pauline material and authority, and theological assessments of its proximity to a supposed "canon within the canon" or its articulation of a supposed "early catholic" perspective.[2]

Commentaries specifically devoted to 1 Peter, on the other hand, might be expected to present a more favorable view of its importance, thereby leading to a greater appreciation of its place within the historical and theological movement of the early church. As anticipated, it is here that we find the document extolled as "a microcosm of Christian faith and duty, the model of a pastoral charge,"[3] a "gallant and high-hearted exhortation which breathes a spirit of undaunted courage and exhibits as noble a type of piety as can be found in any writing of the New Testament outside the gospels,"[4] "one of the most pastorally attractive and vigorously confident documents in the NT."[5] Neither the praise lavished in prefaces nor, as in the case of Selwyn's commentary, the formidable exegesis to follow has been effective, however, in altering the current of prevailing opinion. In fact, one of the most well-known and oft-quoted of the post-World War II commentaries on 1 Peter, rather than undermining such a minimalist appreciation, ironically has contributed to it.

In 1947, only months after the publication of Selwyn's study, the first edition of Francis Wright Beare's *The First Epistle of Peter*[6] made its ap-

---

[2]The influential view of H. Conzelmann (*An Outline of the Theology of the New Testament* [New York: Harper & Row, 1969]) is typical. After an extensive treatment of the primitive, synoptic, and Pauline kerygmas (pp. 29-286), 1 Peter is mentioned in passing as part of "the development after Paul" (pp. 289-317). Classifying 1 Peter "within the sphere of deutero-Paulinism" (p. 295), Conzelmann states: "If we begin from Paul, we shall have to measure post-Pauline theology by Paul's doctrine of justification" (p. 289). The recent introduction of N. Perrin (*The New Testament: An Introduction* [New York: Harcourt-Brace-Jovanovich, 1974]) illustrates a similar approach; see chap. 11, "The Church on the Way to Becoming an Institution: The Literature of Emergent Catholicism" (pp. 253-75, esp. pp. 257-60). For a critique of the "early catholic" classification, see J. H. Elliott, "A Catholic Gospel: Reflections on 'Early Catholicism' in the New Testament," *CBQ* 31 (1969): 213-23.

[3]E. G. Selwyn, *The First Epistle of St. Peter* (London: Macmillan, 1946; 2d ed., 1955) 1.

[4]J. W. C. Wand, *The General Epistles of St. Peter and St. Jude* (London: Methuen, 1934) 1.

[5]J. N. D. Kelley, *The Epistles of Peter and of Jude* (HNTC; New York: Harper & Row, 1969) 1.

[6]Oxford: Basil Blackwell, 1947.

pearance. The novelty, as well as the basic thesis, of Beare's work is described by the author on the first page of the preface: "The English reader is here offered for the first time a commentary based on the thesis, now widely accepted, that First Peter is a pseudonymous work of the post-Apostolic age." Its exegetical precision and thoroughness, stylistic clarity, and apparently popular thesis has gained for the commentary a wide audience. Expanded second and third editions followed in 1958 and 1970, respectively. Reaction to Beare's work, however, has remained mixed, primarily in regard to questions of introduction. Many who sympathize with the positions of the older German exegetes to whom Beare expressed his indebtedness (Gunkel, Knopf, Windisch, Perdelwitz) have welcomed and cited the commentary with enthusiasm. Others who question especially the *religionsgeschichtliche* theories of these early twentieth-century exegetes have found Beare's approach one-sided and dated, especially in the second and third editions fifty and sixty years later. Trends in recent research on 1 Peter, some of them unmentioned by or later than Beare's commentary, also suggest the need for a reassessment, or at least a refinement, of previous "assured" positions.

The purpose of this study is to use the appearance of the third edition of Beare's major commentary on 1 Peter as the occasion for a review of recent trends in Petrine research.[7] Since the text of Beare's third edition, as that of the second edition, is, with few emendations, a photographic reprint of the first, it can safely be assumed that a general description of the content of the commentary is unnecessary.[8] Comment will be restricted to the novel features of the last edition. Attention to some of the important questions raised by Beare's work will then lead to a consideration of different directions taken by other Petrine studies. Strenuous engagement with the work of our teacher and former president of the Society of Biblical Literature is hopefully the most appropriate expression of the esteem in which we hold him as members of the Society and the debt we owe to him as biblical scholars.

THE FIRST EPISTLE OF PETER, THIRD EDITION (1970)

The latest edition of Beare's commentary exceeds the second by twenty-five pages. Most of the new material pertains to recent text-critical developments (pp. 1-24 and pp. 61-64 of the bibliography). This constitutes the

---

[7]This represents a development and expansion of my original intention, viz., a short review of Beare's third edition alone. Because Beare's commentary, however, represents and continues to influence prevailing attitudes toward 1 Peter, it still serves today as a useful point of reference and a logical point of departure for a survey of other research.

[8]For reviews of the 1st ed., see V. Taylor, *Exp Tim* 59 (1947-1948): 90-91; T. W. Manson, *JTS* 49 (1948): 85-86; O. A. Piper, *JR* 29 (1949): 62-63; P. Benoit, *RB* 58 (1951): 125-27. On the 2d ed., see T. Barrosse, *CBQ* 21 (1959): 231-33; M.-E. Boismard, *RB* 66 (1959): 279; F. F. Bruce, *EvQ* 31 (1959): 117-18.

most inclusive and up-to-date description of the text of the epistle, which is now found in three papyri (P^{72}, P^{74}, and P^{81}, the latter being two "meagre fragments"), sixteen uncials (4th-10th cents.), more than 550 minuscules (9th-16th cents.), and certain lectionary passages. Beare has made use of the Beuron edition of the OL and has included a collation of the Athos uncial, Codex 4. An "Additional Note on the Literature Attributed to Peter in the Ancient Church" (pp. 228-29) is another noteworthy *novum*.

The rest of the material on the introduction (pp. 24-60) and the commentary proper (pp. 73-210) is, as in the second edition, with few exceptions a "photographic reprint of the first" (2d ed., p. xi). This is perhaps the disappointing feature of the work. With minor exceptions,[9] little of the new information mentioned or of the additions to the bibliography (pp. 61-71) or of the supplement on "First Peter in Recent Criticism (1946-1969)" (pp. 212-27) has been incorporated into the interpretation of the text itself. The new features of this "new" edition turn out to be unintegrated appendages.

The bibliography and the supplement are themselves somewhat deficient and chronologically misleading.[10] The failure in editorial integration has also resulted in a confusion of cross-references.[11] Other *errata* might also be cited,[12] which are relatively minor points of criticism; but they do raise a more substantive question. In 1958 Beare stated in the foreword to his second edition: "I have seen no reason to modify my main positions on the questions of introduction or on the general interpretation of the document" (p. xi). Twelve years later he is apparently of the same opinion. The question, then, is not simply whether the addition of 20 pages of text-critical material, important as it is, justifies the re-publication of an old text. More fundamentally it must be asked whether the research on and understanding of 1 Peter has been at a virtual standstill since 1947 or whether new studies have not shed some light

---

[9]E.g., the second and third paragraphs on p. 171 and the last paragraphs on pp. 177 and 202.

[10]Under "Commentaries" Beare lists 39 works, including six titles added to the combined lists of the 1st and 2d eds., from the period of the early Church Fathers to 1969. My own (unpublished) bibliography contains 112 from only 1890-1969. Among the "Essays, Articles and Monographs" (from 1890-1965) 45 items are mentioned; a more comprehensive list would include over 220 titles. Since 1969 over 30 studies have appeared. Inasmuch as the supplement duplicates that of the 2d ed., the review of "recent criticism" terminates with 1957, not 1969.

[11]E.g., on p. 214 the reference to "page 170, *supra*" should read "p. 194." On p. 225, where Beare opts for an origin of 1 Peter in Rome (rather than in Asia Minor, as in the 1st ed.), the reference to "p. 31, *supra*" should read "p. 50."

[12]On p. 65 under "Hunter, A. M." etc., read *The Interpreter's Bible* for *The Interpreter's Dictionary of the Bible;* p. 66 under "Schelkle, K. H." etc., read "1966" for "1964"; p. 67 under "The older Introductions" etc., read "Mattill, Jr." for "Maddill, Jr."; under "Brandt, W." etc., read "Witten" for "Wittenberg"; p. 171, fifth line from bottom, read "III.18-IV.6" for "II.18-IV.6."

on old exegetical dogmas. Is recent research to be regarded merely as an appendage to ''assured conclusions''? Or should it not be an *Ansatzpunkt* for fresh thought?

OLD POSITIONS AND NEW PERSPECTIVES

authorship

In the supplements to the second and third editions of his commentary Beare discussed four issues raised in the criticism of 1 Peter since 1947:[13] (1) the document's authenticity and Selwyn's defense of the Silvanus secretarial theory; (2) sources, traditions, and literary affinities; (3) the nature and purpose of the epistle; and (4) its place of composition. For a critique of Beare's own positions and a review of research leading in different directions, they will serve as our point of departure.

The authorship of 1 Peter is closely linked with the question of its sources and its literary affinities with other NT writings. Observations made by scholars concerning the latter become the basis for some conclusions drawn concerning the former. E. G. Selwyn, e.g., used the parallels between 1 Peter and 1-2 Thessalonians[14] to support the theory of an indirect authorship of 1 Peter through the secretarial mediation of Silvanus.[15] Beare, on the other hand, regarded the affinities between 1 Peter and the Pauline corpus as clear evidence of the literary dependence of the former upon the latter. This in turn was submitted as part of the proof of pseudonymous post-apostolic authorship. In fact when evaluating Selwyn's mass of evidence, he goes so far as to say, ''. . . the evidence here presented still seems to me to point to quite different conclusions from those drawn by the Dean of Winchester. It seems to me to establish more clearly than ever the literary dependency of 1 Peter upon several, if not all, of the epistles of the Pauline corpus, and upon a number of other N.T. writings as well.''

A theory of such extensive dependence, however, encounters serious difficulties. For one thing, literary affinity must be distinguished from literary dependence. Beare has noted the former[16] but has not proved the latter. Furthermore, the close relation between 1 Peter, Ephesians, and Romans, in particular, requires a totally fresh assessment. If literary dependence between 1

---

[13]2d ed., pp. 186-204; reprinted, except for the expanded bibliography, in the 3d ed., pp. 212-27.

[14]''Essay II: On the Inter-relation of 1 Peter and Other NT Epistles,'' *First Epistle of St. Peter,* 363-466.

[15]Ibid., 9-17.

[16]See his comments on 1 Pet. 1:3 (*First Epistle of Peter,* 81-82), 2:8 (p. 126), 2:11 (p.135), 2:13-17 (p. 140), 5:1 (p. 197), and 5:12-14 (pp. 208-10).

Common use by both Peter & Paul of parenetic/catechetical/liturgical tradition

Peter and Ephesians is conceivable, then a stronger case could be made for the priority of 1 Peter than vice versa.[17] In the case of Romans the question must be asked whether the author of 1 Peter was dependent less on a letter of *Paul* than on a cherished document of the *Roman community* from which he wrote. The influence, then, would be more Roman than Pauline.[18] The epistolary form of 1 Peter might be cited as an example of at least *indirect* Pauline influence.

For the great majority of parallels between 1 Peter and other NT writings, including several within Romans and Ephesians, a more satisfactory and defensible explanation than that of Beare has been offered. Form criticism and tradition criticism, so infrequent in Beare's work, have demonstrated that the theory of a Petrine dependence upon Paul must now be rejected in favor of a common Petrine and Pauline use of a broadly varied (liturgical, parenetic, and catechetical) tradition. In addition to Petrine parallels to Paul,[19] and the subsequent studies cited by an albeit unconvinced Beare,[20] investigations by J. P. Brown, C. Spicq, R. Gundry, E. Best, and J. H. Elliott[21] have examined the dominical logia of 1 Peter and contacts in terminology and theological

---

[17]As support for Petrine dependence, Beare cites the extensive comparison of the two documents undertaken by C. L. Mitton, "The Relationship between Ephesians and 1 Peter" in *The Epistle to the Ephesians* (Oxford: Clarendon, 1951) 176-97. Although Mitton opts for Ephesian priority, in a final appended paragraph (p. 197) he also concedes the opposite alternative! This would be possible on two conditions: if the author of Ephesians had conflated excerpts from Colossians with those from 1 Peter and if Ephesians were Deutero-Pauline. Both the pseudonymous authorship and at least the conflation technique of the author are now recognized as Ephesian characteristics. For Ephesians' refinement of the common material, compare 1 Pet. 1:3-12/Eph. 1:3-14; 1 Pet. 2:4-5/Eph. 2:19-21. On the latter text, see J. H. Elliott, *The Elect and the Holy: An Exegetical Examination of 1 Peter 2:4-10 and the Phrase Basileion Hierateuma* (NovTSup 12; Leiden: Brill, 1966) 165.

[18]Along these lines, see the suggestive observations of E. Best, *1 Peter* (New Century Bible; London: Oliphants, 1971) 32-36. This approach could also help explain the affinities between 1 Peter and 1 Clement, as well as other documents associated with Rome or Italy, e.g., Hebrews.

[19]Cf. the groundwork laid by E. G. Selwyn, *First Epistle of St. Peter*, 363-466.

[20]*First Epistle of Peter*, 216-20. Cf. also the more recent analyses of the Petrine hymnic material by R. Deichgräber (*Gotteshymnus und Christushymnus in der frühen Christenheit* [SUNT 5; Göttingen: Vandenhoeck & Ruprecht, 1967] esp. pp. 42, 77-78 [1:3-12], 140-43 [2:21-25], 169-73 [1:18-21; 3:18-22]) and K. Wengst (*Christologische Formeln und Lieder des Urchristentums* [Gütersloh: Mohn, 1972] esp. pp. 83-85 and 161-64).

[21]J. P. Brown, "Synoptic Parallels in the Epistles and Form-History," *NTS* 10 (1963-1964): 27-48; C. Spicq, "La Iᵃ Petri et le témoignage évangélique de saint Pierre," *ST* 20 (1966): 37-61; R. Gundry, " 'Verba Christi' in 1 Peter: Their Implications concerning the Authorship of I Peter and the Authenticity of the Gospel Tradition," *NTS* 13 (1966-1967): 336-50; E. Best, "1 Peter and the Gospel Tradition," *NTS* 16 (1969-1970): 95-113; J. H. Elliott, "Ministry and Church Order in the NT: A Traditio-Historical Analysis (1 Pt 5, 1-5 + plls.)," *CBQ* 32 (1970): 367-91.

motifs between 1 Peter and the Gospel traditions, including the common use of a ministry and church-order tradition.[22] There are differences in the conclusions drawn from these studies. My own position[23] assumes a middle ground between that of Spicq and Gundry, on the one hand, and Best and Brown, on the other. The textual affinities demonstrate only commonality of tradition but not authenticity of either sources or Petrine redaction. However, the prominence of Simon Peter in this tradition and the coalescence of the tradition, especially on discipleship and ministry, in 1 Peter clearly suggest the existence and development of a specific Petrine body of material.

Certain features, then, of a fresh approach to 1 Peter are beginning to emerge. A more judicious distinction between tradition and redaction is beginning to clarify the peculiar features of the document. This peculiarity is only obscured by the assumption that its author was a confirmed "Paulinist."[24] It rather argues positively for the liberation of 1 Peter from its "Pauline bondage." Literary affinities and the use of tradition cannot provide the main proof for either apostolic, Silvanine, or pseudonymous authorship. On the other hand, there is compelling evidence to indicate that, whoever the particular author might be, 1 Peter is the product of a Petrine tradition transmitted by Petrine tradents of a Petrine circle. The rich diversity of the sources employed would suggest a central geographical location for this circle in the expansion of the early church (Antioch? Asia Minor? Rome?). In this light the issue of authorship assumes secondary importance.[25] Ultimately, then, the issue of authorship is subordinate to, and should be seen in the context of, the content and the historical-ecclesiastical context of 1 Peter itself.

---

[22]Brown notes 23 Synoptic *topoi* with parallels in the NT epistles. The list of 11 pss. from 1 Peter could be expanded to include at least 15 more. Spicq includes verbal similarities between 1 Peter and the Fourth Gospel. Gundry finds 18 pss. of 1 Peter with parallels in the gospels (esp. in certain "text-plots": the Sermon on the Mount, Olivet discourse, and the scenes of the Upper Room and Gethsemane). "The most striking feature about the *verba Christi* in I Peter," he notes, "is that they refer to contexts in the gospels which are specially associated with the Apostle Peter or treat topics that would especially interest the Apostle Peter according to the gospel tradition concerning him. There is, so to speak, a 'Petrine pattern' in the *verba Christi* reflected in I Peter" (p. 345). Best, in response, rejects Gundry's conclusion that "only Petrine authorship of the epistle and authenticity of the gospel-passages adequately account for the Petrine pattern of the verba Christi" (Gundry, 350) and attributes the similarities to the common "catechetical and liturgical material of the early church" (Best, 112). "Further *Verba on Verba Christi* in First Peter" (*Bib* 55 [1974]: 211-24) is Gundry's latest response to Best.

[23]Elliott, "Ministry," 390-91.

[24]Beare (*First Epistle of Peter,* 54-55) concedes at least one impediment to this theory. But his remarks concerning 1 Peter's doctrine of the Spirit must be qualified. See below.

[25]*Pace* Beare, the theory of pseudonymity makes *more* sense if the content of 1 Peter is more Petrine than Pauline. After all, the document is attributed to Peter, not to Paul! Best (I *Peter,* 59-63) offers some sober reflections on the pseudonymity of 1 Peter and its origin within a Petrine school. See also Elliott, "Ministry," 387-91.

This leads to the third issue of recent Petrine criticism mentioned by Beare, the nature and purpose of 1 Peter: its composition, theology, and historical setting. On this important point, however, Beare has dealt only with the problem of genre.[26] He rejects the elaborate theories of H. Preisker, F. L. Cross, and M.-E. Boismard, who see 1 Peter representative of, or dependent upon, a primitive Christian baptismal-eucharistic liturgy. Nor is it, to Beare's mind, a persecution-document with only incidental references to baptism. It is rather, as he has held since 1947, "a baptismal discourse addressed to a group of recent converts" (1:3-4:11) "intruded into" a later genuine epistolary framework (1:1-2; 4:12-5:14).[27] In recent reassessments, however, the criticism that Beare directed toward other theories has caught up with his own as well.[28] Observations about sources have too quickly become conclusions about genre; supposed indications of disunity (especially the "break" between 4:11 and 12) have been exaggerated; adequate contemporary analogies for distinguishing baptismal homilies or liturgies are lacking.[29] In contrast, analyses of sections of 1 Peter and their relation to the whole, supported by attention to the compositional devices employed,[30] have led to a growing conviction that "in its final form 1 Peter is a piece of genuine correspondence."[31] A thoroughgoing investigation of the literary style, structure, and redactional techniques of 1 Peter has yet to be made. The ground work, however, has been laid.[32] Further observations of such composition-analysis now provide a valuable

---

[26]*First Epistle of Peter*, 220-26.

[27]Ibid., 25-28.

[28]For summaries of the literature on the genre of 1 Peter, see R. P. Martin, "The Composition of 1 Peter in Recent Study," *Vox evangelica: Biblical and Historical Essays by Members of the Faculty of the London Bible College* (ed. R. P. Martin; London: Epworth, 1962) 29-42; W. J. Dalton, *Christ's Proclamation to the Spirits: A Study of 1 Peter 3:18-4:6* (AnBib 23; Rome: Biblical Institute, 1965) 62-71.

[29]Beare himself notes (*First Epistle of Peter*, 221) that "those who take the epistle to be a baptismal document are unanimous in perceiving a significant break after the doxology of 4:11."

[30]Cf. W. J. Dalton, *Christ's Proclamation*, 72-86; J. H. Elliott, *The Elect and the Holy*, 199-218; F. W. Danker, "I Peter 1:24-2:17—A Consolatory Pericope," *ZNW* 58 (1967): 93-102, esp. pp. 101-102; and M.-A. Chevallier, "I Pierre 1/1 à 2/10: Structure littéraire et conséquences exégétiques," *RHPR* 51 (1971): 129-42, esp. pp. 140-42. O. S. Brooks ("I Peter 3:21—The Clue to the Literary Structure of the Epistle," *NovT* 16 [1974]: 290-305) curiously affirms both the homily theory and literary unity.

[31]J. N. D. Kelly, *The Epistle*, 2-3. Cf. also E. Best, *I Peter*, 13, 20-28.

[32]In addition to the works already cited above, the older but valuable analyses of U. Holzmeister should not be overlooked; *Commentarius in epistulas SS. Petri et Iudae apostolorum: Pars I, Epistula prima S. Petri apostoli* (Cursus scripturae sacrae, 3/13; Paris: Lethielleux, 1937) esp. pp. 82-104.

literary control for the determination and interpretation of the document's theology.

Both of the most recent and extensive monographs on 1 Peter have attempted to put this control to good advantage: W. J. Dalton's study of 3:18-22[33] and my own investigation of 2:4-10.[34] The works are similar also in other ways. Each concerns a passage crucial not only to the theology of 1 Peter but also to the christology and ecclesiology of the later church. Each challenges conventional interpretation and use of the passage in question. "1 Peter 3:19," according to Dalton, "has nothing to do with the Descensus [Christi ad inferos]."[35] In relation to the literary and religious background of its day, particularly the apocalyptic perspective of *1 Enoch,* this text refers to Christ's proclamation of victory over hostile angelic powers (the imprisoned spirits) on the occasion of his resurrection-ascension (3:18). First Peter 2:4-10, according to the present writer, has nothing to do with the notion of a "royal or universal priesthood of believers" from which a basis for special ministry might be derived. In continuity with the tradition which it employs, it rather explicates the elect and holy character of the eschatological covenant community, its relation to Jesus, the elect and holy one of God, and its missionary responsibility in the world.[36] Each study, furthermore, while attentive to the sources of 1 Peter, stresses the specific redactional and theological accomplishments of the author. Each has evoked or provoked further research on these texts[37] and thus has led to new perspectives not only on 1 Peter but also on contemporary ecumenical issues.[38] Beare's commentary, unfortunately, takes account of none of this literature.[39]

---

[33]*Christ's Proclamation to the Spirits* (see n. 28 above).

[34]*The Elect and the Holy* (see n. 17 above).

[35]*Christ's Proclamation,* 8.

[36]*The Elect and the Holy,* 219-26. Cf. also J. H. Elliott, "Death of a Slogan: From Royal Priests to Celebrating Community," *Una Sancta* [New York] 25 (1968): 18-31.

[37]Beside Dalton's own follow-up work, "Interpretation and Tradition: An Example from 1 Peter," *Greg* 49 (1967): 17-37, see B. Schwank, "Des éléments mythologiques dans une profession de foi: 1 P 3, 18-22," *Assemblées du Seigneur* 14 (1973): 41-44; F. C. Synge, "I Peter 3:18-21," *Exp Tim* 82 (1971) 311. H. Goldstein, "Die Kirche als Schar derer, die ihrem leidenden Herrn mit dem Ziel der Gottesgemeinschaft nachfolgen: Zum Gemeindeverständnis von 1 Petr 2, 21-25 und 3, 18-22," *Bib Leb* 15 (1974): 38-54. The eschatology of 1 Peter, esp. its apocalyptic coloring, is stressed by G. Dautzenberg, "Σωτηρία ψυχῶν (1 Pt 1,9)," *BZ* ns 8 (1964): 262-76; cf. also J. R. Ramsey, "Eschatology in 1 Peter 3:17," *NTS* 13 (1966-1967): 394-401.

[38]This is particularly the case with regard to *The Elect and the Holy* because of its broad implications. "If," as C. F. D. Moule has noted in his review (*JTS* ns 18 [1967]: 471-74), "Dr. Elliott's thesis stands, a key verse in Reformation teaching, and in modern Roman Catholic ecclesiology also, has gone with the wind" (p. 471). A full list of subsequent studies would be impossible here; the following, therefore, is a representative selection. A detailed discus-

ethics/parenesis

His dissatisfaction with the doctrine of the Holy Spirit in 1 Peter[40] stems from his persistence in measuring Peter by the shape of Paul. In fact, the "undeveloped" pneumatology of 1 Peter constitutes for Beare "clear evidence of affinity with the trends of the second century, not with the first age of the Church."[41] But in 1 Peter the Spirit is inseparably connected with the central theme of holiness and the moral exhortation based upon it.[42] This intricate interrelationship of kerygma and parenesis is one of 1 Peter's most distinguishing features among the epistolary literature of the NT.[43] The moral teaching of the letter, therefore, continues to be a point of focus.[44]

The content of 1 Peter has accurately been described as an "ethics for exiles."[45] A basic influence on the document's message and a further crucial

---

sion will be the subject of a separate study. On 1 Pet. 2:4-10 specifically, see F. W. Danker, "Brief Study," *CTM* 38 (1967): 329-32; E. Best, "I Peter II, 4-10—A Reconsideration," *NovT* 11 (1969): 270-93; J. Coppens, "Le sacerdoce royal des fidèles: Un commentaire de I Petr., II, 4-10," in *Au service de la Parole de Dieu: Mélanges offerts à Msgr. André-Marie Charue* (Gembloux: Duculot, 1969) 61-75; E. Cothenet, "Le sacerdoce des fidèles d'apres la I*a* Petri," *Esprit et Vie* 11 (1969): 169-73; F. F. Ramos, "El sacerdocio de los creyentes (1 Pet 2,4-10)," *Teologia del sacerdocio* (Burgos: Ediciones Aldecoa, 1970) 11-47; N. Hillyer, " 'Rock-Stone' Imagery in I Peter," *Tyndale Bulletin* 22 (1971): 58-81; V. C. Pfitzner, " 'General Priesthood' and Ministry," *Lutheran Theological Journal* (Australia) 5 (1971): 97-110; E. Schüssler Fiorenza, *Priester für Gott* (NTAbh ns 7; Münster: Aschendorff, 1972): 53-59; A. Vanhoye, "La foi qui construit l'église: 1 P 2,4-9," *Assemblées du Seigneur* 26 (1973): 12-17; A. Feuillet, "Les 'sacrifices spirituels' du sacerdoce royal des baptisés (1 P 2,5) et leur préparation dans l'Ancien Testament," *NRT* 96 (1974): 704-28. For studies with wider scope, see R. E. Brown, *Priest and Bishop* (Paramus NJ: Paulist, 1970) 14-20; *Lutherans and Catholics in Dialogue: IV. Eucharist and Ministry* (New York: USA National Committee of the Lutheran World Federation, 1970) 69-100 and 227-82.

[39]Except for one brief descriptive reference to Dalton's thesis (*First Epistle of Peter,* 177).

[40]On this point, however, he concedes that "here certainly our author is no follower of Paul" (Ibid., 54).

[41]Ibid., 55.

[42]See J. H. Elliott, *The Elect and the Holy,* 153-54, 174-85.

[43]As C. Spicq ("La I*a* Petri," 37), along with most commentators, has noticed. On this point the study of E. Lohse is still basic, "Paranese und Kerygma im 1. Petrusbrief," *ZNW* 45 (1954): 68-69.

[44]Cf. L. Kline, "Ethics for the Endtime: An Exegesis of 1 Pe. 4,7-11," *Restoration Quarterly* 7 (1963): 113-23; A. R. Jonsen, "The Moral Teaching of the First Epistle of St. Peter," *Sciences ecclésiastiques* 16 (1964): 93-105; J. W. Thompson, "Be Submissive to Your Masters: A Study of 1 Pt 2:18-25," *Restoration Quarterly* 9 (1966): 66-78; R. Frattallone, "Anthropologia naturale e soprannaturale nella prima lettera di San Pietro," *Studia moralia* 5 (1967): 41-111; L. Goppelt, "Prinzipien neutestamentlicher Sozialethik nach dem 1. Petrusbrief," *Neues Testament und Geschichte* (O. Cullmann Festschrift; eds. H. Baltensweiler and B. Reicke; Zürich: Theologischer Verlag; Tübingen: Mohr, 1972) 285-96; W. Schrage, "Zur Ethik der neutestamentlichen Haustafeln," *NTS* 21 (1974-1975): 1-22.

[45]H. C. Kee, F. W. Young, and K. Froehlich, *Understanding the New Testament,* 2d ed. (Englewood Cliffs: Prentice-Hall, 1965) 355-79.

control for its interpretation is the historical, geographical, and socio-political setting of its author and addressees. This leads us to, but extends beyond Beare's fourth and final issue concerning 1 Peter's place of composition.[46] Beare initially (in the first edition) held that "it was written in the area to which it is addressed," for example, Asia Minor. Now, because of the affinities between 1 Peter and the Roman tradition preserved in Hippolytus' *Apostolic Tradition,* he considers "a Roman origin . . . unquestionable."[47] The place of composition and destination, therefore, are to be distinguished. But this only compounds the already problematic view he presents. For one thing, the doubtful possibility that the author has incorporated in his letter elements of the Anatolian mystery cults, of which he was a past devotee,[48] becomes even more unlikely if he is writing from Rome and employing quite different Roman tradition as well. In regard to the addressees, on the other hand, there are still open questions concerning the specific nature of their imperilled situation.

With many scholars Beare has attempted to relate 1 Pet. 4:12-5:11 to an imperial persecution against Christians undertaken in the reign of Trajan (A.D. 98-117). The location of the addressees in Bithynia-Pontus (1:1) and the supposed affinities between 1 Peter and the correspondence of the governor of this region, Pliny the Younger, with Trajan (*Epistles* 10.96) is offered as corroborating evidence.[49] For a growing number of scholars, however, the evidence is too disputable to prove the theory. There is no agreement among historians as to the inception or extent of the imperial persecution of Christians.[50] Nor is an *imperial* persecution necessarily indicated by the term

---

[46]*First Epistle of Peter,* 226-27.

[47]Ibid., 225. Poor editing, however, fails to make this revision clear. Beare's earlier opinion is still found in the text of the 3d ed. (p. 50).

[48]Ibid., 46 and 35-38, following the dated hypothesis of Perdelwitz and the *religionsgeschichtliche Schule.*

[49]Ibid., 29-34, 188.

[50]In contrast to W. H. C. Frend, *Martyrdom and Persecution in the Early Church* (Garden City: Doubleday, 1967), see N. Lewis and M. Reinhold, eds., *Roman Civilization: Sourcebook II: The Empire* (New York: Harper & Row, 1966) 581-82: In the brief reign of Decius (A.D. 249-251) "the organized imperial persecution of Christianity was begun." E. A. Judge, *The Social Pattern of the Christian Groups in the First Century* (London: Tyndale, 1960) 62-77; and the older collection of sources interpreted by L. H. Canfield, *The Early Persecution of the Christians* (Studies in History, Economics and Public Law, 55/2; New York: Columbia University, 1913; reprinted, New York: AMS Press, 1968) 43-69 (where 1 Peter is associated with the Neronian period). For a recent defense of the Trajan theory, see J. D. McCaughey, "Three 'Persecution Documents' of the New Testament," *AusBR* 17 (1969): 27-40.

πύρωσις in 1 Pet. 4:12.[51] Nor is either the literary or historical "disconti-
nuity" between 1 Pet. 4:11 and 12 at all certain.[52] Nor do the suggested parallels between 1 Peter and Pliny's correspondence prove a common date.[53]
Nor is there evidence that the situation which Pliny describes regarding Bithynia-Pontus is also that of the other provinces addressed in 1 Peter. Nor,
finally, have those scholars favoring the imperial-persecution theory adequately considered or refuted a more likely explanation of the situation, viz.,
the hostility, harassment, and ostracism of a local, social, and "unofficial"
nature. Earlier and more recent studies[54] have cogently argued the latter case.
An important result for the interpretation of 1 Peter is a shift of attention away
from the muddled issue of imperial persecutions to the wider question of the
socio-political status of the Christian communities in the diaspora, their
everyday relations with Jews and Gentiles alike, and the theology which they
developed as an expression of their communal self-understanding and their
existence as disenfranchised "aliens and exiles."[55] As a result of spatial dis-

---

[51]In Prov 27:21 it designates the purifying and testing of metals. According to *Did.* 16:5
the τὴν πύρωσιν τῆς δοκιμασίας is an eschatological sign of the endtime. Cf. also the
eschatological sense of the cognate verb at Eph 6:16 and 2 Pet 3:12.

[52]In fact, J. Knox ("Pliny and 1 Peter: A Note on 1 Pet 4, 14-16 and 3, 15," *JBL* 72
[1953]: 187-89), who also stresses the similarity of 1 Peter and Pliny's letter, presumes the
integrity of the letter in order to make his point.

[53]Pliny's uncertainty about strategy allows for a longer period of confusion after A.D. 70
when Christianity, having separated from Judaism, lost its legal status as a *religio licita.*

[54]E.g., C. F. D. Moule, "The Nature and Purpose of I Peter," *NTS* 3 (1956-1957): 1-11;
W. C. van Unnik, "Peter, First Epistle of," *IDB,* 3. 758-66. More recently, J. N. D. Kelly,
The Epistle, 5-11; E. Best, *I Peter,* 36-42.

[55]Variations on this pregnant theme are diverse. B. Reicke in his "General Introduction"
to *The Epistles of James, Peter and Jude* (AB 37; Garden City: Doubleday, 1964, esp. pp. xv-
xxix) mentions several aspects of the setting of 1 Peter which deserve closer attention. These
include the Church's possible association with the Jewish Zealotic movement as well as with
other social groups which were viewed as potential threats to Roman order (e.g., the *collegia,*
philosophical schools, and circles of nobility). On the latter see also R. Macmullen, *Enemies
of the Roman Order* (Cambridge: Harvard University, 1966). Reicke's too narrow reading of
1 Peter as an admonition against Christian involvement in anti-imperial subversive activity,
however, has been subjected to a careful and convincing criticism by C. F. Sleeper ("Political
Responsibility According to I Peter," *NovT* 10 [1968]: 270-86).

Regarding further concrete aspects of the Church/Judaism/Empire question, see F. M.
Young, "Temple Cult and Law in Early Christianity: A Study in the Relationship Between
Jews and Christians in the Early Centuries," *NTS* 19 (1973): 325-38; H. Goldstein, "Die pol-
itischen Paränesen in 1 Petr und Rom 13," *Bib Leb* 15 (1974): 88-104.

Similarities seen between 1 Peter and the Greek and Roman associations-*collegia* of Asia
Minor (including terminology, practices proscribed in 4:2-4, and mutual sociopolitical vulnerability) contain additional clues concerning the social organization and involvements of the
churches of 1 Peter. Cf. B. Reicke, *The Epistles of James, Peter and Jude,* and earlier *Dia-
konie: Festfreude und Zelos in Verbindung mit der altchristlichen Agapenfeier* (Uppsala Uni-

feeling of homelessness, not belonging

location from the "homeland" (the former Palestinian *klēronomia,* 1 Pet. 1:4), religious and ethnic dissociation from Judaism (2:4-10), and social alienation in the "diaspora" (4:2-4), the Christian mission became a movement of pilgrims and aliens without a geographical home (a *patria*) or the political security of a *polis* or citizenship. It is this situation of acute homelessness and the feeling of not belonging which provides the clearest contours of the *Sitz im Leben* of 1 Peter. And within this situation the theology of the letter appears in sharpest focus. The strangers and aliens of 1 Peter are none other than the "elect and holy people of God." In Christ the homeless ones are members of the *oikos tou Theou.*[56]

One final area of Petrine research, touched upon only obliquely by Beare,[57] concerns the figure and function of Simon Peter in the NT and early church.[58] The fresh questions, especially regarding Peter's location on the NT "trajectory," and the new perspectives gained from the reassessment of old biases hopefully will extend also to the biblical documents bearing his name.

CONCLUSION

Our understanding of 1 Peter and its historical context has grown and shifted considerably in the last two decades. Since Beare's commentary is substantially unmodified from its 1947 form, it is scarcely abreast of the scholarly developments of these decades. The composition, message, and

---

versitets Åarskrift 1951/5; Uppsala: Lundqvist, 1951) 320-38; R. Macmullen, *Enemies,* 173-79, 341-44; C. Spicq, "La I*a* Petri," 58; *idem,* "La place ou le rôle des jeunes dans certaines communautés neotestamentaires," *RB* 76 (1969): 508-27; and E. A. Judge, *Social Pattern,* 40-48.

On the social and theological aspects of the church as a community of pilgrims and exiles, see R. Völkl, *Christ und Welt nach dem Neuen Testament* (Würzburg: Echter Verlag, 1961) 370-80 and M.-A. Chevallier, "Condition et vocation des chrétiens en diaspora: Remarques exégétiques sur la l*re* Epître de Pierre," *RevScRel* 48 (1974): 387-98.

[56]See John H. Elliott, *A Home for the Homeless. A Sociological Exegesis of 1 Peter, Its Situation and Strategy* (Philadelphia: Fortress, 1981).

[57]In his "Additional Note on the Literature Attributed to Peter in the Ancient Church," *The First Epistle,* 228-29.

[58]The literature again is multitudinous. For a basic orientation, see R. E. Brown et al., *Peter in the New Testament: A Collaborative Assessment by Protestant and Roman Catholic Scholars* (Minneapolis: Augsburg; Paramus NJ: Paulist, 1973). Attention to 1 Peter, unfortunately, is minimal; cf. W. G. Thompson and J. H. Elliott, "Peter in the New Testament: Old Theme, New Views," *America* 130 (1974): 53-54. In addition to the "Select Bibliography" (pp. 169-77), see also G. Denzler et al., *Petrusamt und Papsttum* (Stuttgart: Katholisches Bibelwerk, 1970); W. Dietrich, *Das Petrusbild der lukanischen Schriften* (BWANT 5/14(94); Stuttgart: Kohlhammer Verlag, 1972); O. Knoch, *Die 'Testamente' des Petrus und Paulus: Die Sicherung der apostolischen Überlieferung in der spätneutestamentlichen Zeit* (SBS 62; Stuttgart: Katholisches Bibelwerk, 1973).

import of the letter receive less than their due as long as 1 Peter is seen mainly or merely as an appendage of the Pauline corpus. The cultural and cultic links which Beare postulated between 1 Peter and the Cybelene mystery-cults have proved unconvincing. Evidence for a late dating during the Trajanic period has also appeared inconclusive.

Research since 1958 generally has tended to challenge old assumptions while simultaneously raising new questions. Form- and tradition-criticism have uncovered the letter's firm footing in diverse older traditions, some of it probably authentic dominical material. The antiquity of these sources and a comparison of their use in other documents suggest, though they do not prove, the possibility of an earlier dating, perhaps between A.D. 70 and 90. Historical and sociological analysis has pointed to the predicament of homelessness and socio-political alienation rather than an official imperial attack as the setting and occasion of the document. Through redaction criticism the peculiar literary and theological properties of 1 Peter have taken on clearer shape and scope. While further investigation is necessary, there is now sufficient evidence to suggest the existence of a Petrine circle, whose members were responsible for the preservation and propagation of tradition particularly associated with the apostle Peter. This raises new questions concerning the place and significance of such a tradition in the historical and theological development of the early church.

First Peter, together with the historical figure to whom it was ascribed, has for quite some time been the victim of biased oversight and benign neglect. There are lively indications, however, that both apostle and letter have passed their latest exegetical *peirasmos*.

CHAPTER 2

THE CRITICAL EXPLORATION
OF 1 PETER*

DENNIS SYLVA
ST. FRANCIS SEMINARY
MILWAUKEE, WISCONSIN 53207

Critical and comprehensive bibliographies are one of the primary resources for scholars in their attempt to advance their fields of study. They bring together relevant literature from a variety of places. The works of W. Lyons and M. Parvis, B. Metzger, A. J. Mattill and M. B. Mattill, and J. T. Forestell have greatly facilitated scholarly discussion on NT works.[1] This work belongs to this NT bibliographical tradition. I have made a detailed search on critical works on 1 Peter from the nineteenth and twentieth centuries. It is my hope that it will facilitate the study of this "exegetical stepchild." The reader will note that a good number of the studies cited deal with the idea of "Christ's descent among the dead" found in 1 Pet. 3:19-20; 4:6. This tradition is found in other NT and early Christian works. It is only the 1 Peter passages, however, that appear to offer hope of sal-

---

*This article is reprinted with permission from *JETS* 25 (1982): 75-89.

[1]W. Lyons and M. Parvis, *New Testament Literature—An Annotated Bibliography* (Chicago: University Press, 1948); B. Metzger, *Index of Articles on the New Testament Published in Festschriften,* JBL Monograph Series 5 (Philadelphia: SBL, 1951); Idem, *Index to Periodical Literature on the Apostle Paul* (Grand Rapids: Eerdmans, 1960); Idem, *Index to Periodical Literature on Christ and the Gospels* (Leiden: Brill, 1966); A. J. Mattill and M. B. Mattill, *A Classified Bibliography of Literature on the Acts of the Apostles* (Leiden: Brill, 1966); J. T. Forestell, C.S.B., *Targumic Traditions and the New Testament: An Annotated Bibliography with a New Testament Index* (Chico CA: Scholars Press, 1981).

vation to those who have died in their sins. For this reason the passage has occasioned a great deal of exegetical effort.

I. BOOKS AND DISSERTATIONS

Ambroggi, P. De. *Le Epistole cattoliche*. SB 14, 1. Turin: Marietti, 1949.

Andrianopoli, L. *Il mistero di Gesù nelle lettere di San Pietro*. Turin: Societa editrice internazionale, 1935.

Arichea, D. C., and E. A. Nida, *A Translator's Handbook on the First Letter from Peter*. HT. New York/London/Stuttgart: United Bible Societies, 1980.

Augusti, J. C. W. *Die katholischen Briefe, neu übersetzt und erklärt mit Excursen und einleitenden Abhandlungen herausgegeben*. Lemgo: Meyer, 1801-1808.

Balch, D. L. *Let Wives Be Submissive: The Domestic Code in 1 Peter*. SBLMS 26. Chico: Scholars Press, 1981.

Balz, H., and W. Schrage, *Die "katholischen" Briefe. Die Briefe des Jakobus, Petrus, Johannes und Judas*. 11th ed. Göttingen: Vandenhoeck and Ruprecht, 1973.

Barclay, W. *The Letters of James and Peter. Translated with an Introduction and Interpretation*. DSB. 2nd ed. Philadelphia: Westminster, 1976.

Barnes, A. *Notes on the New Testament, Explanatory and Practical-James, Peter, John and Jude*. Grand Rapids: Baker, 1951.

Barnett, A. E. *Paul Becomes a Literary Influence*. Chicago: University Press, 1941.

Bauer, J. B. *Der erste Petrusbrief*. WBK 14. Düsseldorf: Patmos, 1971.

Beare, F. W. *The First Epistle of Peter*. 3rd rev. ed. Oxford: Blackwell, 1970.

Beasley-Murray, G. R. *Die christliche Taufe*. London: n. p., 1962.

Beck, J. T. *Erklärung der Briefe Petri*. Gütersloh: C. Bertelsmann, 1896.

Beelen, J. Th., and A. Van Der Heeren, *De Katholieke Brieven*. Brügge: n. p., 1932.

Bennett, W. H. *The General Epistles: James, Peter, John, Jude*. CB. New York: n. p., 1901.

Besser, W. F. *Die Briefe St. Petri in Bibelstunden für die Gemeinde ausgelegt*. Bibelstunden 8. Halle: n. p., 1854.

Best, E. *1 Peter*. NCB. London: Oliphants, 1971.

Bieder, W. *Die Vorstellung von der Höllenfahrt Jesu Christi. Beiträg zur Entstehungsgeschichte der Vorstellung vom sogenannte Descensus ad inferos*. Zürich: Zwingli, 1949.

_____. *Grund und Kraft der Mission nach dem 1. Petrusbrief*. ThSt 29. Zürich: Evangelischer, 1950.

Bigg, C. *A Critical and Exegetical Commentary on the Epistles of St. Peter and St. Jude*. ICC. 2d ed. Edinburgh: T. & T. Clark, 1910.

Bisping, A. *Erklärung der sieben katholischen Briefe*. EHNT 8. Munich: Aschendorf, 1871.

Blenkin, G. W. *The First Epistle General of Peter*. Cambridge: University Press, 1914.

Boismard, M. E. *Quatre hymnes baptismales dans la première épître de Pierre*. LD 30. Paris: Editions du Cerf, 1961.

Braun, J. *Expository Discourses on the First Epistle of the Apostle Peter*. 3 vols. Marshallton, DE: National Foundation for Christian Education, n. d.

Brown, R. E., K. P. Donfried, and J. Reumann, *Peter in the New Testament*. Minneapolis: Augsburg, 1973.

Brox, N. *Der erste Petrusbrief*. EKKNT 21. Zürich: Benziger, 1979.

Brun, L. *Forste Peters-Brev*. Oslo: Achehoug, 1949.

Bruston, C. *La descente du Christ aux enfers, d'après les apôtres et d'après l'église*. Paris: Fischbacher, 1897.

Bugge, F. W. *Apostlerne Peters og Judas Breve. Indledede, oversatte og forklarede*. N. p.: Christiania, 1885.

Burger, K. *Der erste Brief Petri*. Nördlingen: n. p., 1888.

Caffin, B. C. *The First Epistle General of Peter*. PC. Grand Rapids: Eerdmans, 1950.

Calloud, J. and F. Genuyt, *La première épître de Pierre: Analyse sémiotique*. LD 109. Paris: Cerf, 1982.

Calmes, Th. *Les Epîtres catholiques. L'Apocalypse*. Paris: n. p., 1905.

Camerlynck, A. *Commentarius in Epistolas catholicas*. Brugge: Car. Beyaerte, 1876.

Canes, M. et al. *Les lettres de Paul, de Jacques, Pierre et Jude*. NT-5. Paris: Desclée, 1983.

Charue, A. *Les épîtres catholiques*. La Sainte Bible 12. Paris: Gabalda, 1938.

Clemen, C. *"Niedergefahren zu den Toten," Ein Beitrag zur Würdigung des Apostolikums*. Giessen: J. Riecker, 1900.

Cranfield, C. E. B. *The First Epistle of Peter*. London: SCM, 1950.

—————————. *1 and 2 Peter and Jude*. TBC. London: SCM, 1960.

Cross, F. L. *1 Peter: A Paschal Liturgy*. London: Mowbray, 1954.

Cullmann, O. *Petrus. Jünger-Apostel-Martyrer*. Zürich: Zwingli, 1952.

Dalton, W. J. *Christ's Proclamation to the Spirits: A Study of 1 Peter 3:18-4:6*. AnBib 23. Rome: Biblical Institute, 1965.

Danker, F. W. *Invitation to the New Testament. Epistles IV. A Commentary on Hebrews, 1 and 2 Peter, 1, 2 and 3 John and Jude*. Garden City NY: Image, 1980.

Deering, R. F. "The Humiliation-Exaltation Motif in 1 Peter." Ph.D. dissertation, Southern Baptist Theological Seminary, 1962.

DeHaan, R. W., and H. Vander Lugt. *Good News for Bad Times. A Study of 1 Peter*. Wheaton IL: Victor, 1975.

De Wette, W. M. L. *Kurze Erklärung der Briefe des Petrus, Judas, und Jakobus*. Leipzig: Weidmann, 1847.

Diaz, R. M. *Epistoles Catòliques*. Montserrat: n. p., 1958.

Ebright, H. K. *The Petrine Epistles: A Critical Study of Authorship*. Cincinnati: Methodist Book Concern, 1917.

Eisenschmid, G. B. *Die Briefe des Apostels Petrus übersetzt, erlautert und mit erbaulichen Betrachtungen begleitet*. Ronnenberg: n. p., 1824.

Elliott, J. H. *The Elect and the Holy: An Exegetical Examination of 1 Peter 2:4-10 and the Phrase Basileion Hierateuma*. NovTSup 12. Leiden: Brill, 1966.

——————————. *A Home for the Homeless. A Sociological Exegesis of 1 Peter, Its Situation and Strategy*. Philadelphia: Fortress, 1981.

——————————. *1 Peter. Estrangement and Community*. HBB. Chicago: Franciscan Herald, 1979.

Elliott, J. H. and R. A. v. Martin, *James 1-11 Peter/Jude*. ACNT. Minneapolis: Augsburg, 1982.

Ewald, H. *Sieben Sendschreiben des Neuen Bundes übersetzt und erklärt*. Göttingen: Vandenhoeck & Ruprecht, 1870.

Fabris, R. *Lettera di Giacomo e Prima lettera di Pietro*. LPB 8. Bologna: Dehoniane, 1980.

Felten, J. *Die zwei Briefe des hl. Petrus und der Judasbrief*. Regensburg: n. p., 1929.

Finkbeiner, F. L. "Church and State from Paul to 1 Peter." Ph.D. dissertation, Claremont, 1960.

Foster, O. D. "The Literary Relations of the First Epistle of Peter with their Bearing on Place and Date of Authorship." Ph.D. dissertation, Yale University, 1911.

Franco, R. *Cartas de san Pedro*. Madrid: n. p., 1962.

Frederick, S. C. "The Theme of Obedience in the First Epistle of Peter." Ph.D. dissertation, Duke University, 1975.

Fuller, R. H., et al. *Hebrews, James, 1 and 2 Peter, Jude, Revelation*. PC. Philadelphia: Fortress, 1977.

Gaebelein, F. E. *The Expositor's Bible Commentary: Volume 12 (Hebrews-Revelation)*. Grand Rapids: Zondervan, 1981.

Gewalt, D. "Petrus." Ph.D. dissertation, Heidelberg, 1966.

Goebel, S. *Die Briefe des Petrus, griechisch, mit kurzer Erklärung*. Gotha: n. p., 1983.

Goldstein, H. *Paulinische Gemeinde im Ersten Petrusbrief*. Stüttgart: Katholisches Bibelwerk, 1975.

Gontard, L. *Essai critique et historique sur la première épître de Saint Pierre*. Lyons: n. p., 1905.

Goppelt, L. *Der erste Petrusbrief*. Ed. F. Hahn. MeyerK 12/1. 8th ed. Göttingen: Vandenhoeck and Ruprecht, 1978.

Gourbillon, J. G., and F. M. Buit, *La première épître de S. Pierre*. Paris: n. p., 1963.

Greijdanus, S. *Petrus, Johan en Judas*. CNT 13. Amsterdam: n. p., 1933.

Grillmeier, A. *Der Gottessohn im Totenreich. Soteriologische und christo- logische Motivierung der Descensuslehre in der älteren christlichen Überlieferung*. Freiburg: n. p., 1975.

Gschwind, K. *Die Niederfahrt Christi in die Unterwelt. Ein Beitrag zur Ex- egese des Neuen Testaments und zur Geschichte des Taufsymbols*. NTAbh 2/3-5. Munich: Aschendorff, 1911.

Güder, E. *Die Lehre von der Erscheinung Jesu Christi unter den Toten. In ihrem Zusammenhänge mit der Lehre von den letzten Dingen*. Bern: Jent and Reinert, 1853.

Gunkel, H. *Der erste Brief des Petrus*. Göttingen: n. p., 1906.

Hamblin, R. L. "An Analysis of First Peter with Special Reference to the Greek Participle." Ph.D. dissertation Southwestern Baptist Theological Seminary, 1960.

Hensler, C. G. *Der erste Brief des Apostels Petrus übersetzt und mit einem Kommentar versehen*. Sulzbach: J. E. Seidel, 1813.

Heussi, K. *Die römische Petrustradition in kritischer Sicht*. Tübingen: J. C. B. Mohr, 1955.

Hiebert, D. E. *An Introduction to the New Testament. Vol. 3—The Non-Pau- line Epistles and Revelation*. Rev. ed. Chicago: Moody, 1977.

Hofmann, J. C. K. Von. *Der erste Brief Petri*. Nördlingen: n. p., 1875.

Holmer, U., and DeBoor, W. *Die Briefe des Petrus und der Brief des Judas*. Wuppertal: Brockhaus, 1976.

Holtzmann, O. *Die Petrusbriefe*. NT 2. Giessen: n. p., 1926.

Holzmeister, U. *Commentarius in epistulas SS. Petri et Iudae apostolorum: Pars I. Epistula prima S. Petri apostoli*. CSS 3/13. Paris: Lethielleux, 1937.

Hort, F. G. A. *The First Epistle of St. Peter 1:1-2:17*. London: Macmillan, 1898.

Hottinger, J. I. *Epistolae Jacobi atque Petri cum versione germanica et com- mentario latino*. Leipzig: n. p., 1815.

Huidekopper, F. *The Belief of the First Three Centuries Concerning Christ's Mission to the Underworld*. 8th ed. New York: D. G. Francis, 1890.

Hunter, A. M., and E. G. Homrighausen, *The Epistle of James, The First and Second Epistles of Peter, The First, Second and Third Epistles of John, the Epistle of Jude, The Revelation of St. John the Divine*. IB 12. New York/Nashville: n. p., 1957.

Huther, J. E. *Kritisch-exegetisches Handbuch über den 1. Brief des Petrus, den Brief des Judas und den 2. Brief des Petrus*. Göttingen: Vanden- hoeck and Ruprecht, 1877.

Jachmann, K. R. *Commentar uber die Katholischen Briefe mit genauer Be- rücksichtigung der neusten Auslegungen*. Leipzig: J. A. Barth, 1838.

Jensen, P. *Laeren om Kristi Nedfahrt til de döde. En Fremstilling of Laere- punktets Historie tilligemed et Indloeg i dette*. Copenhagen: n. p., 1903.

Johnstone, R. *The First Epistle of Peter*. Edinburgh: T. & T. Clark, 1888.

Keil, C. F. *Kommentar über die Briefe des Petrus und Judas.* Leipzig: n. p.,
    1883.
Kelly, J. N. D. *The Epistles of Peter and Jude.* HNTC. New York: Harper,
    1969.
Kelly, W. *Preaching to the Spirits in Prison.* London: T. Weston, 1900.
_____. *The First Epistle of Peter.* London: T. Weston, 1904.
Ketter, P. *Hebräerbrief, Jakobusbrief, Petrusbriefe, Judasbrief.* HSLE 16/
    1. Freiburg: Herder, 1950.
Keulers, J. *De Katholieke Brieven en het Boek der Openbaring.* Roermond:
    n. p., 1946.
Knoch, O. *Die "Testaments" des Petrus und Paulus: Die Sicherung der
    apostolischen Überlieferung in der spätneutestamentlichen Zeit.* SBS 62.
    Stuttgart: Katholisches Bibelwerk, 1973.
Knopf, R. *Die Briefe Petri und Juda.* Meyer K. Göttingen: Vandenhoeck &
    Ruprecht, 1912.
König, J. L. *Die Lehre von Christi Höllenfahrt nach der heiligen Schrift, der
    ältesten Kirche, den christlichen Symbolen und nach ihrer vielumfassen-
    den Bedeutung dargestellt.* Frankfurt: H. Zimmer, 1842.
Körber, J. *Die katholische Lehre von der Höllenfahrt Jesu Christi.* Lanshut:
    n. p., 1860.
Kowalski, S. *La Descente de Jésus-Christ aux enfers selon la doctrine de saint
    Pierre.* Roznan: n. p., 1938.
Kroll, J. *Gott und Hölle.* Der Mythos vom descensuskämpfe. SBW 20. Leip-
    zig/Berlin: B. G. Teubner, 1932.
Kuhl, E. *Die Briefe Petri und Judae.* Göttingen: Vandenhoeck & Ruprecht,
    1897.
Leaney, A. R. C. *The Letters of Peter and Jude.* CBC. Cambridge: Univer-
    sity Press, 1967.
Leconte, R. *Les Epîtres catholiques.* Paris: Editions du Cerf, 1953.
Leighton, R. *Commentary on First Peter.* 1853. KRL. Grand Rapids: Kre-
    gel, 1972.
Lenski, R. C. H. *The Interpretation of the Epistles of St. Peter, St. John and
    St. Jude.* Columbus, OH.: Lutheran Book Concern, 1938.
Lewis, J. M. "The Christology of the First Epistle of Peter." Ph.D. disser-
    tation, Southwestern Baptist Theological Seminary, 1952.
Lilje, H. *Die Petrusbriefe und der Judasbrief.* BG 14. Kassel: J. G. Oncken,
    1954.
Lundberg, P. *La Typologie baptismale dans l'ancienne Eglise.* ASNU 10.
    Leipzig/Uppsala: A. Lorentz, 1942.
MacCulloch, J. A. *The Harrowing of Hell.* Edinburgh: n. p., 1930.
Margot, J. C. *Les Epîtres de Pierre.* Genf: n. p., 1960.
Masterman, J. *The First Epistle of S. Peter (Greek Text).* London: Macmil-
    lan, 1900.
Mayerhoff, E. T. *Historisch-kritische Einleitung in die petrinischen Schrif-
    ten.* Hamburg: F. Perthes, 1835.

Michl, H. *Die katholischen Briefe.* RNT 8/2. Regensburg: F. Pustet, 1953.

Millauer, H. *Leiden als Gnade. Eine traditionsgeschichtliche Untersuchung zur Leidenstheologie des ersten Petrusbriefes.* Bern: H. Lang, 1976.

Moffatt, J. *The General Epistles—James, Peter and Judas.* MNTC. London: Hodder and Stoughton, 1947.

Monnier, J. *La descente aux enfers. Etude de pensée religieuse, d'art et de littérature.* Paris: Fischbacher, 1904.

——————. *La première Epître de l'Apôtre Pierre.* Macon: Protat freres, 1900.

Moorehead, W. G. *Outline Studies in the New Testament. Catholic Epistles—James, 1 and 2 Peter, 1, 2, 3 John and Jude.* New York: Revell, 1910.

Munro, W. *Authority in Peter and Paul: The Identification of a Pastoral Stratum in the Pauline Corpus and 1 Peter.* SNTSMS 45. Cambridge: Cambridge University Press, 1983.

——————. ''Authority and Subjection in early Christian 'Paidea' with Particular Reference to the Pauline Corpus and 1 Peter.'' Ph.D. dissertation, Columbia, University, 1974.

Norblad, C. *Föreställningen om Kristi hadesförd undersökt till sitt ursprung. En religionshistorisk studie.* Uppsala: n. p., 1912.

Olson, V. E. ''The Atonement in 1 Peter.'' Ph.D. dissertation. Union Theological Seminary in Virginia, 1979.

Olsson, B. *Forsta Petrusbrevet.* KNT 17. Stockholm: EFS-farlaget, 1982.

Penna, A. S. *Pietro.* Brescia: Morcelliana, 1954.

Perdelwitz, E. R. *Die Mysterienreligion und das Problem des 1. Petrusbriefes.* Giessen: A. Töpelmann, 1911.

Pesch, R. *Die Echtheit aures Glaubens.* Freiburg: Herder, 1980.

Philipps, K. *Kirche und Gesellschaft nach dem 1. Petrusbrief.* Gütersloh: Mohn, 1971.

Plumptre, E. H. *The General Epistles of St. Peter and St. Jude.* Cambridge: University Press, 1893.

——————. *Spirits in Prison and Other Studies On Life After Death.* London: W. Isbister, 1884.

Preisker, H. *Die Katholischen Briefe.* HNT 15. Tübingen: J. C. B. Mohr, 1951.

Price, J. J. H. ''Submission-Humility in 1 Peter: An Exegetical Study.'' Ph.D. dissertation, Vanderbilt University, 1977.

Purkiser, W. T. *Hebrews. James. Peter.* BBL 11. Kansas City MO: Beacon Hill, 1974.

Pury, R. *Ein Petrusbrief in der Gefangniszelle.* Zollikon-Zürich: Evangelischer, 1944.

Quanbeck, W. A. et al. *Revelation and The General Epistles. A Commentary on Hebrews, James, I & II Peter, I, II, & III John, Jude, Revelation.* ICC 8; Nashville: Abingdon, 1983.

Rees, P. S. *Triumphant in Trouble. Studies in 1 Peter*. Westwood NJ: Revell, 1962.

Reicke, B. *The Disobedient Spirits and Christian Baptism. A Study of 1 Pt. 3:19 and Its Context*. ASNU 13. Copenhagen: E. Munksgaard, 1946.

Rendtorff, H. *Getrostes Wandern, Eine Einführung in den ersten Brief des Petrus*. Hamburg: Furche, 1951.

Reuss, J. *Die Katholischen Briefe*. Wurzburg: n. p., 1959.

Rissi, M. *Die Taufe für die Toten*. ATANT 42. Zürich: n. p., 1962.

Rolston, H. *The Apostle Peter Speaks to Us Today*. Atlanta: John Knox, 1977.

Ryan, T. J. "The Word of God in First Peter; A Critical Study of 1 Peter 2:1-3." Ph.D. dissertation, Catholic University of America, 1973.

Salguerro, J. *Epistolas Catholicas*. Madrid: n. p., 1965.

Sander, E. T. "Purosis and the First Epistle of Peter 4:12." Ph.D. dissertation, Harvard University Press, 1967.

Scharfe, E. *Die Petrinische Strömung der Neutestamentlichen Literatur*. Berlin: Reuther and Richard, 1893.

Schelkle, K. H. *Die Petrusbriefe. Der Judasbrief*. Freiburg: Herder, 1963.

Schiwy, G. *Weg ins NT. Kommentar und Material. Bd. IV: Nach-Paulinen*. Wurzburg: Echter, 1970.

_____. *Die katholischen Briefe*. Aschaffenburg: Pattloch, 1973.

Schlatter, A. *Die Briefe des Petrus. Erläuterungen zum NT*. Berlin: n. p., 1953.

_____. *Petrus und Paulus nach dem ersten Petrusbrief*. Stüttgart: Calwer, 1937.

Schmidt, B. *Die Vorstellungen von der Höllenfahrt Christi in der alten Kirche*. N. p., 1906/07.

Schmidt, D. H. "The Peter Writings: Their Redactors and their Relationship." Ph.D. dissertation, Northwestern University, 1972.

Schmidt, K. W. Ch. *Die Darstellung von Christi Höllenfahrt in den deutschen und den ihnen verwandten Spielen des Mittelalters*. Marburg: n. p., 1915.

Schneider, J. *Die Kirchenbriefe*. NTD 10. Göttingen: Vandenhoeck and Ruprecht, 1967.

Schott, T. *Der Erste Brief Petri erklärt*. Erlangen: A. Deichert, 1861.

Schroger, F. *Gemeinde in 1. Petrusbrief*. RKT 1. Passau: Passavia, 1981.

Schutz, H. G. " 'Kirche' in spät-neutestamentlichen Zeit. Untersuchungen über das Selbstverständnis des Urchristentums an der Wende vom 1. zum 2. Jahrhundert anhand des 1 Petr., des Hebr. und der Past." Ph.D. dissertation, Bonn, 1964.

Schweizer, A. *Hinabgefahren zur Hölle als Mythus ohne biblische Begrundung durch Auslegung der Stelle 1 Petr. 3:17-22 nachgewiesen*. Zürich: n. p., 1868.

Schweizer, E. *Der erste Petrusbrief*. 3d ed. Zürich: Theologischer, 1973.

Selwyn, E. G. *The First Epistle of St. Peter*. 2d ed. London: Macmillan, 1946.

Senior, D. *1 and 2 Peter*. Wilmington DE: Glazier, 1980.

Shimada, K. "The Formulary Material in First Peter." Ph.D. dissertation, Union Theological Seminary, NY, 1966.

Skrade, C. E. "The Descent of the Servant: A Study of 1 Peter 3:13-4:6." Ph.D. dissertation, Union Theological Seminary in Virginia, 1966.

Soden, H. von. *Briefe des Petrus*. HKNT. Freiburg: J. C. B. Mohr, 1899.

Speyr, A. von. *Die Katholischen Briefe*. 2 vols. Einsiedeln: n. p., 1961.

——————. *Kreuz und Hölle*. Einsiedeln: n. p., 1966.

Spitta, F. *Die Predigt an die Geister (1 Petr. 3:19)*. Göttingen: Vandenhoeck & Ruprecht, 1890.

Sporri, T. *Der Gemeindegedanke im ersten Petrusbrief: Ein Beitrag zur Structur des urchristlichen Kirchenbegriffs*. Gutersloh: C. Bertelsmann, 1925.

Spoto, D. M. "Christ's Preaching to the Dead: An Exegesis of 1 Peter 3,19 and 4,6." Ph.D. dissertation, Fordham University, 1971.

Staffelbach, G. *Die Briefe der Apostel Jakobus, Judas, Petrus, und Johannes*. Lucerne: Räber, 1941.

Stegmann, A. *Silvanus als Missionar und "Hagiograph."* Rottenburg: W. Bader, 1917.

Steiger, W. *Der Erste Brief Petri mit Berücksichtigung des ganzen biblischen Lehrbegriffes ausgelegt*. Berlin: L. Oehmigke, 1832.

Stibbs, A. M., and A. F. Walls, *The First Epistle General of Peter*. London: Tyndale, 1959.

Stoeckhardt, G. *Kommentar über den ersten Brief Petri*. St. Louis: Concordia, 1912.

Stoger, A. *Bauleute Gottes. Der 1. Petrusbrief als Grundlegung des Laienapostolats*. LW 3. Munich: n. p., 1954.

Strynkowski, J. J. "The Descent of Christ among the Dead." Ph.D. dissertation, Pont. Univ. Gregorianae, 1972.

Testuz, M. *Papyrus Bodmer VII-IX: L'Epître de Jude. Les Epîtres de Pierre. Les Psaumes 33 et 34*. Cologne/Geneva: n. p., 1959.

Trempela, P. N. *Hypomnēma eis to epistolas tēs kainēs diathēkēs, tomos III: Hē pros Hebraious kai hai hepta katholikai*. Athens: n. p., 1956.

Turmel, J. *La descente du Christ aux Enfers*. Paris: Bloud et cie., 1908.

Unnik, W. C., Van. *De verlossing I Petrus 1:18, 19 en het probleem van den eersten Petrusbrief*. Amsterdam: Noord-hollandische. uitg mij., 1942.

Usteri, J. M. *"Hinabgefahren zur Hölle." Eine Wiedererwagung der Schriftstellen: 1 Petr. 3:18-22 und Kap. 4, Vers 6*. Zürich: S. Höhr, 1886.

——————. *Wissenschaftlicher und praktischer Kommentar über den ersten Petrusbrief*. Zürich: S. Höhr, 1887.

Vaccari, A. *Le Lettere cattoliche*. SB 9. Rome: n. p., 1958.

Valentine, F. *Hebrews, James, 1 & 2 Peter*. LBBC 23. Nashville: Broadman, 1981.

Van Kasteren. *De eerste brief van den apostel Petrus*. Hertogenbosch: n. p., 1911.

Vogels, H. J. *Christi Abstieg ins Totenreich und das Lauterungsgericht and den Toten.* Freiburg: Herder, 1976.

Volter, D. *Der erste Petrusbrief, seine Entstehung und Stellung in der Geschichte des Urchristentums.* Strassburg: Heitz and Mündel, 1906.

Von Balthasar, H. U. *Theologie der drei Tage.* Einsiedeln/Zürich: n. p., 1969.

Wand, J. W. C. *The General Epistles of St. Peter and St. Jude.* London: Methuen, 1934.

Watson, D. L. "The Implications of Christology and Eschatology for a Christian Attitude Toward the State in 1 Peter." Ph.D. dissertation, Hartford Seminary, 1970.

Weiss, B. *Der petrinische Lehrbegriff.* Berlin: n. p., 1855.

Wexels, W. A. *Aaben erklaering til mine Medkristne om min Anskuelse og Bekjendfelse angaaende Christi Nedfahrt till Helvede og Muligheden af en Omvendelse efter Doden.* N. p.: Christiania, 1845.

Wichmann, W. *Die Leidenstheologie. Eine Form der Leidensdeutung im Spätjudentum.* Stuttgart: W. Kohlhammer, 1930.

Wiesinger, A. *Der Erste Brief des Apostels Petrus.* Königsberg: n. p., 1856.

Wilson, C. A. *New Light on New Testament Letters.* Grand Rapids: Baker, 1975.

Windisch, H. *Die Katholischen Briefe.* 3rd ed. HNT. Tübingen: Mohr, 1951.

Wohlenberg, G. *Der erste und zweite Petrusbrief.* KNT. Leipzig: n. p., 1923.

Zezschwitz, C. A. G. von. *Petri Apostole de Christi ad inferas descensu sententia ex loco nobilissimo. I ep. III, 19 erata, exacta and epistolae argumentum.* Lipsiae: Ackermanni et Glaseri, 1857.

II. ARTICLES

Aalen, S. "Oversettelsen av ortet *eperōtēma* i dapstedet 1 Petr. 3:21." *TTKi* 43 (1972): 161-75.

Agnew, F. H. "1 Peter 1:2—An Alternative Translation." *CBQ* 45:1 (1983): 68-73.

Arvedson, "*Syneideseos agathēs eperōtēma* (1 Petr. 3:21). "*SEA* 15 (1950): 55-61.

Ashcraft, M. "Theological Themes in I Peter." *TE* 13:1 (1982): 55-62.

Bammel, E. "The Commands in 1 Peter 2:17." *NTS* 11 (1964-1965): 279-81.

Barr, J. "*b'rs-molis:* Prov. 9:31, 1 Pet. 4:18." *JSS* 20 (1975): 149-64.

Bauer, J. B. "Aut maleficius aut alieni speculator (1 Petr. 4, 15)." *BZ* 22 (1978): 109-15.

Beare, F. W. "The Teaching of First Peter." *ATR* 26 (1944/1945): 284-96.

Bernhard, J. H. "The Descent into Hades and Christian Baptism (A Study of 1 Peter 3:19ff.)." *Expositor* 8/11 (1916): 241-74.

Best, E. "Spiritual Sacrifice. General Priesthood in the New Testament." *Int* 14 (1960): 273-99.

——————. "1 Peter 2:4-10—A Reconsideration." *NovT* 11 (1969): 270-93.

——————. "1 Peter and the Gospel Tradition." *NTS* 16 (1969/1970): 95-113.

Biser, E. "Abgestiegen zu der Hölle." MTZ 9 (1959): 205-11.

Bishop, E. F. "*Oligoi* in 1 Peter 3:20." *CBQ* 13 (1951): 44-45.

Blagen, I. T. "Suffering and Cessation from Sin According to 1 Peter 4:1." *AUSS* 21:1 (1983): 27-50.

Blevins, J. L. "Introduction to 1 Peter." *RevExp* 79:3 (1982): 401-13.

Blinzer, J. "*Perateuma*. Zur Exegese von 1 Petr. 2:5 u. 9." *Episcopus*. Regensburg: n. p., 1949, 49-65.

Boismard, M. E. "Une Liturgie baptismale dans la Prima Petri." *RB* 63 (1956): 182-208; 64 (1957): 161-83.

——————. "Pierre (Première épître de)." *DBSup* 7 (1966): 1415-55.

Bojorge, H. "Fundamentacion y narmas de la conducta cristiana segun la la carta de Pedro." *RevistB* 37 (1975): 269-77.

Bolkestein, M. H. "De Kerk in haar vremdelingschap volgens de eerste brief van Petrus." *NieuweTS* 25 (1942): 181-94.

Boolyer, G. H. "The Indebtedness of 2 Peter to 1 Peter." *New Testament Essays: Studies in Memory of T. W. Manson* (ed. A. J. B. Higgins; Manchester: n. p., 1959).

Borchert, G. L. "The Conduct of Christians in the Face of The 'Fiery Ordeal' (4:2-5:11)." *RE* 79:3 (1982): 451-62.

Bornemann, W. "Der erste Petrusbrief—eine Taufrede des Silvanus?" *ZNW* 19 (1919/20): 143-65.

Bornhauser, K. "Jesus Predigt für die Geister." *Allg. Evangel. Luth. Kirchen-Zeitung* 54 (1921): cols. 322-24.

Bousset, W. "Zur Hadesfahrt Christi." *ZNW* 19 (1919/1920): 50-66.

Bovon, F. "Foi chrétienne et religion populaire dans la première épître de Pierre." *ETR* 53 (1978): 25-41.

Brandt, W. "Wandel als Zeugnis nach dem 1. Petrusbrief." *Verbum Dei manet in aeternum*. Witten: n. p., 1953.

Brooks, O. S. "1 Peter 3:21—The Clue to the Literary Structure of the Epistle." *NovT* 16 (1974): 290-305.

Brown, J. P. "Synoptic Parallels in the Epistles and Form-History." *NTS* 10 (1963/1964): 27-48.

Brox, N. "Zur pseudepigraphischen Rahmung des ersten Petrusbriefes." *BZ* 19 (1975): 78-96.

——————. "Situation und Sprache der Minderheit im ersten Petrusbrief." *Kairos* 19 (1977): 1-13.

——————. "Tendenz und Pseudepigraphie im ersten Petrusbrief." *Kairos* 20 (1978): 110-20.

——————. "Der erste Petrusbrief in der literarischen Tradition des Urchristentums." *Kairos* 20 (1978): 182-92.

Bruni, G. "La communita christiana nella prima lettera di Petro." *Servitium* 7 (1973): 278-86.

Bultmann, R. "Bekenntnis und Liedfragmente im 1. Petrusbrief." *ConNT* 11 (1947): 1-14.

Cabrol, F. "Descente du Christ aux enfers d'après la liturgie." *DACL* 4:1 (Paris: n. p., 1920): cols. 682-93.

Carrington, P. "St. Peter's Epistle." *The Joy of Study (Papers on New Testament and Related Subjects Presented to F. C. Grant)*. NY: n. p., 1951, 57-63.

Cerfaux, L. "Regale sacerdotium." *Recueil Lucien Cerfaux II.BETL* 7 (Gembloux: n. p., 1954): 283-315.

Chase, F. H. "Peter, First Epistle of." *Dictionary of the Bible* (ed. J. Hastings; n. p.), 3. 1898-1904.

Chevallier, M. A. "1 Pierre 1/1 à 2/10: structure littéraire et conséquences exégétiques." *RHPR* 51 (1971): 129-42.

——————. "Condition et vocation des chrétiens en diaspora: remarques exégétiques sur la lre épître de Pierre." *RSR* 48 (1974): 387-400.

Choine, J. "Descente du Christ aux enfers." *DBSup* 2 (Paris: n. p., 1934): cols. 395-431.

Clark, S. D. "Persecution and the Christian Faith." *TE* 13:1 (1982): 72-82.

Clemen, C. "Die Einheitlichkeit des 1. Petrusbriefes verteidigt." *TSK* 77 (1905): 619-28.

Colecchia, L. F. "Rilievi su 1 Piet. 2:4-10." *RevistB* 25 (1977): 179-94.

Combrink, H. J. B. "The Structure of 1 Peter." *Neot* 9 (1975): 34-63.

Cook, D. "1 Peter 3:20: An Unnecessary Problem." *JTS* 31 (1980): 72-78.

Coppens, J. "Le sacerdoce royal des fidèles: Un commentaire de 1 Pie. 2:4-10." *Au service de la Parole de Dieu: Mélanges offerts à Msgr. André-Marie Charue*. Gembloux: Duculot, 1969, 61-75.

Cothenet, E. "Le sacerdoce des fidèles d'après la la Petrie." *Esprit et Vie* 11 (1969): 169-73.

——————. "Liturgie et vie chrétienne d'après 1 Pierre." *Conférences Saint-Serge* 25 (n. d.) 97-113.

——————. "Le realisme de l'esperance chretienne selon I Pierre." *NTS* 27:4 (1981): 564-72.

Coutts, J. "Ephesians 1:3-14 and 1 Peter 1:3-12." *NTS* 3 (1956): 115-27.

Cramer, J. "Exegetica et critica. Het glossematisch karacter van 1. Petr. 3:19-21 en 4:6." *Nieuwe Bijdragen* 7 (1891): 73-149.

Cranfield, C. E. B. "The Interpretation of 1 Peter 3:19 and 4:6." *ExpTim* 62 (1957/1958): 369-72.

Dalton, W. J. "Interpretation and Tradition: An Example from 1 Peter." *Greg* 49 (1967): 17-37.

——————. "The Interpretation of 1 Peter 3:19 and 4:6: Light from 2 Peter." *Bib* 60 (1979): 547-55.

——————. "The Church in 1 Peter." *TY* (1981-1982): 79-91.

Danker, F. "1 Peter 1:24-2:17—A Consolatory Pericope." *ZNW* 58 (1967): 93-102.

———. "Brief Study." *CTM* 38 (1967): 329-32.

Daube, D. "*Kerdainō* as a Missionary Term." *HTR* 40 (1947): 109-20.

Dautzenberg, G. "*Sōtēria psychōn* (1 Pet. 1:9)." *BZ* 8 (1964): 262-76.

Davies, P. E. "Primitive Christology in 1 Peter." *Festschrift to Honor F. W. Gingrich.* Leiden: n. p., 1972, 115-22.

Delling, G. "Der Bezug der christlichen Existenz auf das Heilshandeln Gottes nach dem ersten Petrusbrief." *Neues Testament und christliche Existenz.* Tübingen: n. p., 1973, 95-113.

DeVilliers, J. L. "Joy and Suffering in 1 Peter." *Neot* 9 (1975): 64-86.

Diest, F. E. "Van die duisternis tot sy merkwaardige lig' (1 Petr. 2:9) in die lig van Elephantine." *WGTT* 11 (1970): 44-48.

Dinkler, E. "Die Taufaussagen des Neuen Testaments." *Zu Karl Barths Lehre von der Taufe.* Gütersloh: n. p., 1971, 60-153.

Elliott, J. H. "Death of a Slogan: From Royal Priests to Celebrating Community." *US* 25 (1968): 18-31.

———. "Ministry and Church Order in the NT: A Traditio-Historical Analysis (1 Pt. 5:15 & plls.)." *CBQ* 32 (1970): 367-91.

———. "The Rehabilitation of an Exegetical Step-Child: 1 Peter in Recent Research." *JBL* 95 (1976): 243-54.

———. "Salvation and Exhortation to Christian Behavior on the Basis of God's Blessings (1:1-2:10)." *RE* 79:3 (1982): 415-25.

Fascher, E. "Petrus" *Sokrates und Christus.* Beiträge zur Religionsgeschichte. Leipzig: n. p., 1959, 175-223.

Felten, J. "Zur predigt Jesu an 'die Geister im Gefängnis,' 1 Petr. 3:19 und 4:6." *Festschrift der Vereinigung katholischer Theologen "Aurelia."* Bonn: n. p., 1926.

Feuillet, A. "Les 'sacrifices spirituels' du sacerdoce royal des baptistes (1 P. 2:5) et leur préparation dans l'Ancien Testament." *NRT* 96 (1974): 704-28.

Filson, F. "Partakers with Christ. Suffering in First Peter." *Int* 9 (1955): 400-12.

Fitzmyer, J., S.J. "The First Epistle of Peter." *JBC* (1968): 362-68.

Foster, O. D. "The Literary Relations of 'The First Epistle of Peter,' with their Bearings on Date and Place of Authorship." *Trans. Conn. Aca. Ar. Sc.* 18 (n. d.) n. pp.

Fransen, I. "Une homélie chrétienne: la première Epître de Pierre." *BVC* (1960): 28-38.

Frattallone, R. "Anthropologia naturale e suprannaturale nella prima lettera di San Pietro." *Studia Moralia* 5 (1967): 41-111.

Fridrichsen, A. "1 Peter 3:7." *SEA* 12 (1947): 143-47.

Frings, J. "Zu 1 Petr. 3:19 und 4:6." *BZ* 17 (1925/26): 75-88.

Fronmuller, G. F. C. "The First Epistle General of Peter." *Langes Commentary on the Holy Scriptures.* Grand Rapids: Zondervan, n. d.

Furnish, V. "Elect Sojourners in Christ: An Approach to the Theology of 1 Peter." *PSTJ* 28 (1975): 1-11.

Gamba, G. G. "L'Evangelista Marco Segretario-'Interprete' della prima lettera di Petro?" *Sal* 44:1-2 (1982): 61-70.

Ganschinietz, R. "*Katabasis*." *PW* (1919): cols. 2359-449.

Glaze, R. E. "Introduction to 1 Peter." *TE* 13:1 (1982): 23-34.

Goldstein, H. "Die politischen Paranesen in 1 Petr. 3 und Rom. 13" *BibLeb* 14 (1973): 88-104.

_____. "Die Kirche als Schar derer, die ihrem leidenden Herrn mit dem Ziel der Gottesgemeinschaft nachfolgen. Zum Gemeinderverständnis von 1 Petr. 2:21-25 und 3:18-22." *BibLeb* 15 (1974): 38-54.

Goppelt, L. "Prinzipien neutestamentlicher Sozialethik nach dem 1. Petrusbrief." *Neues Testament und Geschichte* (ed. H. Baltensweiler and B. Reicke; Zürich: Theologischer; Tübingen: Mohr, 1972) 285-96.

Gundry, R. "Verba Christi in 1 Peter: Their Implications Concerning the Authorship of 1 Peter and the Authenticity of the Gospel Tradition." *NTS* 13 (1966/1967): 336-50.

_____. "Further Verba on Verba Christi in First Peter." *Bib* 55 (1974): 211-32.

Hall, R. "For to This You Have Been Called: The Cross and Suffering in 1 Peter." *RestorQuart* 19 (1976): 137-47.

Hanson, A. T. "Salvation Proclaimed: I. 1 Peter 3:18-22." *ET* 93:4 (1982): 100-105.

Harris, J. R. "A Further Note on the Use of Enoch in 1 Peter." *Expositor* 6 (1901): 346-49.

_____. "On a Recent Emendation in the Text of St. Peter." *Expositor* 6 (1902): 317-20.

_____. "Two Flood Hymns of the Early Church." *Expositor* 8 (1911): 405-17.

Hart, J. H. "The First Epistle of Peter." *Expositor's Greek Testament*. Grand Rapids: Eerdmans, 1961, n. pp.

Hatas, S. "Sens dynamique de l'expression *laos eis peripoiēsin* en 1 P 2, 9." *Bib* 65:2 (1984): 254-58.

Heimer, C. J. "The Address of 1 Peter." *ExpTim* 89 (1978): 239-43.

Hiebert, D. E. "Peter's Thanksgiving for Our Salvation." *SM* 29 (1980): 85-103.

_____. "Selected Studies from 1 Peter. Part 1: Following Christ's Example: An Exposition of 1 Peter 2:21-25." *BSac* 139:553 (1982): 32-45.

_____. "Selected Studies from 1 Peter. Part 2: The Suffering and Triumphant Christ: An Examination of 1 Peter 3:18-22." *BSac* 139:554 (1982): 146-58.

_____. "Selected Studies from 1 Peter. Part 3: Living in the Light of Christ's Return: An Exposition of 1 Peter 4:7-11." *BSac* 139:555 (1982): 243-54.

_____. "Selected Studies from 1 Peter. Part 4: Counsel for Christ's Undershepherds: An Exposition of 1 Peter 5:1-14." *BSac* 139:556 (1982): 330-41.

Hill, D. "On Suffering and Baptism in 1 Peter." *NovT* 18 (1976): 181-89.

_____. " 'To Offer Spiritual Sacrifices . . . ' (1 Peter 2:5): Liturgical Formulations and Christian Paraenesis in 1 Peter." *JSNT* 16 (1982): 45-63.

Hillyer, N. "First Peter and the Feast of Tabernacles." *TB* 21 (1970): 39-70.

_____. " 'Rock-Stone' Imagery in 1 Peter." *TB* 22 (1971): 58-81.

Holtzmann, H. "Höllenfahrt im Neuen Testament." *ARW* 11 (1908): 285-97.

Hunzinger, C. H. "Babylon als Deckname für Rom und die Datierung des 1. Petrusbriefes." *Gottes Wort und Gottes Land*. Göttingen: n. p., 1965, 67-77.

_____. "Zur Struktur der Christus-Hymnen in Phil. 2 und 1 Petr. 3." *Der Ruf Jesu und die Antwort der Gemeinde*. Göttingen: n. p. 1970, 142-56.

Huther, J. E. "Epistles of Peter and Jude." *Kommentar zum Neuen Testament* (ed. H. A. W. Meyer; n. p., 1873-1880) n. pp.

Jeremias, J. "Zwischen Kartfreitag und Ostern. Descensus und Ascensus in der Kartfreitagstheologie des Neuen Testaments." *ZNW* 42 (1949): 194-201.

Johnson, S. E. "Preaching to the Dead." *JBL* 79 (1960): 48-51.

Jones, P. R. "Teaching First Peter." *RevExp* 79:3 (1982): 463-72.

Jonsen, A. R. "The Moral Teaching of the First Epistle of St. Peter." *Sciences Ecclesiastiques* 16 (1964): 93-105.

Josephson, H. "Niedergefahren zur Hölle." *Der Beweis des Glaubens* 33 (1897): 400-18.

Kasemann, E. "Eine urchristliche Taufliturgie." *Festschrift für Rudolf Bultmann*. Stuttgart: n. p., 1949, 133-48.

Kayalaparampil, T. "Christian Suffering in 1 Peter." *Biblehashyam* 3 (1977): 7-19.

Ketter, P. "Das allgemeine Priestertum der Glaubigen nach dem 1. Petrusbrief." *TTZ* 56 (1947): 43-51.

Kirkpatrick, W. D. "The Theology of First Peter." *SWJT* 25:1 (1982): 58-81.

Kline, L. "Ethics for the Endtime: An Exegesis of 1 Pt. 4:7-11." *RestorQuar* 7 (1963): 113-23.

Knapp. P. "1 Petri 3:17ff. und die Höllenfahrt Jesu Christi." *Jahrbücher fur Deutsche Theologie* 23 (1978): 177-228.

Knox, J. "Pliny and 1 Peter: A Note on 1 Pt. 4:14-16 and 3:15." *JBL* 72 (1953): 187-89.

Kohler, M. E. "La communauté des chrétiens selon la première épître de Pierre." *RTP* 114:1 (1982): 1-21.

Kokot, M. "Znaczenie 'nasienia niezniszizalnego' w 1 P. 1:23." *CT* 44 (1974): 35-44.

Krafft, E. "Christologie und Anthropologie im 1. Petrusbrief." *EvT* 10 (1950/1951): 120-26.

Kramer, S. N. "Innana's Descent to the Nether World. The Sumerian Version of 'Istar's Descent'." *RA* 34 (1937): 93-134.

Kühschelm, R. " 'Lebendige Hoffnung' (1 Petr. 1, 3-12)." *BL* 56:4 (1983): 202-206.

Kuss, O. "Zur paulinischen und nachpaulinischen Tauflehre im Neuen Testament." *Auslegung und Verkundigung I*. Regensburg: n. p., 1963, 121-50.

Lauterburg, M. "Höllenfahrt Christi." *RE* (3d rd.; Leipzig: n. p., 1900) 7. 199-206.

La Verdiere, E. A. "A Grammatical Ambiguity in 1 Pet. 1:23." *CBQ* 36 (1974): 89-94.

Lea, T. "1 Peter-Outline and Exposition." *SWJT* 1 (1982): 17-45.

Leaney, A. R. C. "1 Peter and the Passover: An Interpretation." *NTS* 10 (1963/1964): 238-51.

Lippert, P. "Leben als Zeugnis. Ein Beiträg des ersten Petrusbriefes zur pastoral-theologischen Problematik der Gegenwart." *Studia Moralia* III. Rome: n. p., 1965, 226-68.

Lohse, E. "Paranese und Kerygma im 1 Petrusbrief." *ZNW* 45 (1954): 68-89.

Loofs, F. "Descent to Hades (Christ's)." *Encyclopedia of Religion and Ethics IV*. NY: Charles Scribner & Sons, 1924.

Love, J. P. "The First Epistle of Peter." *Int* 8 (1954): 63-87.

Lumly, J. R. "1 Peter 3:17." *Expositor* 1 (1890): 142-47.

Malherbe, A. J. "The Apologetic Theology of the Preaching of Peter." *RQ* 13 (1970): 205-23.

Manns, F. "Sara, modele de la femme obeissante. Etude de l'Arriere-Plan Juif de 1 Pierre 3, 5-6." *BO* 26:2 (1984): 65-73.

Manson, T. W. "Review of E. G. Selwyn, *The First Epistle of Peter*." *JTS* 47 (1946): 218-27.

Martin, R. P. "The Composition of 1 Peter in Recent Study." *Vox Evangelica: Biblical and Historical Essays by Members of the Faculty of the London Bible College,* ed. R. P. Martin (London: Epworth, 1962) 29-42.

Massaux, E. "Le Texte de la la Petri du Papyrus Bodmer viii." *Melanges G. Rychmans*. Louvain: n. p., 1963, n. pp.

McCaughey, J. D. "Three 'Persecution Documents' of the New Testament." *AusBR* 17 (1969): 27-40.

_____. "On Re-Reading 1 Peter." *ABR* 31 (1983): 33-44.

Miller, D. G. "Deliverance and Destiny. Salvation in First Peter." *Int* 9 (1955): 413-25.

Minear, P. S. "The House of Living Stones. A Study of 1 Peter 2:4-12." *ER* 34:3 (1982): 238-48.

Mitton, C. L. "The Relationship Between 1 Peter and Ephesians." *JTS* 1 (1950): 67-73.

Moule, C. F. D. "Some Reflections on the 'Stone Testimonia' in Relation to the Name Peter." *NTS* 2 (1955/1956): 56-59.

—————. "The Nature and Purpose of 1 Peter." *NTS* 3 (1956/1957): 1-11.

Mounce, R. H. *A Living Hope: A Commentary on 1 and 2 Peter*. Grand Rapids: Eerdmans, 1982.

Nauck, W. "Freude im Leiden, Zum Problem einer urchristlichen Verfolgungstradition." *ZNW* 46 (1955): 68-80.

—————. "Probleme des frühchristlichen Amtverständnisses (1 Petr. 5:2 ff.)." *ZNW* 48 (1957): 200-20.

Neugebauer, F. "Zur Deutung und Bedeutung des 1. Petrusbriefes." *NTS* 26 (1979): 61-86.

Neyrey, J. H. "First Peter and Converts." *BibTod* 22:1 (1984): 13-18.

Nixon, R. E. "The Meaning of 'Baptism' in 1 Peter 3:21." *SE* 4 (1968): 437-41.

Odeberg, H. "Nederstigen till dodsriket." *Bibliskt Manadshafte* 18:12 (1944): 357-59.

Odland, S. "Kristi praediken for 'aanderne i forvaring' (1 Petr. 3:19)." *NorTT* 2 (1901): 116-44, 185-229.

Omanson, R. "Suffering for Righteousness' Sake (3:13-4:11) *RE* 79:3 (1982): 439-50.

Osborne, T. P. "L'utilisation des citations de l'Ancien Testament dans la première épître de Pierre." *RTL* 12:1 (1981): 64-77.

—————. "Guidelines for Christian Suffering: A Source-Critical and Theological Study of 1 Peter 2, 21-25." *Bib* 64:3 (1983): 381-408.

Patsch, H. "Zum alttestamentlichen Hintergrund von Rom. 4:25 und 1. Petrus 2:24." *ZNW* 60 (1969): 273-79.

Patterson, D. K. "Roles in Marriage: A Study in Submission: 1 Peter 3:1-7." *TE* 13:2 (1983): 70-79.

Perkins, D. W. "Simon Rock: An Appraisal of Peter in the New Testament Witness." *TE* 13:1 (1982): 42-54.

Pfitzner, V. C. " 'General Priesthood' and Ministry." *LTJ* 5 (1971): 97-110.

Piper, J. "Hope as the Motivation of Love: 1 Peter 3:9-12." *NTS* 26 (1980): 212-31.

Plooij, D. "De Descensus in 1 Petrus 3:19 en 4:6." *TT* 47 (1913): 145-62.

Quillet, H. "Descente de Jesus aux enfers." *DTC* (Paris: n. p., 1911): 4. cols. 565-619.

Radermacher, L. "Der erste Petrusbrief und Silvanus." *ZNW* 25 (1926): 287-99.

Ramos, F. F. "El sacerdocio de los creyentes (1 Pet. 2:4-10)." *Teologia del sacerdocio*. Burgos: Ediciones Aldecoa, 1970, 11-47.

Ramsey, J. R. "Eschatology in 1 Peter 3:17." *NTS* 13 (1966/1967): 394-401.

Refoule, F. "Bible et éthique sociale. Lire aujourd'hui 1 Pierre." *Supple-ment* 131 (1979): 457-82.

Reicke, B. "Die Gnosis der Manner nach 1 Petr. 3:17." Neutestamentliche Studien für R. Bultmann. *BZNW* 21 (Berlin: n. p., 1954): 296-304.

Richards, G. C. "1 Pet. 3:21." *JTS* 32 (1931): 77.

Robertson, P. E. "Is 1 Peter a Sermon?" *TE* 13:1 (1982): 35-41.

Rodding, G. "Descendit ad inferna." *Kerygma und Melos.* Berlin/Hamburg: n. p., 1970, 95-102.

Rubinkiewicz, R. " 'Duchy Zamkniete w urezieniu. Interpretacja 1 P 3, 19 w swielte Hen 10, 4.12." *RTK* 28:1 (1981): 77-86.

Russell, B. "Eschatology and Ethics in 1 Peter." *EvQ* 47 (1975): 78-84.

Scharlemann, M. H. "Why the *Kyriou* in 1 Peter 1:25?" *CMT* 30:5 (1959): 352-56.

Schattenmann, J. "The Little Apocalypse of the Synoptics and the First Epis-tle of Peter." *Today* 11 (1954): 193-98.

Schelkle, K. H. "Das Leiden des Gottes-Knechtes als Form christlichen Le-bens (nachdem 1 Petrusbrief). *Wort und Schrift.* Düsseldorf: n. p., 1966, 162-65.

Schlosser, J. "1 Pierre 3, 5b-6." *Bib* 64:3 (1983): 409-10.

Schmidt, P. "Zwei Fragen zum ersten Petrusbrief." *ZWT* 1 (1908): 24-52.

Schnackenburg, R. "Episkopos und Hirtenamt." *Schriften zum Neuen Tes-tament.* Munich: n. p., 1971, 247-67.

Schroger, F. "Die Verfassung der Gemeinde des ersten Petrusbriefes." *Kirche im Werden,* ed. J. Hainz (Munich: n. p., 1976): 239-52.

Schwank, B. "Wie Freiaber als Sklaven Gottes (1 Petr. 2:16) Das Verhältnis der Christen zur Staatsmacht nach dem ersten Petrusbrief." *Erbe und Auftrag* 36 (1960): 5-12.

——————. "Diabolus tamquam leo rugiens (1 Petr. 5:8)." *Erbe und Auftrag* 38 (1962): 15-20.

——————. "Le 'chretien normal' selon le Nouveau Testament. 1 P. 4:13-16." *AsSeign* 29 (1973): 26-30.

——————. "Des elements mythologiques dans une profession de foi. 1 P. 3:18-22." *AsSeign* 29 (1973): 41-44.

Schweizer, E. "1 Petrus 4:6." *TZ* 8 (1952): 152-54.

Scott, C. A. "The 'Suffering of Christ.' A Note on 1 Peter 1:11." *Expositor* 6:12 (1905): 234-40.

Selwyn, E. G. "Unsolved New Testament Problems: The Problem of the Au-thorship of 1 Peter." *ExpTim* 59 (1948): 256-59.

——————. "Eschatology in 1 Peter." *The Background of the New Testament and Its Eschatology,* ed. W. D. Davies & D. Daube. Cam-bridge: University Press, 1964, 374-401.

——————. "The Persecutions in 1 Peter." *SNTS* (1950): 39-45.

Senior, D. "The Conduct of Christians in the World (2:11-3:12) *RE* 79:3 (1982): 427-38.

——————. "The First Letter of Peter." *BibTod* 22:1 (1984): 5-12.

Shimada, K. "The Christological Creedal Formula in 1 Peter 3:18-22—Reconsidered." *AnnJapanBibInst* 5 (1979): 154-76.

——————. "A Critical Note on 1 Peter 1, 12." *AJBI* 7 (1981): 146-50.

Sieffert, E. A. "Die Heilsbedeutung des Leidens und Sterbens Christi nach dem ersten Briefe des Petrus." *Jahrbucher für Deutsche Theol.* 20 (1975): 371-440.

Sleeper, C. F. "Political Responsibility According to 1 Peter." *NovT* 10 (1968): 270-86.

Smith, M. L. "1 Peter 3:21. *Eperōtēma.*" *ET* 24 (1912/1913): 46-49.

Snodgrass, K. R. "1 Peter 2:1-10: Its Formation and Literary Affinities." *NTS* 24 (1977): 97-106.

Soltau, W. "Die Einheitlichkeit des 1 Petrusbriefes." *TSK* 79 (1906): 456-60.

Soucek, J. B. "Das Gegenüber von Gemeinde und Welt nach dem ersten Petrusbrief." *Communio Viatorum* 3 (1960): 5-13.

Spicq, C. "*Agapē, agapaō* dans les Epîtres de saint Pierre et de saint Jude." *Agapē dans le Nouveau Testament: Analyse des Textes,* ed. C. Spicq. Paris: n. p., 1959, 2, chap. 5.

——————. "La la Petri et la temoignage evangelique de saint Pierre." *ST* 20 (1966): 37-61.

Stolt, J. "Isogogiske problemer verdrørende 1. Petersbrev." *DTT* 44:3 (1981): 166-73.

Streeter, B. H. "First Peter." B. H. Streeter, *The Primitive Church* (London: Macmillan, 1929).

Strobel, A. "Macht Leiden von Sunde frei? Zur problematik von 1 Petr. 4:1 f." *ThZ* 19 (1963): 412-25.

Sylva, D. "1 Peter Studies: The State of the Discipline." *BTB* 10 (1980): 155-63.

——————. "Translating and Interpreting 1 Peter 3:2." *BT* 34:1 (1983): 144-47.

——————. "A 1 Peter Bibliography." *JETS* 25:1 (1982): 75-89.

Synge, F. C. "1 Peter 3:18-21." *ExpTim* 82:10 (1971): 311.

Tarrech, A. P. "Le milieu de la Première épître de Pierre." *RCT* 5:1 (1980): 95-129.

——————. "Le milieu de la première épître de pierre (continuation)." *RCT* 5:1 (1980): 331-402.

Thils, G. "L'enseignement de S. Pierre." *EBib* (Paris: n. p., 1943), n. pp.

Thompson, J. W. and Elliott, J. H. "Peter in the New Testament: Old Theme, New Views." *America* 130 (1974): 53-54.

Thornton, T. C. G. "1 Peter, a Paschal Liturgy?" *JTS* 12 (1961): 14-26.

Thurston, R. W. "Interpreting First Peter." *JETS* 17 (1974): 171-82.

Tiede, D. L. "An Easter Catechesis: The Lessons of 1 Peter." *WW* 4:2 (1984): 192-201.

Tripp. D. H. "*Eperōtēma* (1 Peter 3:21). A Liturgist's Note." *ET* 92:9 (1981): 267-70.

Unnik, W. C. van. "Peter, First Epistle of." *IDB*, 3. 758-66.

_____. "The Teaching of Good Works in 1 Peter." *NTS* 1 (1954/1955): 92-110.

_____. "A Classical Parallel to 1 Peter 2:14 and 20." *NTS* 2 (1955/1956): 198-202.

_____. "Christianity According to 1 Peter." *ExpTim* 68 (1956/1957): 79-83.

_____. "The Critique of Paganism in 1 Peter 1:18." *Neotestamentica et Semitica*, ed. E. Ellis and M. Wilcox (Edinburgh: T. & T. Clark, 1969) 129-42.

Vallauri, E. " 'Succencti lumbos mentis vestrae (1 Piet. 1, 13) nota per una traduzione." *BO* 24:1 (1982): 19-22.

Vanhoye, A. "La foi qui construit l'Eglise. 1 P. 2:4-9." *AsSeign* 26 (1973): 12-17.

Vidigal, J. R. "A Catequese Baptismal no Primeira de Sao Oedro." *RCB* S:19-20 (1981): 76-84.

Vitti, A. "Eschatologia in Petri epistula prima." *VD* 11 (1931): 298-306.

Volkmar, G. "Über die katholischen Briefe und Henoch." *ZWT* 4 (1961): 422-36.

Von Balthasar, H. U. "Abstieg zur Hölle." *TQ* 150 (1970): 193-201.

Vrede, W. "Miscellen, 3: Bemerkungen zu Harnacks Hypothese über die Addresse des 1. Petrusbriefs." *ZNW* 1 (1900): 75-85.

_____. "Der erste Petrusbrief," *Die katholischen Briefe*, ed. M. Meinertz and W. Vrede. (Bonn: n. p., 1932) n. pp.

Wand, J. W. C. "The Lessons of First Peter. A Survey of Recent Interpretation." *Int* 9 (1959): 387-99.

Wifstrand, A. "Stylistic Problems in the Epistles of James and Peter." *ST* 1 (1948): 170-82.

Willmering, H. "The First Epistle of St. Peter." *A Catholic Commentary on Holy Scripture*, ed. B. Orchard et al. (London; n. p., 1953) 1177-80.

Winberry, C. L. "Ethical Issues in 1 Peter." *TE* 13:1 (1982): 63-71.

_____. "Introduction to the First Letter of Peter." *SWJT* 25:1 (1982): 3-16.

Wolff, C. "Christ und Welt im 1 Petrusbrief." *TLZ* 100 (1975): 333-42.

CHAPTER 3

"PARENESIS AND KERYGMA IN 1 PETER"

EDUARD LOHSE
EVANGELICAL CHURCH OF HANOVER
HANOVER, GERMANY

TRANSLATED BY JOHN STEELY

In recent years three new scholarly commentaries on 1 Peter have appeared, altogether independent of each other.[1] In addition to these, there have been several briefer studies and essays[2] that are devoted to specific problems in 1 Peter. The views and conclusions that are set forth in those works are so sharply divergent from each other on specific points that the question must be raised once again as to the proper way to interpret the content and the character of this epistle.

Zeitschrift für die neutestamentliche Wissenschaft 45 (1954): 68-89.

[1]E. G. Selwyn, *The First Epistle of St. Peter,* London 1946, 2d, 3d ed., 1949; F. W. Beare, *The First Epistle of Peter,* Oxford 1947; H. Windisch, *Die katholischen Briefe,* 3d ed., significantly revised by H. Preisker, Tübingen 1951.

[2]Here mention may be made, among others, of R. Bultmann, "Bekenntnis- und Liedfragmente im I Petrus," *ConNT* 11 (1947): 1-14; W. Bieder, "Grund und Kraft der Mission nach dem I Petrus," *Theologische Studien* 29, Zürich 1950; E. Krafft, "Christologie und Anthropologie im 1. Petrusbrief," *EvT* (1950): 120-26; L. Mitton, "The Relationship between 1 Peter and Ephesians," *JTS* (1950): 67-73; T. Aroedson, "Syneideseos agathes eperotema, En studie till I Ptr 3:21," *SEÅ* (1950): 55-61. On Christ's descent into Hades: Bo Reicke, "The Disobedient Spirits and Christian Baptism," *Act. Sem. Neot. Upsal. XIII,* Lund 1946; J. Jeremias, "Zwischen Karfreitag und Ostern," *ZNW* (1949): 194-201; W. Bieder, *Die Vorstellung von der Höllenfahrt Jesu Christi* (ATANT 19; Zürich, 1949).

I

Earlier exegesis thrust the question of authenticity into the foreground of interest. The question then was usually answered by the view that Silvanus had composed the epistle under the commission of the apostle (5:12); on this point one should consult the very detailed statements in Theodor Zahn's *Einleitung in das Neue Testament* (3rd ed.; Leipzig/Erlangen, 1924, II, 1-43). Alongside this, the problem of what material lies back of the writing and how this material has been reworked was first taken up by R. Perdelwitz.[3] Citing documentation from the mystery religions, Perdelwitz advanced the thesis that the writing is composed of two originally independent parts; 1:3-4:11 formed a baptismal sermon that has been expanded in 1:1-2 and 4:12-5:14 with a later hortatory writing which the same author addressed to the suffering Christians in Asia Minor. This thesis has been widely accepted,[4] adopted—though with some reservations—by such commentators as H. Windisch,[5] F. Hauck,[6] and, most recently, F. W. Beare. Beare sees the basic element of the writing as a baptismal discourse that is of slightly earlier origin than the epistle, which was composed in Rome *circa* A.D. 111/112 in view of the threatened persecutions that we know about from Pliny's letter to Trajan.[7] The baptismal discourse has been utilized and revised for this purpose. In his exegesis Beare sees it as his task to offer to the English reader for the first time a commentary maintaining the thesis "that First Peter is a pseudonymous work of the post-apostolic age" (IX). What this commentary achieves is the mediation to other countries of the position of earlier exegesis in Germany, but it does not go

---

[3]"Die Mysterienreligion und das Problem des I. Petrusbriefes," Religionsgeschichtliche Versuche und Vorarbeiten XI, 3, Giessen 1911. On the debate with Perdelwitz's argument cf. most recently Selwyn, *First Peter,* 305-11: "1 Peter and the Mystery Religions."

[4]On the problem of the baptismal sermon cf. W. Bornemann, "Der I Ptr—eine Taufpredigt des Silvanus?" *ZNW* (1919/20): 143-65; 1 Pet. 1:3-5:11 is thought to represent a baptismal discourse of Silvanus which he delivered about the year A.D. 90 in a city in Asia Minor, in connection with Psalm 34. That is a construction that has been formulated with a lively imagination indeed!—In England, B. H. Streeter (*The Primitive Church,* London 1929, 115ff., esp. 123ff.) has adopted the theory of a baptismal address. He thinks that it arose somewhere in Asia Minor.

[5]*Die katholischen Briefe* (2d ed., Tübingen, 1930).

[6]*Die Kirchenbriefe* (NTD; 4th ed., Göttingen 1947). Likewise, A. Adam ("Das Sintflutgebet in der Taufliturgie," *Jahrbuch der Theologischen Schule Bethel,* 1952, 20-21) agrees with the thesis of a baptismal discourse.

[7]*First Peter* 14. On this cf. the review by T. W. Manson, in *JTS* 49 (1948): 85-86. In the study cited in note 2, above, Bieder agrees with Beare (*First Peter* p. 3, n. 1), though to be sure he is somewhat more reserved toward the thesis that would understand the entire epistle as a baptismal discourse.

beyond the present status of research as it is represented by Perdelwitz and Windisch.

Most recently, H. Preisker has adopted the suggestions that date back to Perdelwitz, but he has modified them in one respect; according to him, in our epistle a primitive Christian worship service of a baptizing community (1:3-4:11) has been put into written form. This service then was ended with the concluding service of the entire community (4:12-5:11).[8] The baptismal act itself, which was omitted for reasons of arcane discipline, supposedly would come in between 1:22 and 1:23. The administration of baptism was preceded by an introductory psalm (1:3-12), followed by an instructional discourse (1:13-21). Attached to baptism is a brief baptismal vow (1:22-25) including an exhortation to brotherly love, and then in 2:1-10 a festal hymn is sung. The parenesis in 2:11-3:12, which is stylistically distinguished from the preceding parts of the worship service, is put in the mouth of a preacher who only here appears on the scene, while in a so-called revelatory discourse in 3:13-4:7a an apocalyptist is speaking. Chapter 4:7b-11c forms the concluding prayer of the baptismal service. Of course, Preisker must undertake some emendations of the text in order to draw a prayer out of the parenesis. In 4:12 the baptismal service is followed by a concluding service for the entire community. From this point on, suffering is spoken of as an already experienced reality, in distinction from the hypothetical mention of suffering in the baptismal service. According to Preisker, these outlines of a baptismal service of the Roman church were later bracketed with introductory and concluding salutations and then sent to the churches of Asia Minor.

Nevertheless, Preisker still is unable to provide conclusive proof of this thesis that purports to find in First Peter a baptismal service.[9] Where else in the literature of primitive Christianity would we find a somewhat comparable liturgical formulary for a baptismal service in the style of First Peter? It is suggested that the individual prophets set down in writing what they offered to the community by way of pareneses and revelations and that ψαλμός, διδαχή, ὕμνος, παράκλησις, and ἀποκάλυψις occurred alternately in the worship services,[10] but this declaration is not sufficient to supply a basis for the theory of a baptismal service here. Even apart from this, however, it must be asked whether the main part of the epistle after all actually is correctly

---

[8]*Die katholischen Briefe,* 156-62.

[9]Preisker's position on the question of authenticity must be regarded as extremely dubious when he suggests that the Roman church wanted to set forth the course of a worship service "as it was conducted in Rome in (as they believed) the spirit of Peter" (*Die katholischen Briefe* 161). For a critique of Preisker's thesis cf. F. Hauck, *TLZ* (1952) cols. 34-35; E. Käsemann, *VF* (1952): 192; G. Delling, *Der Gottesdienst im Neuen Testament* (Göttingen 1952) 59.

[10]*Die katholischen Briefe,* 161.

understood in terms of the theme of baptism.[11] The references to baptism are limited almost exclusively to the first part of the epistle, 1:3-2:10, and they are echoed in the following chapters only occasionally.[12]

Before we undertake the task of inquiring into the leading ideas and the subject of the epistle, a further word must be said about the relationship of 1 Peter to the rest of the epistolary literature of the NT. Earlier exegetes attempted to explain the unquestionable closeness to Pauline theology by assuming a literary dependence. It is true that 1 Peter does not have such important theologoumena as justification by faith, the question of the relationship of faith and works, the problem of the law, the church as the body of Christ, and several others; but the reciprocal echoes in ideas and formulas are indeed numerous. However, these echoes are not limited to the Pauline epistles, but connections can also be shown with James, Hebrews, the book of Revelation, the Synoptics, and the book of Acts. Though H. J. Holtzmann[13] once thought that 1 Peter is literarily dependent upon all these writings, the recently published new edition of the Feine-Behm introduction to the NT significantly limits this view, though it expresses the opinion that a relationship of literary dependence must be assumed at least to the epistles to the Romans and the Ephesians.[14]

E. G. Selwyn, on the other hand, in his splendid commentary, has undertaken to apply to the exegesis of 1 Peter the form-critical studies of the catechetical material of the New Testament epistolary literature. These studies were first undertaken by A. Seeberg in his *Katechismus der Urchristen-*

---

[11]Cf. Dibelius, *TRu* (1931): 232.

[12]In 4:1 we probably have a reference to baptism. See below. On this point cf. Selwyn, *First Peter* 41. The words about the conversion of Christians, for example in 2:25 and 4:2-3, are too narrowly understood when one tries to relate them only to baptism. Chapter 3:20-21 stands in an old confession of faith into which a baptismal instruction was inserted. (In opposition to other views I am in agreement here with Oscar Cullmann, *The Earliest Christian Confessions,* London 1949, 20). This confession, however, is not quoted with reference to baptism; instead, it is connected with the statements about the sufferings of Christians and Christ's expiatory suffering. The baptismal reference in vv 20-21 had already been combined with the confession before the latter was incorporated into 1 Peter.

[13]*Einleitung in das Neue Testament* (3d ed. Freiburg, 1892) 313ff.

[14]Ninth ed. Heidelberg 1950, 247. Even Beare acknowledges a literary dependence of 1 Peter on several Pauline and deutero-Pauline epistles (*First Peter* 9). E. Percy (*Die Probleme der Kolosser- und Epheserbriefe,* Lund 1946) on the other hand has demonstrated in a careful study that there is no literary dependence between Ephesians and 1 Peter. The close similarities between the two epistles are explained instead by the fact "that in both epistles we have to do in large measure with widely held liturgical material as well as paraenesis" (440; cf. 433-40). Finally, E. L. Mitton ("Relationship") has once again defended the thesis that 1 Peter is dependent upon Ephesians.

heit (Leipzig: 1903)[15] and then were significantly advanced by M. Dibelius[16] as well as by A. M. Hunter[17] and P. Carrington.[18] Unfortunately, Selwyn's thoroughgoing studies, which in fact blaze new ways for the understanding of 1 Peter, are burdened by two points of view that careful specific expositions are not able to fit into a correct overall picture: first, form-critical work is unhappily linked to the question of authenticity, since Selwyn is constantly concerned with proving that either Peter or Silvanus is the author.[19] Then in association with Carrington he attempts to arrange the catechetical material and to reconstruct the main parts of the primitive Christian catechism under five headings.[20] There will always be weighty objections that must be raised against such an attempt at reconstruction, because in doing this one too easily ventures into the realm of hypotheses that cannot be proven. The form-critical study of the parenetic pieces therefore will have to be conducted even more cautiously, and on specifics one will have to be more tentative and careful in pronouncing judgment. While in the Synoptics we can identify with great probability, even down to parts of verses, the Markan or the Logia material as the resource on which Matthew and Luke drew, the connections that can be demonstrated between the parenetic portions of the epistles do not suf-

---

[15]Developed further in his works: *Das Evangelium Christi* (Leipzig, 1905); *Die beiden Wege und das Aposteldekret* (Leipzig, 1906); and *Die Didache des Judentums und der Urchristenheit* (Leipzig, 1908).

[16]*Der Brief des Jakobus,* Göttingen 1921, esp. 1-10; "Zur Formgeschichte des Neuen Testamentes (ausserhalb der Evangelien)," *TRu* (1931): 207-42; *Die Formgeschichte des Evangeliums* (2d ed., Tübingen, 1933), esp. 234-65 (Die Paränese); cf. also the commentaries in Lietzmann's *Handbuch* series: *An die Epheser, Kolosser, Philemon* (2d ed., Tübingen, 1927); *Die Pastoralbriefe* (2d ed., 1931); *An die Thessalonicher I, II, An die Philipper* (3d ed., Tübingen, 1937).

[17]*St. Paul and his Predecessors* (London, 1940).

[18]*The Primitive Christian Catechism* (Cambridge, 1940).

[19]Thus Selwyn would like to show (Essay II, pp. 369-84) that 1 Peter is especially closely related to 1 and 2 Thessalonians, and for all three epistles he takes Silvanus to be the apostle's stenographer. But the similarities between these epistles are not especially striking, and even statistics of vocabulary cannot prove anything. Indeed, it has to prompt some reservations when one observes that, for example, θλῖψις and διωγμός, which are frequently used in the Thessalonian epistles, are entirely absent from 1 Peter. On the other hand, the Thessalonian epistles do not have the term πειρασμός, which 1 Peter uses twice (1:6; 4:12). The weight of vocabulary statistics certainly should not be overestimated. But in the last analysis, one can use the stenographer hypothesis to prove the genuineness of any epistle. One unknown is replaced by another. But what is gained thereby? Can Silvanus, a member of the original community, actually have authored our epistle? Then why not Peter himself? Such hypotheses do not provide much help for exegesis. Cf. the problem of the authorship of the Pastoral Epistles.

[20]Cf. *First Peter* 389: 1. The entry in the new life at baptism; 2. The new life: its negative implications (Deponentes); 3. The new life: its faith and worship; 4. The new life: its social virtues and duties (Subjecti); 5. Teaching called out by crisis (Vigilate; State/Resistite).

fice to identify written sources as a common model for them. This much, however, may be taken as certain: the epistles of the NT, too, in much greater measure than was previously assumed, made use of traditional material that had been handed down orally (or perhaps occasionally in written form?) and applied this material to the concrete situation of the church that was being addressed. For this reason, then, the way of form-critical study can prove fruitful for the exegesis of the NT epistles in twofold fashion: for one thing, we learn to get a clearer, sharper picture of the question as to the source of the material; and then thereby we are able to recognize more clearly the distinctiveness of the individual passage in the utilization of traditional material. Along this path the exegesis of 1 Peter too can be further advanced. For the differences in style in the different parts of the epistle that H. Preisker has correctly observed and brought out[21] are not to be explained by the sequence of a service of worship in which several preachers speak, but they must be derived from the diverse sources of the traditional material.[22] A few examples will be given now to show briefly how this task is to be undertaken.[23]

II

The epistle is addressed to Christians who are suffering and afflicted. It is the author's aim to strengthen and comfort them in this time of trial. He seeks to employ in this task the parenetic material that has been handed down, and in so doing he subordinates it to a unitary leading thought, the preservation of the Christians in their suffering.[24]

---

[21]*Die katholischen Briefe,* 156-61.

[22]As an analogous example one might here point to the Manual of Discipline, which will be mentioned more frequently below and which combines in itself diverse elements—liturgically framed pieces, doctrinal portions, legal prescriptions, and hymnic passages.

[23]We need not go into the earlier attempts, under the assumption of numerous interpolations in 1 Peter, to reconstruct the original form of the epistle, since today these attempts generally have been abandoned. Daniel Völter (*Der I. Petrusbrief—seine Entstehung und Stellung in der Geschichte des Urchristentums,* Strassburg 1906) undertook, by means of arbitrary excisions, to purge an originally Jewish-Christian epistle of later revisions made by a Pauline theologian. One detects in Völter's study that he had somehow sensed the problem of tradition and the use of tradition. To seek to employ literary-critical operations on 1 Peter, however, certainly means to miss the mark.

[24]Cf. A. Schlatter, *Petrus und Paulus nach dem I. Petrusbrief* (Stuttgart, 1937) 13: "He [Peter] was prompted to write his epistle precisely because the church must be instructed in how to suffer." Cf. also pp. 30-31. This perspective is correctly recognized also by Beare, though he does not employ it in the entire task of interpretation: "It is a message sent to the churches of Asia Minor to help them meet the first demoralising shock of a sudden and violent outburst of persecution, to reassure them of the truth of their faith, and to encourage them to remain firm in their allegiance to Jesus Christ whatever the cost" (p. 6).

household code – hypotassesthai

a) The passage 2:11-3:12, in which a so-called *Haustafel* is employed, stands out from the epistle as a whole, as a relatively complete unit. In the introduction, 2:11-12, which is clearly identified as a new beginning by the address (ἀγαπητοί),[25] the entire congregation is challenged, in spite of the slanders that they must endure, to hold without wavering to a life of good conduct, so that the heathen will see their good works and praise God in the day of tribulation.[26] Under the rubric of ὑποτάσσεσθαι (2:13, 18; 3:1, 5; cf. 5:5), in 2:13-17 the church is exhorted to be obedient to authority. In the main body of this passage then various individual situations are addressed— slaves, women, men—and finally in summary fashion a word is addressed to all of them (3:8-12).

The closest parallel to the utterance about authority is found in Rom. 13:1-7.[27] In both passages we find the word ὑποτάσσεσθαι (1 Pet. 2:13; Rom. 13:1, 5). In both places the divine authority of civil officials is emphasized (1 Pet. 2:13, 15; Rom. 13:4). Both of them stress the fact that the civil officials reward the good and punish the wicked and therefore have a divinely appointed task to perform (1 Pet. 2:14; Rom. 13:3, 4). Romans 13:5 demands ὑποτάσσεσθαι διὰ τὴν συνείδησιν, 1 Pet. 2:13 διὰ τὸν κύριον.[28] First Pet. 2:17 concludes with the admonition πάντας τιμήσατε, while Rom. 13:7 says, ἀπόδοτε πᾶσιν τὰς ὀφειλάς . . . τῷ τὴν τιμὴν τὴν τιμήν. Corresponding to the brief admonition in 1 Pet. 2:17, τὴν ἀδελφότητα ἀγαπᾶτε are the verses Rom. 13:8-10, where the commandment to love is intensified because love is the fulfilling of the law. These ideas that are enunciated in both passages, however, do not allow the conclusion that one epistle is literarily dependent upon the other; instead, both of them go back, independent of each other, to traditional material that was handed down (probably orally). In 1 Peter this is subordinated to the topic of the entire epistle: through their good deeds the suffering Christians are to silence the ignorance of foolish men (2:15; cf. 2:12 in the superscription to this entire section).

The words to the slaves are to be compared with Col. 3:22-4:1, Eph. 6:5-9, 1 Tim. 6:1-2, and Titus 2:9-10. The traditional exhortation to submissive obedience ἐν φόβῳ (1 Pet. 2:18, Col. 3:22, Eph. 6:5—add κυρίου, cf. Col.

---

[25]On ὡς παροίκους καὶ παρεπιδήμους cf. 1:1.

[26]D. Daube ("Jewish Missionary Maxims in Paul," *ST* 1948: 158-69) identifies, as a model for the missionary feature of the parenesis, some examples of Jewish rules concerning behavior in relationship to proselytes and Gentiles (*y. B. Mes.* 8c, et al.). For 1 Pet. 2:12, too, he offers an illuminating conjecture that Jewish prototypes lie back of this passage (p. 160).

[27]One should also compare 1 Tim. 2:1-3 and Titus 3:1-3.

[28]The expression διὰ συνείδησιν θεοῦ is used in 2:19 in the parenesis addressed to slaves.

3:22) is again applied in 1 Peter to the special situation: obedience is to be shown even to the eccentric masters (2:18). Doing right and suffering is the way indicated for the Christian slaves (2:20), for Christ too has suffered (2:21-25).[29] Christian women are admonished to be obedient to their husbands, as also in Col. 3:18f., Eph. 5:22-24, 1 Tim. 2:9-15, and Titus 2:3-5, among which 1 Timothy 2 is the closest parallel to 1 Pet. 3:1-6. In both passages one finds an explicit position taken against outward adornment, though—as O. Michel has shown[30]—the form of the catalog in 1 Peter is more strongly hellenized than that in 1 Timothy 2. The two passages, however, are independent of each other, and they even use different Old Testament examples—1 Peter cites Sarah, but 1 Timothy cites Adam and Eve. Therefore, for this passage too we shall have to assume the prototype of traditional parenesis which was reshaped in accordance with the situation of the local church: the husbands of whom 1 Peter speaks are pagans. Just as the persecuted Christians through their works of love bear witness to the truth of the gospel before the pagans who slander them, so also the women, by means of their conduct without words—in silent service as missionary behavior—are to win their husbands. As the final word addressed to a group in the church[31] it is said to the Christian husbands that they are to show proper honor to their wives (3:7). Such a brief sentence suffices here because this admonition, as will be seen, remains without reference to the situation of suffering. Precisely for this reason there is missing even a demand addressed to the masters that they treat their slaves well.

The concluding words in 3:8-12 are addressed once again to the entire church and in so doing they employ a saying of the Lord (3:9; cf. Matt. 5:39, 44) and a detailed quotation from Ps. 34:13-17. Here once again parenetic traditional[32] material has been placed within the special point of view of the entire epistle; in their suffering[33] the Christians are not to allow themselves to be led astray into returning evil for evil, but instead of this should bless. For God looks upon the righteous, but he turns his face against those who do evil.

---

[29]On the parenesis to slaves cf. the expression, ὡς δοῦλοι Χριστοῦ . . . δουλεύοντες τῷ κυρίῳ καὶ οὐκ ἀνθρώπους (Eph. 6:6-7; cf. Col. 3:23-24).

[30]"Grundfragen der Pastoralbriefe," in *Festschrift für Th. Wurm* (Stuttgart, 1948) 90.

[31]Note the serial use of ὁμοίως in 3:1, 7; 5:5, which is also found in hellenistic lists. Cf. L. Radermacher, "Der I Petrusbrief und Silvanus" (*ZNW* 25, 1926) 290ff.

[32]Cf. 1 Thess. 5:13-22; Rom. 12:9-19. On this subject see Selwyn, *First Peter* 412-13.

[33]Cf. Schlatter, *Petrus und Paulus* 130: "The exhortation (scil., of the *Haustafel*) applies to those who are suffering in their straitened circumstances who endure even more sufferings because of their being Christians."

If we ask now about the *source* of the catechetical materials utilized here, first of all the hellenistic character of the *Haustafeln* should be observed.[34] The style of the parenesis is hellenistic, and the OT is everywhere cited exactly in agreement with the LXX. Of course, the related passages in Tobit 4 and 12, in the Testaments of the Twelve Patriarchs, in Ecclesiasticus, and in Pseudo-Phocylides are also to be compared with the *Haustafeln*.[35] In any case, the answer to our question is not given merely by our perceiving the hellenistic clothing of the parenesis. For the exegetes have always had some difficulty in explaining why participial forms are used instead of imperatives in a number of passages in 1 Peter that speak of the conduct of Christians: for example, 2:18, οἱ οἰκέται, ὑποτασσόμενοι ἐν παντὶ φόβῳ τοῖς δεσπόταις; 3:1, ὁμοίως γυναῖκες, ὑποτασσόμεναι τοῖς ἰδίοις ἀνδράσιν; 3:7, οἱ ἄνδρες ὁμοίως, συνοικοῦντες; cf. also 3:8-9, 4:8, and 1:13-14. David Daube has recently given the explanation for this use of the imperative participle in a highly instructive article on "Participle and Imperative in I Peter."[36] After his convincing presentation showing that there are no extant hellenistic parallels for this usage,[37] Daube refers to numerous examples showing that in Tannaitic Hebrew the participle can occupy the place of the imperative. Thus, for example, *m. Ber.* VI:6, אחד ואחד מברך לעצמו כל = "each one is to say the benediction for himself." The use of the participle in the imperative sense, nevertheless, is limited to a particular group of ordinances and commandments. It is used primarily in general rules, not in a direction given to a specific person in a particular situation as, for example, "Go and bring me my coat." In the direct address in which the wisdom literature speaks, when the father is instructing the son the imperative or the imperfect is preferred, rather than the impersonal participle. Just as is the case in the Tannaitic Hebrew of the Mishna, now also in the NT the use of the imperative participles is limited to rules and general instructions.[38] Whereas in Hebrew, participles, imperatives, and infinitives can replace each other in

---

[34]Cf. K. Weidinger, *Die Haustafel* (UNT, Heft 14; Leipzig, 1928) 40ff.; on 1 Pet. 2:11-3:12 see pp. 62-66.

[35]Cf. Selwyn, *First Peter,* 421-22.

[36]As an appended note to Selwyn's commentary, *First Peter,* 467-88. Blass-Debrunner-Funk (*A Greek Grammar of the New Testament and Other Early Christian Literature,* Chicago/London: University of Chicago, 1961, section 468.2, pp. 245-46) is unable to provide any suitable explanation.

[37]Pages 467-71, in a discussion with J. H. Moulton, *A Grammar of New Testament Greek,* I (3d ed., 1908) 180ff., 232ff. I have checked Daube's evidence in Ecclesiasticus and in the Wisdom of Solomon. Not a single imperative participle is to be found in these books.

[38]Cf. ibid., page 477: "The participles of the New Testament are confined to rules, general directions."

a single passage and all of them can have the imperative force,[39] in NT Greek adjectives are added to this group, since the Greek exhibits a much greater wealth of adjectives than does the Hebrew. On this point, one should consult the context of Rom. 12:9-19, where adjectives,[40] participles,[41] imperatives,[42] and infinitives[43] are found together, all of them with an imperative meaning. The whole passage, which can be translated without difficulty into smooth Hebrew, presents traditional parenetic material that has as its content the proper conduct of the members of the community.

The same holds true also for the use of the imperative participle in 1 Peter. It is not necessary for us to go through each one of the passages. Instead, only a couple of points pertinent to the matter should be noted here: (1) 1 Pet. 1:14 contains the imperative participle μὴ συσχηματιζόμενοι ταῖς πρότερον ἐν τῇ ἀγνοίᾳ ἐπιθυμίαις, while the parallel in Rom. 12:2 has the regular imperative μὴ συσχηματίζεσθε. It would be conceivable that this expression once formed the beginning of a series of prescriptions. But Paul and 1 Peter made use of it in their pareneses independent of each other. This is demonstrated by the fact that in 1 Peter, which consistently uses better Greek than Paul uses, we find variously formed imperative participles where they are lacking in the Pauline parallels.[44] (2) As far as the question of a prototype that was common to both of them is concerned, one will have to be very cautious in the assumption of written sources.[45] But since the use of the imperative participle is restricted exclusively to rules that refer to the life within the community, it is of considerable significance that in the recently discovered Manual of Discipline, in col. 1, we also find infinitives, imperfects, and participles in alternation, where the participles have an imperative meaning.[46] It may be expected that after the Dead Sea Scrolls have become better

---

[39]E.g., *m. Hag.* II.1, 2; cf. Daube, in the appended note to Selwyn's *First Peter,* 473-74.

[40]V 9, ἡ ἀγάπη ἀνυπόκριτος, et passim.

[41]V 9 ἀποστυγοῦντες τὸ πονηρόν, κολλώμενοι τῷ ἀγαθῷ, et passim.

[42]V 14, εὐλογεῖτε τοὺς διώκοντας; v 16, μὴ γίνεσθε φρόνιμοι.

[43]V 15, χαίρειν μετὰ χαιρόντων, κλαίειν μετὰ κλαιόντων.

[44]Cf., e.g., 1 Pet. 3:1 with Eph. 5:22 and Col. 3:18; 1 Pet. 2:18 with Eph. 6:5 and Col. 3:22.

[45]On this, in my opinion, Daube (appended note to Selwyn's *First Peter,* 484-88) goes too far in his conjectures.

[46]In the prescription concerning admission to the covenant it is said in lines 18ff. (M. Burrows, *The Dead Sea Scrolls* II, New Haven 1951):

והיו הכוהנים

והלויים מברכים את אל ישועות ואת כול מעשי אמתו וכול

העוברים בברית *אומרים אחריהם אמן אמן

והכוהנים מספרים את צדקות אל במעשי גבורתים

מעוברים בברית מודים 1.24, והלויים מספרים 1.22 cf. ,.etc

known and have been more thoroughly studied we shall be able to gain a clearer insight into the origin and development of the primitive Christian congregational parenesis.[47] In any case, there is good reason for presuming that like the Jew who entered into the fellowship of the Qumran community, the Christian had to submit to a definite order which was fixed in binding prescriptions.[48]

Consequently, from these statements about the *Haustafel* in 1 Pet. 2:11-3:12 we perceive that—as in the case of the Pastoral Epistles, for which this task has already been undertaken[49]—exegetical work must give attention to the question as to Palestinian and hellenistic material. This material that has been handed down certainly has undergone a hellenistic revision and reshaping in our present epistle. But when we learn better to understand the traditional material in terms of its origin—as is shown in the example of the *Haustafel*—it can also be demonstrated more clearly in particular that our epistle adopts rules for the life of the community that have been handed down and sharpens them for the specific situation of the suffering community.

Just as was the case in 2:11-3:12, now in a form-critical analysis of the remaining parts of the epistle it could be shown in what way the traditional material that has been handed down has also been reworked. However, since this task could be fulfilled only in a thoroughgoing investigation, here the matter must be allowed to rest with only a few comments and suggestions.

1. The passage 1:3-12 forms a single sentence. In the compiling of adjectives, participles, appositions, and subordinate clauses it is clearly distinguished from the rest of the epistle in style. In the introductory formula of praise εὐλογητὸς ὁ θεὸς καὶ πατὴρ τοῦ κυρίου ἡμῶν Ἰησοῦ Χρισ-

---

* No longer dependent on והיו in line 19.

On the significance of the Scrolls cf. especially K. G. Kuhn, "Die in Palästina gefundenen hebräischen Texte und das Neue Testament," *ZTK* (1950): 192-211.—On page 487 Daube points to a similar parallel: *m. Dem.* 2.3 contains prescriptions for those who belong to the Chaberim and have separated themselves from the 'Am-ha-'aretz: חבר אינו מוכר לעם הארץ המפקב עליו להיות "Anyone who undertakes to be a *Chaber* may not sell to an 'Am-ha-'aretz."

[47]Here we may cite only two examples: 1. While heretofore the catalogs of virtues and vices in the New Testament have been traced back to hellenistic material, now we find in the Manual of Discipline (1QS IV.9ff.) a detailed enumeration of all the vices that grow out of the spirit of corruption. Cf. Gal. 5:19ff. 2. On the contending of the fleshly lusts against the ψυχή (1 Pet. 2:11) cf. 1QS IV.23: so long as the end has not yet arrived, "the spirits of truth and of wickedness contend in the hearts of men." But at the end there stands the ἡμέρα ἐπισκοπῆς that is created by God (cf. 1QS IV.26).

[48]On this topic now cf. also E. Stauffer, "Der 'Geist der Freiheit' in der Ordensregel von Jericho," *TLZ* (1952) cols. 527-32.

[49]Cf. O. Michel, "Grundfragen der Pastoralbriefe," *Festschrift für Th. Wurm* (Stuttgart 1948) 83-99; W. Nauck, *Die Herkunft des Verfassers der Pastoralbriefe, ein Beitrag zur Frage der Auslegung der Pastoralbriefe* (Dissertation, Göttingen 1950).

τοῦ it is reminiscent of 2 Corinthians 1 and Ephesians 1. The parenesis, which clearly is repeatedly connected with baptism,[50] is introduced with a psalm of prayer. The entire passage 1:3-2:10 is dominated by the idea of the holy people of God, to which the Christians now belong. But according to Lev. 19:2, there is an obligation for this people of God: ἅγιοι ἔσεσθε, ὅτι ἐγὼ ἅγιος (1:16).[51] This dominant idea of the holy people of God now once again recalls, in striking fashion, the community of the new covenant which has become familiar to us from the Palestinian texts and the Damascus Document. Some examples may serve to show briefly how their ideas appear to have influenced primitive Christian parenesis. The Christians are ἐκλεκτοί (1:1; 2:9), while the members of the Qumran sect call themselves בחורי אל[52] or קדושים,[53] which should be compared with the ἅγιοι in 1:16. While the Palestinian community identifies itself as עם קדושכה (= ''thy holy people''),[54] the Christians understand themselves to be ἔθνος ἅγιον (2:9) that forms the new priesthood and is to perform priestly functions. While the Christian community is founded upon Jesus Christ as the cornerstone, the fellowship of the Qumran document is conscious of being ''firmly grounded in the truth, an everlasting planting, a holy house for Israel. . . . They will be a 'tested bulwark,' a 'precious cornerstone'; the foundations that he has laid will remain unshaken, nor will they be removed from their place''—thus clearly echoing Isa. 28:16.[55] In both places membership in the community means gaining a

---

[50]1 Pet. 1:3, 13ff., 18, 23; 2:1-2, 10. The repeated reference to baptism is obvious in the parenesis. Chap. 1:3 speaks of the rebirth as an already accomplished fact: ὁ ἀναγεννήσας. Therefore we should refrain from the attempt to reconstruct a baptismal service. See above.

[51]J. Danielou (*Sacramentum futuri*, Paris 1950) has explored the typological connections between 1 Pet. 1:13-2:10 and the book of Exodus. In that process he has called attention above all to the following passages (cf. J. Jeremias, *TLZ* 1952, col. 40): those who are baptized are the new people of God who set out on their pilgrimage (1:17) with their loins girded (1:13). They are redeemed by the blood of the Lamb (1:18-19) and may drink from the rock that flows with the life-giving water (2:5). Still without justification is Danielou's conjecture that in 1 Pet. 1:13-2:10 we have to do with a baptismal homily that was delivered during the paschal week. It is appropriate to ask, however, whether 1 Peter has adopted traditional material that was used in baptismal homilies in order to utilize it in a discourse to the suffering churches.— Like Danielou, J. Hempel (*ZAW* 63, 1951, page 132, note 9) also has expressed the conjecture that 1 Pet. 1:3-2:12 presupposes a Christian Easter sermon which on its own part had its prototype in a Jewish Passover homily.

[52]1QpHab 10.13 (M. Burrows, *The Dead Sea Scrolls* I; New Haven: Yale University, 1950).

[53]1QH III, 22; IV, 25; cf. K. G. Kuhn, ''Die hebräischen Texte'' 199.

[54]Documentation in Kuhn, *TDNT* V, 299.

[55]1QS VIII.5-8. On the German translation of this passage cf. H. Bardtke (*Die Handschriftenfunde am Toten Meer*, Berlin 1952, p. 100). On this point one should also compare 1QS IX.6, where the community is characterized as ''a holy house for Aaron . . . a house of community for Israel, who walks in perfection.''

share in the κληρονομία (1:4).[56] The contrast between light and darkness that pervades the writings of the Qumran sect is also adopted in 1 Pet. 2:9: God has called the Christians out of darkness εἰς τὸ θαυμαστὸν αὐτοῦ φῶς and therewith made them his people.[57] This event that occurs in baptism is eschatologically understood, for what the prophets one time awaited has now been proclaimed (1:10-12, 20).[58] The ἀποκάλυψις Ἰησοῦ Χριστοῦ (1:13) has been granted to the believers; they have received the knowledge of God's secrets.[59] Membership in the community implies renunciation and abandonment of the old way of life (1:14; 2:1: ἀποθέμενοι) and a new beginning in one's behavior as τέκνα ὑπακοῆς (1:14).[60] Thus in 1 Peter as in the Palestinian texts the dualism of light and darkness is ethically understood;[61] God's commandments are to be observed, and one's neighbor is to be loved (1:22; cf. CD 6:20-21; cf. 4:1; 5:5). The Christian who has laid aside the old way is challenged to put on the Christian armor[62] (1:13) and soberly to keep watch at his post of duty (1:13; cf. 4:7; 5:8).[63]

These points of similarity between 1 Pet. 1:3-2:10 and the Qumran texts, of which we have given some examples here, certainly are not to be traced to a direct appropriation by 1 Peter. Instead, as a comparison with numerous parallels in other NT writings, particularly James, can show[64]—1 Peter refers

---

[56]The persons who belonged to the sect are called אנשי גורל אל (1QS 2.2). Cf. Kuhn, *ZTK* (1950): 200.

[57]It should be noted that φωτισθῆναι becomes a *terminus technicus* for baptism; cf. Heb. 6:4; 10:32; Eph. 5:14; Justin, *Apol.* I.61.12-13; 65.1; *Dial.* 122.1.

[58]Cf. the documentation in Kuhn, "Die hebräischen Texte," 208-209, concerning the eschatological understanding of the nature of the community.

[59]On the concept רז/μυστήριον in the Qumran texts see 1QpHab 7.5, 8, 14, and cf. Kuhn, "Die hebräischen Texte," 204-205.

[60]Cf. בני אור etc.

[61]Cf. Selwyn, *First Peter,* 379 n. 1.

[62]Cf. Isa. 59:17; Wisd. Sol. 5:17ff.; Odes. Sol. 10:6ff., et passim.

[63]Cf. 1QS 1.18 and the documentation in Kuhn, "Die hebräischen Texte," 202-203, and *TDNT* V, 298ff.

[64]The demonstrable parallels in our passage to the epistle of James stand in the same sequence in the two epistles. Cf. 1 Pet. 1:1-Jas. 1:1; 1 Pet. 1:6-7-Jas. 1:2-3; 1 Pet. 1:24-Jas.1:10-11; 1 Pet. 1:23-2:2-Jas. 1:18-22. On the connections between the two epistles cf. A. Schlatter, *Der Brief des Jakobus* (Stuttgart, 1932) 67-73; further, M. Dibelius, *Der Brief des Jakobus* (Göttingen 1921) 29-30; F. Hauck, *Der Brief des Jakobus* (Erlangen/Leipzig, 1926) 14. The fixed sequence of the pareneses shows that the oral tradition was already being passed on in a definite form. We are not to think of any literary dependence between the two epistles. One should compare, e.g., 1 Pet. 1:7 with Jas. 1:3 and Rom. 5:3. On this point see Grundmann, *TDNT* II, 258, n. 14.

to traditional material that is appropriated in already christianized form.[65] The conflictual situation into which the Christian is placed in the world now causes the parenesis that has been handed down to appear under the theme of the entire epistle: for a short time, if it is God's will, the Christians undergo suffering in various kinds of πειρασμοί (1:6-8), but the suffering is superseded by the eschatological rejoicing that is already being sounded in the church. The church knows that Christ is the cornerstone on Mount Zion that supports her, and she knows that those who do not believe the Word and are disobedient must according to God's will be ashamed because of him (2:6-8).

2. The actual *theme* of the epistle now is explicitly treated from 3:13 on to the conclusion of the epistle, in order *to comfort the suffering Christians*. Even though these passages are determined to a large extent by the concrete situation of the congregations in Asia Minor—the Christians are questioned as to the basis of their hope (3:15), they are slandered (3:16; 4:3-4, 14) and hauled into court (4:15-16)—still even here the parenesis that has been handed down comes into play. The individual pieces follow in a loose connection; 3:13 is attached in a series of key words to the quotation from the Psalms at the end of the *Haustafel* (κακά/κακώσων),[66] and 4:11 forms, together with a doxology, a certain insertion, but by no means a conclusion, as in other epistles also doxologies are found within the epistles themselves.[67] The weightiness of the parenesis is heightened, the more nearly it approaches the end of the writing: 5:8-9 speaks in conclusion of the διάβολος as the real adversary who attacks the Christians in their sufferings.[68]

---

[65]In our passage, too, the Old Testament sayings are consistently cited following the LXX. To be sure, 1 Pet. 2:6 cites Isa. 28:16 in a version different from the LXX, as does Rom. 9:33. But Rom. 9:33 and 1 Pet. 2:6, again, do not agree with each other in the wording, so that one is not to think of any mutual literary dependence, but rather of traditional material that was available to both of them. In this traditional version apparently Isa. 28:16 and 8:14 had been combined. 1 Pet. 2:7 adds Ps. 118:22; this passage is likewise connected in Luke 20:17-18 with Isa. 8:14. The fact that Hos. 1:9 and 2:23 are quoted in 1 Pet. 2:10 and similarly in Rom. 9:25 (here preceding the words of Isaiah) again does no prove anything about any direct literary dependence. Form-critical study will strive here to get back to their shared model. Of course, it is at least doubtful whether in so early a time this model could already have had the written form of a book of testimonies, as many think. It seems to be that Selwyn's statements (*First Peter* 281) where he attempts to reconstruct a hymn wherein the aforementioned quotations were used is worthy of consideration.

[66]Cf. the arrangement of key words in 2:4ff.: λίθος; 2:20-21: πάσχοντες/ἔπαθεν; 3:17-18: πάσχειν/ἔπαθεν.

[67]Cf. Selwyn on this passage (*First Peter* 220). Only in Rom. 16:27, Jude 25, and 2 Pet. 3:18 does the doxology close the epistle. One should compare the doxologies in 1 Clement, which by no means always form a conclusion: 1 Clem. 20:12; 32:4; 38:4; 43:6; 45:7-8; 50:7; 58:2; 61:3; 64; 65:2.

[68]Nevertheless I would not consider it correct to think that from 4:12 on one must presuppose a different situation from that of 1:1-4:11. While in 4:12 the sufferings are called a

Even though Selwyn goes too far in his attempt to reconstruct a kind of catechism for those being persecuted, one that is based upon words of the Lord like the collection in Matt. 10:24-41,[69] still a look at the concordance will show that the parenesis with reference to suffering in 1 Peter was not formulated *ad hoc,* but rather uses traditional material in abundant measure. Here we may cite only a few of the key words that will serve to clarify:[70] ἀγαλλιᾶσθαι (1:6),[71] πειρασμός (1:6),[72] δοκιμάζειν (1:7),[73] φοβεῖσθαι (3:14f.),[74] κρίμα (4:17),[75] νήφειν and γρηγορεῖν (1:13; 4:7; 5:8),[76] and ἀντιστῆναι (5:9);[77] and the series could be further expanded significantly.[78]

As far as the *source* of the material that is utilized is concerned, a distinction must be made here as well as in the other parts of the epistle between Palestinian and hellenistic material.[79] First Peter 4:1, in a parenthesis[80] of the parenesis that challenges the readers to arm themselves (ὁπλίσασθε), makes use of the idea, which can be documented only in Palestinian Judaism, that the dying person, especially the martyr, through his suffering and death secures atonement for his sins or even for those of another.[81] The sentence, "For he who has suffered in the flesh is free from sin" (ὅτι ὁ παθὼν σαρκὶ πέπαυται ἁμαρτίας) points to an event in the past (παθών, πέπαυται) and apparently is to be understood in a figurative sense. The clear parallelism to

---

πύρωσις, in 1:6, 7 sufferings had already been characterized as a testing. In 1:6, 7, as well as in 3:14, 17, and 4:1, the author speaks of suffering not only as a hypothetical possibility but as an event that has already come upon the Christians: λυπηθέντες (1:6)! It is in the very nature of the subject of this epistle that the weight of the statements is heightened as one approaches the end of the epistle.

[69]Selwyn, *First Peter,* 439-58.

[70]A comparison of 1 Pet. 4:14-19 with 2 Thess. 1:4-12 also is instructive.

[71]Cf. 1 Thess. 1:6.

[72]Cf. Jas. 1:2, 12.

[73]Cf. 1 Thess. 2:4; Jas. 1:3.

[74]Cf. Matt. 10:28.

[75]Cf. 2 Thess. 1:5.

[76]Cf. 1 Thess. 5:6; 1 Cor. 16:13; Col. 4:2.

[77]Cf. 1 Thess. 3:8; 1 Cor. 16:13; Phil. 4:1; Col. 4:12; Eph. 6:11-14.

[78]Cf. also e.g., 1 Pet. 5:5-9 with Jas. 4:6-7: in both passages Prov. 3:34 is quoted, humility before God is called for, and resistance to the devil is urged.

[79]Schlatter at various points in his commentary (cf. e.g., *Petrus und Paulus* 66-67) calls attention to the problem that is presented by the christianizing or hellenizing of Palestinian ideas.

[80]To relate the ὅτι to the ἔννοιαν as explicative would make no sense, because it is not speaking of Christ's breaking with sin.

[81]Specific evidence is given in my work "Märtyrer und gottesknecht" (Göttingen, 1955).

the participial usage that forms the beginning of the sentence (Χριστοῦ οὖν παθόντος σαρϰί)[82] should be observed. In baptism the Christian has died with Christ, so that the old way of life is renounced and the new attitude must be put on. The figure of putting on the weaponry and armor, however, is meant to strengthen the Christians in situations of suffering (4:1-6). For this reason, in the midst of persecutions they are reminded that the break with sin, which has already taken place in baptism, puts them under obligation not to fall back again into the old pagan way of life. We are not to think here of an influence exerted by Rom. 6:7,[83] as Knopf and Bornemann thought;[84] instead, First Peter adopts the Palestinian concept of the expiatory power of suffering and death, and in this figurative application of this idea to the break with sin that is accomplished in baptism the epistle is independent of Pauline influence.

Just as in the case of 4:1, so also with reference to 4:17-18 it can be shown that the idea of the judgment that begins at the house of God is of Palestinian-Jewish origin: the Lord will first discipline Israel, in order thereby to pay the penalty for her sins; then, after this beginning of the judgment upon the ungodly, the judgment upon the righteous also will intervene.[85] First Peter employs these ideas: now judgment is beginning with the house of God, with us. But all the more dreadful will be the end of those who do not obey God's gospel! Thus the author of our epistle adopts Jewish and Christian thought-material that has been handed down and employs it in the parenesis related to sufferings: παραϰαλῶν ϰαὶ ἐπιμαρτυρῶν ταύτην εἶναι ἀληθῆν χάριν τοῦ θεοῦ, εἰς ἣν στῆτε (5:12).

In our reflections on this material we have intentionally and entirely left aside the problem of who then wrote 1 Peter, and instead of this we have attempted to elicit an understanding of the epistle from its contents. Even if it could be demonstrated that Peter or Silvanus wrote our document, still this would not provide for exegesis an answer to the question as to the source and

---

[82]1 Peter frequently speaks of Christ's having suffered, and thereby Christ's death is meant. On this point cf. W. Michaelis, *Herkunft und Bedeutung des Ausdrucks "Leiden und Sterben Jesu Christi"* (Bern, 1945) 6-7.

[83]On the meaning of Rom. 6:7 cf. K. G. Kuhn, "Zu Römerbrief 6:7" *ZNW* 30 (1931): 305-10.

[84]R. Knopf, *Die Briefe Petri und Juda* (Göttingen, 1912) 162; W. Bornemann, *ZNW* 19 (1919/20): 157-58. Perdelwitz's attempt to trace the clause in 4:1b back to the mystery religions is not convincing.

[85]T. Benj. 10; rabbinic documentation is given in Strack-Billerbeck III 767. On this point cf. also W. Wichmann, *Die Leidenstheologie* (BWANT IV, 2; Stuttgart, 1930) 29-30.

origin of the transmitted parenesis and the nature of its use.[86] From the epistle itself, however, we can conclude that the author, who adopted parenetic tradition for framing his work of consolation and comfort, must have stood in relatively close proximity to Pauline theology.[87] We shall have to hold firmly to this persuasion even if—as a precise and detailed exegesis would have to show—we cannot think of a literary dependence of 1 Peter upon the Pauline epistles. It can even be said with certainty that the epistle must have issued from Rome. This conclusion is justified not only by the mention of Babylon as a cover-name for Rome (5:13), but also by the proximity and affinity of 1 Peter to 1 Clement. The manifold connections between these two writings show that both epistles refer to similar traditional material, and indeed both have their origin in the Roman Christian community. For the connections between the two epistles cannot be explained by arguing that 1 Clement quoted from 1 Peter. Instead, Polycarp of Smyrna is the first one who certainly knew and used our epistle (Pol. *Phil.* 8:1 et passim).

The two epistles agree in characterizing the church as an alien company in the world and begin with the same liturgical introductory greeting: χάρις ὑμῖν καὶ εἰρήνη πληθυνθείη,[88] though 1 Clement, to be sure, inserts, following the word χάρις the expression ἀπὸ παντοκράτορος θεοῦ διὰ Ἰησοῦ Χριστοῦ. In both epistles, traditional parenesis has been appropriated and reworked, and in 1 Clement it has been applied to the controversy in Corinth.[89] In 1 Clement 16 as in 1 Peter, the meekness of Christ is docu-

---

[86]To be sure, Selwyn tries repeatedly to adduce evidence for apostolic authorship. He will hardly be successful in that undertaking, however, when he writes for example (*First Peter* 27): "What we know of St. Peter from the Gospels accords well with a strain of poetry in his temperament; the fisherman's life on the Lake of Gennesaret with its long vigils under the stars and its opportunities for fostering the gift of wonder, the swift intuitions which so often took him ahead of his fellow-disciples, and the steady disciplining of these under the Master's eye and word before intuition could pass through penitence into faith—all these things are consonant with such a view. They do not give him the style of I Peter, but they would give him the qualities of mind which would have made him see in the cultured Silvanus a kindred soul after his own heart."

[87]For example, ἐν Χριστῷ in 3:16, 5:10, 14; χάρισμα in 4:10, otherwise only in the Pauline epistles; καλεῖν meaning "to call," and several others. It should be noted that 1 Clement similarly appropriates Pauline expressions (thus χάρισμα, ἐν Χριστῷ, καλεῖν, etc.).

[88]1 Pet. 1:1-2 is independent of the Pauline epistolary formula. It should be noted that this form of greeting follows the Oriental, not the Greek epistolary formula. Here 1 Peter stands in the Jewish tradition, which is defined by the division of the introduction to the epistle into two parts. In the first half the names of the writer and the readers adorned with abundant attributes, and in the second half devout wishes are attached. On this matter cf. E. Lohmeyer, *ZNW* 26 (1927): 160-61. In addition to the inscription of 1 Clement, 2 Pet. 1:1-2 and Jude 1-2 should be compared with 1 Pet. 1:1-2.

[89]1 Clem. 13-15 shows how here too Old Testament citations, sayings of the Lord, and traditional material are adduced for the parenesis.

mented, not by pointing to the passion narrative but with an explicit quotation from Isaiah 53, in order to set before the Corinthians the example of Christ (ὑπογραμμός), 1 Clem. 16:7; cf. 1 Pet. 2:21). In both epistles the patriarchs are seen as fathers even of the Gentile Christians (1 Pet. 3:6; 1 Clem. 4:8; 31:2; et passim). According to both epistles, the prophets prophesied in the Holy Spirit (1 Pet. 1:11; 1 Clem. 8:1). First Peter too must take the occasion to exhort the younger members of the community to be obedient to the elders (5:1-5; 1 Clem. 57:1). Both 1 Clem. 30:2 and 1 Pet. 5:5 in quoting Prov. 3:34 put θεός in place of κύριος, which is the LXX reading. First Clem. 49:5, like 1 Pet. 4:8, quotes Prov. 10:12 in a form that agrees with neither the Hebrew text nor the LXX. In both 1 Pet. 2:9 and 1 Clem. 59:2 (cf. 36:2) we find ἐκάλεσεν ἡμᾶς ἀπὸ τοῦ σκότους εἰς φῶς. The statistical study of vocabulary, finally, can adduce a whole series of expressions that in the rest of the literature of primitive Christianity are used rarely or not at all but are employed in 1 Peter as well as in 1 Clement.[90] It should be noted in conclusion that 1 Clem. 5:4-5 names Peter and Paul in close association as the great martyr-apostles of the Roman community, while 1 Peter, as a writing issued under the authority of Peter, appears to wear Pauline clothing, and thus likewise places Peter and Paul close to each other.

One should not make too much of the connections that have been compiled here, for it is to be observed on the other hand that 1 Clement writes a more elegant kind of Greek than 1 Peter, whose Greek style has often been over-estimated,[91] and that Clement has a far better mastery of the forms of contemporary discourse than the author of 1 Peter. Since there are also various other distinctions between the two epistles to be noted—in particular, 1 Clement is influenced in far greater measure than 1 Peter by hellenistic, and especially Stoic, trains of thought—one should avoid taking the reciprocal connections between the two epistles as an occasion for posing a new hypothesis about the presumed author of the epistle. Only this much may be affirmed as a conclusion: the connections between the two epistles that have been set forth confirm the assumption that was expressed earlier, that 1 Peter

---

[90]As examples I note the following: ἀδελφότης, 1 Clem. 2:4-1 Pet. 2:17; 5:9; ἀγαθωποιεῖν/ἀγαθωποιία, 1 Clem. 2:7; 33:1; 34:2-1 Pet. 2:14-15, 20; 3:17; 4:19; ἀπροσωπολήμπτως, 1 Clem. 1:3-1 Pet. 1:17; ἐπισκοπή (day of judgment), 1 Clem. 50:3-1 Pet. 2:12; ἐποπτεύω/ἐπόπτης, 1 Clem. 59:3-1 Pet. 2:12; 3:2; God as κτίστης, 1 Clem. 19:2; 59:3; 62:2-1 Pet. 4:19; κραταιὰ χείρ, 1 Clem. 28:2; 60:3-1 Pet. 5:6; ποίμνιον, 1 Clem. 44:3; 54:2; 57:2-1 Pet. 5:2, 3; τιμὴν ἀπονέμειν, 1 Clem. 1:3-1 Pet. 3:7; φιλαδελφία, 1 Clem. 47:5; 48:1-1 Pet. 1:22; φιλοξενία, 1 Clem. 1:2; 10:7; 11:1; 12:1-1 Pet. 4:9—The list of parallels could be expanded significantly. However, since in the earlier discussion about the question of authorship the weight of vocabulary statistics was greatly exaggerated, we propose here only to point to this path and not to follow it further.

[91]On the style of 1 Peter cf. the essay by Radermacher (see above, note 31).

likewise comes from the Roman church which is writing under the authority of the apostle who is called the rock, addressing the Christians in Asia Minor who are under attack.

III

Thus, as 1 Peter shows, primitive Christian parenesis is compiled from various elements.[92] Old Testament quotations, particularly Wisdom psalms and the proverbs, Palestinian and hellenistic conceptions and traditions, and isolated sayings of the Lord[93] stand side-by-side and are adduced according to the specific needs of the moment. The growth of the parenetic tradition-material must have proceeded at first along the lines of oral tradition. Therefore it is a highly questionable undertaking to seek to detach from the abundance of material a fixed schema of a catechism.[94] Just as the Logia material in Matthew and Luke appears in different arrangement and sequence and therefore can hardly be traced back to a written source,[95] the parenetic tradition is not defined by a rigid framework, but by oral repetition.

Now while the parenesis in James and in Romans 12-13 is fitted into the epistles in a closed set of sayings and a fixed arrangement and it is preserved in blocks in these epistles in spite of being adopted, in 1 Peter the traditional material is more loosely preserved, having been expanded through the addition of applications and explanations. Especially characteristic of the parenesis of our epistle is the way in which it is combined with the kerygma, which like the parenesis is taken over from the tradition. Here we do not have the imperative deduced from the previously unfolded indicative, as is done in Paul's writings, but the parenesis comes first and then is justified by means of the appended reference to the will and the acts of God. Thus the challenge addressed to the πρεσβύτεροι to feed the flock of God (5:2) is followed in v 4 by a saying about the ἀρχιποιμήν Jesus Christ, who as the true shepherd also presents the model of proper shepherding. And wherever it appears in the epistle the causal ὅτι indicates the basis for the ethical admonition that is voiced.[96] In 1:15-16 the challenge to lead a holy life is validated by the quo-

---

[92]Cf. Selwyn, *First Peter,* 438.

[93]On 1:22 cf. Jesus' commandment to love; on 3:9 cf. the prohibition of revenge, Matt. 5:39-44 (cf. Rom. 12:17; 1 Thess. 5:15).

[94]On these efforts cf. above.

[95]On this question cf. J. Jeremias, "Zur Hypothese einer schriftlichen Logienquelle Q," *ZNW* 29 (1930): 147-49.

[96]On this point see Selwyn, *First Peter,* 217.

Is 53, χological justification for admonition to suffer

tation from Lev. 19:2, ''You shall be holy, for I am holy.''[97] In 5:5 the saying from Prov. 3:34, ''God resists the proud but gives grace to the humble,'' provides the undergirding for the word addressed to all to manifest humility in their conduct toward one another. In other passages a brief statement like ''Love covers a multitude of sins'' (4:8)[98] or a reference to the will of God (2:15, 21; 3:9) provides the justification for the parenesis.[99] Finally, it is characteristic of the way in which 1 Peter employs OT quotations for its exhortations that in 3:10-12, the verses from Ps. 34:13-17, which with only minor divergences follow the LXX,[100] are slightly altered with the insertion of a ὅτι in v 12. Thereby the theological rationale which in the psalm follows the preceding imperative without any connecting link is underscored: God's eyes look upon the righteous and his ears hear their cry, but the face of the Lord is against those who do evil.

The ultimate and actual rationale that 1 Peter offers for the ethical admonitions, however, is of a christological nature. Just as in the Pauline epistles the traditional parenesis occasionally is christianized only by an added ἐν Χριστῷ or ἐν κυρίῳ, so also 1 Peter inserts a brief theological rationale into the admonitions by the addition of διὰ τὸν κύριον (2:13) or διὰ συνείδησιν θεοῦ (2:19). A detailed justification for the parenesis is frequently given, however, by the combination of confessions and hymns with the parenetic pieces.[101] Thus it is said that the Christians' manner of life should be conducted in fear, because they know that they were not redeemed from the futile manner of life inherited from their fathers with perishable things such as silver and gold, but with the precious blood of Christ as a lamb without spot or blemish (1:17ff.). The entire community is charged rather to suffer because of good deeds, if that should be God's will, than to be punished for evil deeds (3:17). For Christ has suffered once because of sins, the just for the unjust. This saying, which is reminiscent of Isaiah 53, is followed now by a hymn about Christ that describes his saving work beginning with his death, continuing through his descent into Hades, the resurrection, the ascension, and his being seated at the right hand of the Father, to the universal

---

[97]ὅτι is employed to introduce quotations of Scripture also in 1:24 and 2:6.

[98]Similarly cf. 4:1—4:8 is a free quotation of Prov. 10:12; on this cf. Jas. 5:20.

[99]On the use of the causal ὅτι cf. further 4:14, 17.

[100]The second person of the LXX text has been transposed into the third person in 1 Peter.

[101]A. Seeberg (Der Katechismus der Urchristenheit, Leipzig 1903, 86-96) was the first to call attention to the use of formula-like material in 1 Peter. On this point cf. especially R. Bultmann, ''Bekenntnis- und Liedfragmente im I Petrusbrief'' ConNT XI (1947): 1-14.

Lordship of Christ.[102] Thus the parenesis finds its actual anchoring by being traced back to the kerygma.

The slaves who must suffer at the hands of their masters are pointed to Christ's sufferings which he bore patiently and obediently. Even here, though (2:21ff.), we do not have passages from the story of Jesus' passion; instead, the justification for the parenesis is provided by a hymn that portrays Jesus' suffering and death in a style reminiscent of Isaiah 53.[103]

The hymn begins with an explanatory ὅτι. Since its original application was not to slaves who were in distress, but rather it was sung by the entire congregation, v 24 speaks of "our sins,"[104] and it is to be presumed that in the hymn v 21 originally said ὑπὲρ ἡμῶν.[105] Since the writer of the epistle, however, now is applying this hymn to the situation of his readers, instead of the expression in the first person we have the direct address in the second person. The following verses (22-23) portray in four clauses the patient suffering of Jesus:[106] the first cites Isa. 53:9;[107] the two in the middle employ antitheses to show that Jesus endured everything without complaining: "When he was reviled, he did not revile in return; when he suffered, he did not threaten"

---

[102]On the character of the hymn cf. the commentaries on this passage. Further, cf. R. Bultmann, "Bekenntnis und Liedfragmente"; O. Cullmann, *Earliest Christian Confessions,* 20; W. Bieder, *Die Vorstellung von der Höllenfahrt Jesu Christi* (Zurich, 1949); J. Jeremias, "Zwischen Karfreitag und Ostern" (*ZNW,* 1949) 194ff. The verses 3:18-22 break the connection, for the train of thought of 3:13-17 is not taken up again until 4:1. Thus we are dealing with the quotation of some fixed formulations that are cited here because they begin with an utterance about Christ's sufferings. Bultmann's attempt at reconstructing a hymn from 1:20 and 3:18-22 is not convincing, since it requires too drastic emendations of the text and moreover proceeds from the unproven assertion that originally the hymn dealt with the gnostic idea of the redeemer's preaching to the spirits in the air.

[103]Vv. 21ff. are more ancient than the parenesis that precedes them. This is evident from the fact that the reference to the example of Christ would cause us to expect a precise correspondence to what was said just before this. Instead of a clause like ὅτι καὶ Χριστὸς ἀγαθωποιῶν καὶ πάσχων ὑπέμεινεν (cf. A. Knopf. *Die Briefe Petri und Juda* 114), however, it is Jesus' vicarious suffering that is the theme here.

[104]Codex B, assimilated here to v. 21, has τὰς ἁμαρτίας ὑμῶν.

[105]P, the Byzantine (Koine) text, and the Clementine Vulgate read ἡμῶν and ὑμῖν; 2 and the Peshitta Syriac read ἡμῶν and ἡμῖν. This textual attestation, however, carries no weight. The change into the second person must have been preferred by the writer of the epistle.

[106]Our division of the clauses differs from that of R. Bultmann ("Bekenntnis- und Liedfragmente" 13).

[107]LXX Isa. 53:9: ὅτι ἀνομίαν οὐκ ἐποίησεν οὐδὲ δόλον ἐν τῷ στόματι αὐτοῦ. 1 Clem. 16:10 has the same variant text as 1 Pet. 2:21: ὅτι ἀνομίαν οὐκ ἐποίησεν οὐδὲ εὑρέθη δόλος ἐν τῷ στόματι αὐτοῦ. This probably is a variant of the LXX text which perhaps arose under the influence of Zeph. 3:13.

hymn is used as parenesis rather than kerygma

(RSV).[108] The fourth clause says, in an effective contrast to the silence that Jesus maintained with reference to men, that he did, however, commit it all to him who judges righteously.[109] Verse 24 again borrows from Isaiah 53 and concludes the portrayal of Christ's suffering by pointing to its atoning effect. Thus two statements about Jesus' atoning death provide a frame for the brief account of the passion that is shaped in accordance with Isaiah 53, and thereby they emphasize for whose benefit all this has happened. Even in v 25 there is no reference to the context in which the entire *Haustafel* stands. Instead, the hymn ends here with a reminder to the church that on the basis of the forgiveness of sins that has been wrought by Jesus' suffering and dying, they, once wandering sheep, have been gathered into a flock under the one shepherd and bishop of their souls. Thus even from these last words of the hymn it emerges that here we are not dealing with expressions that are formulated *ad hoc,* but with a quotation from a hymn about Christ.

καὶ Χριστὸς ἔπαθεν ὑπὲρ ὑμῶν (ἡμῶν)—the hymn begins with this confessional sentence and follows the parenesis. In the prefixed καί the slaves and Christ are joined together in a fellowship of suffering. In this brief declaration that Christ's passion was suffered for us the theme of the hymn is indicated. In v 21b, however, this theme has been changed by the author of the hymn, by his setting Christ before the slaves as an example. They are challenged to follow in his footsteps. Consequently, the subject is no longer Christ's vicarious atoning death; instead, Christ's sufferings are understood as exemplary.[110] Thus the kerygmatic accent of the hymn has been thrust aside in favor of the parenesis, so that v 21b must not have belonged to the hymn originally.

By its being linked to the kerygma, however, the parenesis is provided with a stout justification. For through Christ's atoning death we have died to sin, in order to live unto righteousness. Through Christ's wounds healing is accomplished,[111] so that the believers have been set free to a new life (2:24).

---

[108]This portrayal of Jesus' patient suffering must have been the reason for the citing of the hymn in connection with the parenesis to the slaves, in order to set before the suffering slaves the example of Christ. Therefore we are not to assume that these clauses were first formulated by the author of the epistle. (contra Bultmann, ''Bekenntnis- und Liedfragmente'' 13).

[109]The παρεδίδου of Jesus stands over against the παρεδόθη of Isa. 53:12. He let himself be sacrificed and left everything to God's hands.

[110]On the exemplary character of Jesus' sufferings cf. Heb. 12:2; Mark 10:45. It is in keeping with the high estimate of Christ's sufferings as an example that in the second century there is increasingly frequent mention of Christ's ὑπομένειν in suffering. This ὑπομένειν functions as an example for the Christians' patient suffering. Cf. *Barn.* 5:1, 6, 12; Ign. *Pol.* 3:2; Pol. *Phil.* 1:2; 8:1-2; Justin *Apol.* I.50.1; 63.10, 16; *Dial.* 68.1; 121.2.

[111]Cf. Isa. 53:5: ἰάθημεν however has been changed into ἰάθητε, in order to address the community directly.

In their sufferings now they are referred to their Lord; they are comforted because the dying and resurrection of Jesus Christ has already taken place for their sake. The eschatological event that has dawned with his death and resurrection also includes the suffering of the Christians. The judgment that is now breaking in upon the house of God, however, will soon and inescapably be followed by the judgment of the living and the dead (4:17-19; 4:5). On the basis of this eschatological understanding the suffering of the Christians is comprehended as a participation in Christ's sufferings (4:13),[112] and for this very reason, joy prevails in the Christian community (4:13-14; 1:6-7). Blessed is that person who is reproached for Christ's sake (4:14). But on the other hand, precisely because these are the last times (4:7), the ethical obligation that is laid upon the Christians is to be taken with double seriousness. By their love and good deeds they are to bear witness to the truth of their faith (2:12, 15, 20; 3:1, 6, 17; 4:7-11, 15; et passim), always ready to give to anyone who asks an account of the hope that is in them (3:15).

The confessional and hymnic pieces that are used by 1 Peter treat—as we have seen—of Christ's sufferings (cf. 1:18-21; 2:21-25; 3:18-22) and are cited because of these contents. In this way the parenesis finds its anchoring in the kerygma, and the inherited material of varied origin is tuned to the one basic tone that sounds through the epistle from beginning to end. Christ has suffered, and the Christians are called upon to follow in his steps. As strangers and sojourners in this world, however, they are on the way to their heavenly home with joyous hope.

---

[112]On this point cf. H. Braun, *Das Leiden Christi* (Theologische Existenz heute 69; München, 1940).

CHAPTER 4

1 PETER, ITS SITUATION AND STRATEGY: A DISCUSSION WITH DAVID BALCH

JOHN H. ELLIOTT
UNIVERSITY OF SAN FRANCISCO
SAN FRANCISCO, CALIFORNIA

The following represents an expanded version of my contribution to a dialogue with David Balch on 1 Peter held in December 1982. This discussion was part of the program of the joint annual meeting of the American Academy of Religion and the Society of Biblical Literature that took place on 19-22 December 1982 in New York City. Our dialogue and its theme, "1 Peter: Social Separation or Acculturation?" had been prompted by the opposing conclusions that we had reached concerning the situation and strategy of 1 Peter in our recently published works, *A Home for the Homeless*[1] and *Let Wives Be Submissive*.[2]

---

[1]John H. Elliott, *A Home for the Homeless: A Sociological Exegesis of 1 Peter, Its Situation and Strategy* (Philadelphia: Fortress, 1981); see also my *1 Peter: Estrangement and Community* (Herald Biblical Booklets, Chicago: Franciscan Herald Press, 1979) and my popular-level commentary that appeared following our discussion, *James* (R. A. Martin), *I-II Peter/Jude* (John H. Elliott) (Augsburg Commentary on the New Testament, Minneapolis: Augsburg, 1982).

[2]David L. Balch, *Let Wives Be Submissive: The Domestic Code in 1 Peter* (Society of

As is the case with many such dialogues, this one too had its history of previous exchanges. In my study, *A Home for the Homeless,* I had referred to Balch's original 1974 Yale dissertation.[3] In his dissertation as well as in its published version (1981) he had commented on my earlier treatment of 1 Peter 2:4-10, *The Elect and the Holy* (1966).[4] This published work, containing both striking agreements and sharp divergences, set the background for our 1982 discussion. By agreeing to summarize our views on 1 Peter and critique each other's conclusions we hoped to shed some light on the complex social dynamics implied by this text and ultimately to advance the understanding of early Christianity's engagement with its environment. The positive response of those attending our friendly debate has encouraged us to make this discussion available to a wider audience.

Unfortunately, no recording was made of the proceedings and much of the exchange was oral. Professor Balch summarized a paper that he had prepared, and my response was based on a summary of its main points, which he had sent me in advance of the meeting. The remainder of the discussion consisted in oral exchange between ourselves and the audience. With Professor Balch's 1982 paper now at my disposal, I can offer in this article a more extensive response to his comments. First I shall summarize major points on which we agree. Next some minor misunderstandings or misreadings will be clarified. Then the remainder of this article will treat areas and issues of major disagreement.

POINTS OF AGREEMENT

1. Regarding the general time frame of 1 Peter and the social situation it presumes, we agree that the letter was written in the last third of the first century (Balch, *Wives,* 138: "65-90 A.D."; Elliott, *Home,* 87: "73-92 C.E."). It was addressed to Christians suffering not as a result of an official persecution of Christianity instigated by Rome but as a consequence of sporadic outbursts of local suspicion, resentment, and hostility.

2. We agree that 1 Peter incorporates and modifies a traditional hellenistic household code though there is disagreement over the purpose of its employment (*Home,* 207-37; *Wives,* 1-20, 81-116; Paper, 1-3 and passim).

Biblical Literature Monograph Series, 26; Chico: Scholars Press, 1981). For a recent assessment of both works see the review essay of Antoinette Wire in *Religious Studies Review* 10:3 (1984): 209-16.

[3]David L. Balch, *"Let Wives Be Submissive . . . " The Origin, Form and Apologetic Function of the Household Duty Code (Haustafel) in 1 Peter* (Ann Arbor: University Microfilms International, 1976).

[4]John H. Elliott, *The Elect and the Holy. An Exegetical Examination of 1 Peter 2:4-10 and the phrase Basileion Hierateuma* (NovT Supplements 12; Leiden: E. J. Brill, 1966).

3. We agree that the historical origin of this domestic code can be traced back to Aristotle's comments on the household in the first book of his *Politics* (*Home*, 213-20; *Wives*, 33-59.)

4. In our respective studies both of us have also noted the antiquity, continuity, and universality of the association between discussions concerning household management (*oikonomia*) and management of the city or state (*politeia*). The roles and relations of the household provided an apposite model for conceptualizing and legitimating roles and status in the political sphere. The use and elaboration of the "*oikonomia* tradition" (*Home*, 214) served as a vehicle for promoting order and harmony in both *oikos* and *polis* by embodying a set of shared values concerning the central importance of the *oikos* as the primary instance of human association, its structure and its effective management.

From these common observations, however, the differing focuses of our research in *Wives* and *Home* have taken us on diverging paths and ultimately led us to conflicting conclusions concerning the function of the proximate origin and intended function of the household code in 1 Peter. Balch (*Wives*, paper) restricts his attention exclusively to the material and purpose of the code in 1 Peter and sees the use of the code as evidence that the letter is advocating a program of Christian assimilation to secular society. On the other hand, I am concerned with the totality of 1 Peter and the manner in which the household code serves the letter's overall strategy of encouraging and exhorting its addressees as the brotherhood of faith (2:17, 5:9) and household of God (2:5, 4:17).

CLARIFICATIONS

As my colleague has pointed out (Paper, 4), unclarity concerning the issue under question had led to some misunderstandings and misrepresentations. I welcome and accept his criticism that I have erroneously mistaken his interpretation of the aim of the Petrine household code in *Wives* for an interpretation of the general aim of the letter as a whole. It is a hermeneutical truism, however, that the function of any of the parts of a writing can only be adequately determined by examination of its total literary context and of its role within the total line of argument from commencement to close. One of my major contentions is that in neglecting to analyze and explain in *Wives* how the household code relates to and serves the general strategy of the letter, Balch has forfeited an essential control over his interpretation. He thus has produced an incomplete and unbalanced assessment of the code, its context, and of the social dynamics implied by the letter. The remarks of his present paper, however, involve a "necessarily broader" view of the pertinent issues for discussion (Paper, 5). This will require a consideration of 1 Peter in its totality.

Before turning to points of major disagreement, I too should like to clarify some minor misreadings or misimpressions. Among the many instances in 1 Peter of social polarity and conflict that I cite, I nowhere claim that the letter sets "the rural house of God over against the evil city" (paper, 5, 9). My point in *Home* (59-65) is that the intended recipients of the letter included inhabitants of the predominantly rural regions of the Anatolian interior and that the letter reflects awareness of their rural location.[5] The fundamental contrast to which I call attention is that drawn between the Christian community and external non-Christian society, life within the *oikos* of God as contrasted with resident alien status (*paroikia*) within secular society (*Home,* 21-58, 118-32, 200-37).

Balch also wonders how I can "read the domestic code and conclude that the letter encourages the termination of past familial ties" (Paper, 8). Here I suggest, he is confusing his reading of the domestic code with my interpretation of such passages as 1:3-5, 10-12, 13-21; 2:4-10, 11; 4:1-6. Finally, Balch curiously sees me implying that Christian sectarians "swallow[ed] Roman politics whole" (Paper, 22, n. 42) when a major concern of my study is to demonstrate the measures urged in 1 Peter for *resisting* external pressures to conform (*Home,* 101-64 and passim).

With this final clarification we are already touching on areas of substantive disagreement.

MAJOR DISAGREEMENTS

Our first methodological disagreement involves more than the differing focal points of our interests, his in the household code and mine in the letter as a whole. It rather concerns the scope of the material to be taken into consideration when attempting to ascertain the strategy[6] of a biblical writing or

---

[5]For a more extensive treatment of this issue see Armand Piug Tarrech, "Le Milieu de la première Epître de Pierre," *Revista Catalana de Teologia* 5 (1980): 95-129, 331-402. This study is an expansion of his research paper for a course on 1 Peter that I taught at the Pontifical Biblical Institute in Rome in the Spring semester, 1978. It is in relation to Luke-Acts, not 1 Peter, that attention was called to the contrast between the household and the temple and its urban base (*Home,* 193-94). On the well-known ancient contrast between rurality and *urbanitas* see Ramsay MacMullen, *Roman Social Relations 50 B.C. to A.D. 284* (New Haven: Yale University Press, 1974) esp. pp. 28-56 and G. E. M. de Ste. Croix, *The Class Struggle in the Ancient Greek World from the Archaic Age to the Arab Conquests* (Ithaca: Cornell University Press, 1981) esp. pp. 9-19.

[6]On the meaning and use of the term "strategy" see Elliott, *Home,* 10-11, 19 n. 22, 106-107.

the function of any of its component parts. Ignoring all but the code material in 1 Peter, Balch thinks that a social function of this code can be determined solely on the basis of its content and its previous history and use. I, on the other hand, maintain that a determination of the function of this or any other traditional material incorporated in 1 Peter requires analysis not only of its content, shape, history and function *prior* to its incorporation in 1 Peter, but also of the manner in which this tradition has been adapted to fit and serve the general strategy of the letter.

Restriction of attention to the Petrine household code alone, in my opinion, constitutes an unjustifiable isolation of the part from the whole. All subunits of the Petrine letter, except for demonstrable later interpolations (which Balch does not claim the code to be), are controlled in their semantic, syntactic, and pragmatic (functional) aspects by their larger context, the text as a whole. Accordingly, the function of the household code in 1 Peter may be expected to be consonant with the argument and aim of the letter in its totality. Through an investigation of the entire content of 1 Peter, I have attempted in *Home* to elucidate the part played by the domestic code material in the overall strategy of the letter. Balch, on the other hand, in focusing exclusively on the code itself has neglected to examine the relation of this material to its total context. This difference in method and the scope of the material examined has led us to divergent conclusions regarding both the significance of the code in 1 Peter in particular and the strategy of the letter in general. His theory that the code has been employed to indicate and urge Christian assimilation to secular values appears diametrically opposed to my theory that the code provides a schema in 1 Peter for instructing Christians concerning the conduct and commitments typical of the Christian brotherhood, the household of God (*Home,* 200-37). The first view, I would contend, assigns to the household code in 1 Peter an aim incompatible with the letter's general strategy. The second view sees the code as part of a coherent argument developed throughout the letter.

Though *Wives* contains an analysis of the structure of 1 Peter (123-31), it remains unclear to me how Balch understands the letter's overall strategy. Since I have already treated this question at length (*Home,* 101-64), a summary of my view may suffice at this point. In general the letter offers consolation and encouragement to Christian resident aliens and strangers suffering from local hostility, slander, and unjustifiable abuse. The strategy of the letter was to counteract the demoralizing and disintegrating impact that such social tension and suffering had upon the Christian sect by reassuring the intended recipients of the distinctive elect and holy community to which they belonged and the new dignity they shared by virtue of their call by God, their sanctification through baptismal rebirth, and their faith in Jesus Christ, the elect and holy suffering servant of God. As obedient children subject to the

divine Father's will, these holy people are urged to lead a holy way of life
that specifically involves not only the avoidance of evil and the doing of good
but also nonconformity "to the passions of your former ignorance" (1:14)
and "futile ways inherited from your fathers"(1:17), renunciation of Gentile
(that is, non-Christian) patterns of behavior (2:11, 4:1-3), severance of de-
bilitating social ties (4:4) and vigilant resistance of the devilish adversary
seeking to devour them (5:8-9). In general the injunctions, contrasts, imagery, and traditions in 1 Peter all served the common aim of reinforcing a
sense of distinctive communal identity, promoting the internal cohesion of
the community, and providing it with a persuasive sustaining rationale for
continued faith, commitment, and hope.

Within this conceptual framework and consonant with the letter's general
aim, the household code (2:13-3:12; 5:1-5) provides a schema for delineating
behavior, norms, and values typical of persons belonging to the household of
God. At some points Christian and secular valuations of behavior converge
(for example, respect for just civil rulers, 2:13-14; avoiding evil and doing
good, 2:12, 14, 15, 20; 3:6, 10-12, 13-17; 4:12-19; subordination of domestic slaves to owners, wives to husbands and younger men to elders, 2:18-20,
3:1-6, 5:5). At other key points, on the other hand, a distinctive Christian perspective and rationale is evident and a clear distinction of allegiance and ethos
is stressed. The ultimate reason for Christian subordination, for instance, is
obedience to the will of God as his servants (2:15-16, 19-20; cf. 3:17; 4:2,
19) consistent with the obedience of the servant Lord (2:13, 21-25, cf. 1:2).
In 2:18-20 the traditional order of domestic roles is reversed so that domestic
servants are *first* addressed and thereby made examples of the entire household of God to which then the connected christological material applies (2:21-
25). In their subordination to their husbands, wives are Sarah's children and
God's subjects in the doing of good (3:6). Conjugal life is motivated by the
fact that *both* believing husbands and wives are "co-heirs of the grace of God"
(3:7). Mutual humility of *all* members of God's household, superordinates
and subordinates alike, is a sign of a common subordination to the will of God
(3:8-9, 5:5-7). In 2:17 a clear distinction is drawn between the honor due the
emperor as to all men on the one hand, and on the other, the love that binds
only the brotherhood (cf. 1:22, 3:8, 4:8, 5:14) and the fear (awe and reverence) that is reserved for God alone (cf. 1:17; 2:17-18; 3:2, 6, 14, 16).

This similarity and yet dissimilarity in Christian and secular values and
ethos brings us to the important question raised in Balch's paper concerning
"separation, boundaries, and linkages." Before proceeding, however, first
a word of summary is in order. Thus far a comparison of our two analyses of
1 Peter presents us with the following alternatives. As a rather unlikely possibility for which I see no textual justification, it might be suggested that there
is no coherence between the strategy of the letter in general and the function

of the code in particular. In this case, Balch's hypothesis concerning the function of the code material might be correct, my interpretation of the general strategy of the letter might also be correct, but my proposal regarding the function of the code might be erroneous. If, however, as seems much more likely, there is a coherence between the aim of the letter in general and that of the code in particular, then: (A) either Balch's interpretation of the code's function is correct and my interpretation of the letter's overall strategy is incorrect; or (B) my interpretation is correct on both counts and his conclusions regarding the code's function is incorrect.

Balch's present paper, while still directing attention to the material of the Petrine code, has the merit of broadening the field of discussion. The questions he raises require examination of the entire text of 1 Peter and of the sociological theories most useful for discerning its situation and strategy. Since the theory underlying his string of arguments in pages 5-11 becomes evident in his comments on ''Separation, Boundaries, and Linkages'' (11-13), I shall begin here and consider his earlier points when they become pertinent.

First Peter bears witness to the difficulties encountered by the early Christian movement in its interaction with non-Christian society. On the one hand, by the time of 1 Peter this messianic movement in Christianity constituted a movement distinguishable from both its parent Judaism and other Mediterranean cults. Its adherents bore the distinctive label of *christianoi* (4:16). Attracting Jews and Gentiles alike to its vision of a universal salvation, it saw itself as the covenant community of the end time, God's special elect and holy people (2:4-10). It was constituted by God's merciful election and call (1:2, 15; 2:4-10; 5:10, 13) and faith in Jesus Christ and his resurrection that conferred new life and hope (1:3, 13, 21; 3:15, 21; 5:10). These distinctive beliefs involved a distinctive set of loyalties to God, Jesus Christ, and the brotherhood and required a distinctive mode of behavior. As the God who calls is holy, so believers are to be holy and ''not to conform to the passions of your former ignorance'' (1:14-16; 2:11; 4:1-3). As obedient children born anew to a living hope (1:3, 14, 22), believers were subject to God's will. In their hearts they were to reverence Christ as Lord (3:15) and await his coming with hope and confidence (1:5, 7, 13; 4:13; 5:1).

On the other hand, this sectarian community did not and could not live in a social vacuum. In contrast to the Qumran sect, for example, its conception of a universal salvation was embodied in a universal mission. The brotherhood reached throughout the world (5:9). Its goal was to convert nonbelievers to the faith and to the glorification of God (2:12, 3:2). This exotic movement from the East, however, was perceived to be a dangerous cancer within the body politic and was treated accordingly. Within its ranks were many strangers and resident aliens (*parepidemoi, paroikoi,* 1:2, 2:11) who had no permanent roots in the local communities and whose strange language, habits, and customs already called into question their civic loyalties. In the Christian community these marginalized and displaced strangers in society had sought a place of belonging, and a salvation that involved a new and inclusive form of human brotherhood. But the exclusive allegiance to God and the severance of social ties which conversion to Christianity required (1:14-19, 4:4) only exacerbated the social tensions. Branded with the opprobrious label "Christians" (4:16, literally, "Christ-lackeys"), the followers of Jesus had begun to suffer from discrimination, slander, and reproach of a hostile society comprising Jews and pagans alike (1:6; 2:12, 19-20; 3:9, 13-17; 4:4, 12-15; 5:1, 8-10). Suffering caused by the social tensions with outsiders would eventually undermine confidence, cohesion, and commitment within the community. Discouragement could also lead to defection and the disintegration of the sect. Suffering and the opprobrium of "strangeness" could have been minimized or eliminated through the simple step of social conformity or assimilation. But this would have resulted in the sacrifice of the distinctiveness and exclusiveness to which the sect owed its existence. The crisis that the Christians of Asia Minor faced was not simply coping with suffering in itself but maintaining those elements of their communal life which suffering threatened to undermine: a common sense of identity and mission nurtured by a unifying faith and hope that involved unswerving loyalty to God, Jesus Christ, and the brotherhood.[7]

This foregoing analysis of the situation addressed in 1 Peter is based upon material in the letter. The reconstruction of the social dynamics and the underlying social issues at stake, however, is made with the help of social scientific research on sects. The social conditions, tensions, and strategies evident in 1 Peter are typical of sects or analogous religious movements in formative stages of their development, particularly those groups adopting what has been described as a "conversionist response to the world."[8]

Professor Balch rejects the conversionist sect as an appropriate model for analyzing the character and condition of the Petrine community and instead contends that "the Petrine communities are more acculturated than Professor Elliott suggests" (Paper, 12). He proposes the case of the Mennonites in North American society as a more appropriate social analogue for conceptualizing

---

[7]For similar assessments of the situation of the Petrine situation see, inter alia, the literature cited in *Home,* 57-58, nn. 87 and 88; Marc E. Kohler, "La communauté des Chrétiens selon la premier Épître de Pierre," *Revue de Théologie et de Philosophie* 114 (1982): 1-21; and especially the commentaries of Leonard Goppelt, *Der erste Petrusbrief* (KEK 12/1, ed. Ferdinand Hahn, 1. ed.; Göttingen: Vandenhoeck und Ruprecht, 1978) and Norbert Brox, *Der erste Petrusbrief* (Evangelisch-Katholischer Kommentar zum Neuen Testament 21; Zürich: Benzinger, and Neukirchen-Vluyn: Neukirchner Verlag, 1979).

[8]Elliott, *Home,* 73-84, 107-18.

the situation of the Petrine communities in first century Asia Minor.[9] Within the limits imposed by any such cross-cultural comparison,[10] the value of Balch's suggestion is to call attention to the related dynamics of group "boundary maintenance" and "linkage" of some group members with elements of the external social system.[11]

As with any subsociety within the total social system, this tension between boundary maintenance (preservation of distinctive group values, beliefs, norms, identity, and limits set on intergroup contacts) and system linkage (contacts and interdependency among groups) aptly characterizes a dilemma reflected also in 1 Peter and the early Christian movement. J. Howard Kauffman's description of the Mennonite dilemma which Balch quotes (Paper, 13-14), in fact, is strikingly similar to my analysis of the dilemma facing the Petrine community (*Home*, 107-108). I have attempted to show how the strategy of 1 Peter *in its entirety* was designed to deal with *both* horns of this dilemma. While advocating means for preserving the distinctive identity, internal cohesion, and continued commitment of the addressees (that is, effective steps toward boundary maintenance), the letter also encourages behavior, principally the avoidance of evil and the doing of good (2:12, 14, 15; 3:6, 10-12, 13-17; 4:19), or a holy way of life in obedience to God's will (1:14-17, 22; 2:1, 19; 3:1-6, 13-17; 4:1-4, 12-19) which will enlighten and silence Gentile (that is, outsiders') ignorance (2:15, 3:15), put the lie to their slander (2:12, 3:16, 4:14-16) and ultimately be effective in even "winning" such outsiders to the faith (3:1-2) and leading them to glorify God (2:12, cf. *Home*, 118-29).

Balch, unfortunately, examines only one of the two horns of this dilemma. As a consequence he draws unbalanced conclusions concerning the situation addressed in this letter and the letter's overall aim.

---

[9]Balch makes use of J. Howard Kauffman's study, "Boundary Maintenance and Cultural Assimilation of Contemporary Mennonites," *Mennonite Quarterly Review* 51 (1977): 227-40.

[10]The comparison of firmly established independent Mennonite groups in the United States and Canada with an emergent Christian sectarian movement in Asia Minor has serious limitations. In any such cross-cultural comparison differing historical, economic, social, political, and cultural conditions must be weighed. Furthermore, the groups Balch compares are in different stages of development and face different modes of response from their "host societies." The problem of "stagnation" facing the Mennonites according to Kauffman varies greatly from the problem of hostile abuse encountered by the Asia Minor Christians. Finally, while both groups seek to maintain identity and cohesion through boundary control, I see no evidence in 1 Peter of the further goal that Kauffman attributes to the Mennonites, namely that of "making socio-political contributions to the larger world and receiving beneficial value inputs from the larger world" (235). The value of Kauffman's study for our purposes lies chiefly in the attention it calls to the concepts of "boundary maintenance" and "linkage."

[11]On "boundary maintenance" and "systemic linkage" see Charles P. Loomis, *Social Systems: Essays on Their Persistence and Change* (Princeton: D. Van Nostrand, 1960) 31-34, and Marvin E. Olsen, *The Process of Social Organization: Power in Social Systems*, 2d ed. (New York: Holt, Rinehart and Winston, 1978) 74-75.

His case for the supposition that "the Jewish author of 1 Peter is assimilating" (Paper, 15), is based on two questionable suppositions: (1) that the household code is employed in 1 Peter to urge "a systemic linkage between Christian sectarians and Roman society" (Paper, 14, 15) and (2) that this shows a preference for Greco-Roman domestic values and structures which were "radically different" from those of Old Testament Israelite society (Paper, 15).

The second supposition is even weaker than the first. Is Balch seriously suggesting that wives and slaves did not occupy subordinate positions in ancient Israelite patriarchal society (Paper, 15)? Furthermore why compare 1 Peter to the domestic structures and values of ancient Israel when the arrangements and culture of hellenistic Judaism are closer to hand? As Balch himself has shown in *Wives*,[12] both Philo and Josephus give eloquent testimony to diaspora Judaism's adoption of the hellenistic structure and rationale of household management. The close affinities between hellenistic-Jewish and hellenistic-Christian reflections on household management point to the former as *the most immediate source* of influence upon the latter. Thus it appears unwarranted to conclude that "the pattern of household submission" in 1 Peter indicates *direct* Christian adoption of Greco-Roman culture and a calculated step toward social assimilation (Balch, Paper, 3, 4-15).[13] Christianity emerged in a social context where these patriarchal structures were already in place. Its choice was not whether or not to "adopt" domestic patterns in which its members already found themselves, but whether or not to encourage behavior within these structures which would embody a new set of values typical of a new vision of human community.

First Peter advocated the latter course. In religiously divided households slaves and wives were to remain subordinate, but for the same reason that in the communal household of faith subordination was appropriate. Subordination now signified submission to *God's will* and solidarity with the obedient servant Lord (2:18-25). In this brotherhood all members are co-heirs and household stewards of God's grace (3:7, 4:10). While this represents no frontal assault on the institution of the hellenistic household, it also constitutes no case of total capitulation to pagan values.

---

[12]Balch, *Wives*, 8, 52-56. See also James E. Crouch, *The Origin and Intention of the Colossian Haustafel* (FRLANT 109: Göttingen: Vandenhoeck und Ruprecht, 1972) passim, and Goppelt, *Der erste Petrusbrief*, 166-68.

[13]Earlier in *Wives* Balch took a more cautious position. Here he considered it "*a priori* probable" that influence came "through Hellenistic Judaism rather than through pagan sources" and states: "the ultimate origin of the ethic is to be found in Greek political thought, but I cannot draw firm conclusions about the immediate source of the code in 1 Peter" (120).

Balch's first supposition relates his theory concerning assimilation to the issue of social linkage. He defines "assimilation" as "the process of replacing traditional . . . norms of belief and behavior with alternative norms borrowed or adopted from the surrounding society and cultures" (Paper, 13, 14). The phenomenon and process of assimilation is actually more complex than this, involving not only the change of cultural patterns to those of [the] host society ("acculturation"), but also "large-scale entrance into cliques, clubs, and institutions of the host society ("identificational assimilation"), absence of prejudice ("attitude receptional assimilation"), absence of discrimination (behavior receptional assimilation), and the absence of value and power conflict ("civic assimilation").[14] A thorough consideration of 1 Peter as reflecting a situation of Christian assimilation to Greco-Roman society would require examination of all these factors in the assimilation process, an enterprise that at this point must be reserved for another time. For the present discussion I will restrict myself to the following observations.

The material in 1 Peter upon which Balch concentrates does indeed illustrate some points of system linkage (contacts between Christian slaves and wives with non-Christian owners and husbands, 2:18-25, 3:1-6). I do not find this cogent evidence, however, for the contention that this material "urges the Christian sectarians in one social system to maintain systemic linkages to pagans in another, Roman, social-political system" (Paper, 14). Slaves and wives were not advised to terminate their relations with unbelieving owners and husbands because slaves had no legal power or right to do so, and because of Christian valuation of the marital bond and the envisioned possibility of spousal conversion (3:1-2 and 1 Cor. 7:10-16).

Moreover, even here in the letter, the valuation of domestic order (and its institutionalization through super- and subordination) shared by Christian and non-Christian alike is conditioned by Christian motives attached to such behavior ("for the Lord's sake, 2:13, and 2:18-20 followed by 2:21-25; as children of Sarah and the holy women who "hoped in God," 3:5-6). In the case of the wives, furthermore, the expectation is that such subordination may gain their husbands for the Christian community (3:1-2). Where Christians' relations with non-Christians cannot or need not be terminated, as in the case of these slaves and wives, the believers should use the situation as an opportunity for demonstrating the distinctive beliefs, values, and commitments of the Christian brotherhood, including steadfastness in faith and unjust suffering in mindfulness of God and in solidarity with the suffering Lord (2:18-25),

---

[14]Milton M. Gordon, *Assimilation in American Life. The Role of Race, Religion, and National Origins* (New York: Oxford University Press, 1964) esp. 60-83. I am grateful to my colleague Ralph Lane, Jr. for referring me to this study.

and "reverent, chaste and confident conduct" in solidarity with the holy women of old (3:1-6) and in hope of spousal conversion.

Keeping open the channels of communication between believers and nonbelievers ought not to be confused with an advocacy of social assimilation. Nor has it been shown that 1 Peter anywhere urges an *increase* in system linkages which a program of social assimilation would require. The hope of *converting* nonbelievers through exemplary Christian behavior points rather in an opposite direction. Contacts between insiders and outsiders are to be utilized as an opportunity for recruitment to the Christian faith and "proclaiming the mighty saving deeds of him who called you out of darkness into his marvelous light" (2:9).

Thus, even the material upon which Balch exclusively focuses fails to demonstrate the theory that the maintenance of Christian and non-Christian contacts is evidence of 1 Peter's interest in social assimilation. This theory appears even more implausible when we consider the related factor that Balch mentions but fails to examine.

As has been previously noted by Balch himself following Kauffman, interaction between groups involves the dilemma of *both* system linkages *and* boundary maintenance. What he states about the problem facing the Mennonites applies equally to the Petrine community:

> The old dilemma shows itself again. If they were to tighten their boundaries and reduce their linkages with other groups, Mennonites would give less, and receive less from, other groups. On the other hand, if they abandoned their boundaries and greatly increased their linkages, Mennonites would lose their present identity and no longer have any contribution to make to themselves or to other groups. The goal has to be to keep up enough communication linkages to allow the flow of benefits inward and outward, but also to maintain boundaries effective enough to prevent the loss of whatever unique identity Mennonites have, or whatever contribution they can make to the world around them. (Paper, 14)

Balch's analysis of 1 Peter, however, gives no attention to the other horn of this dilemma, namely, its concern for the maintenance of Christian group boundaries. In focusing exclusively on the household code and the issue of social linkage, he fails to examine the evidence of a predominant stress upon the necessity for dissociation and nonconformity, a stress that is bolstered by emphasis upon the believers' distinctive communal identity and divinely conferred status as the elect and holy household of faith. Any adequate explanation of the letter's situation and strategy must take into account all its content. Balch's interpretation does not. In his analysis it remains unclear whether or how both horns of the dilemma were addressed in 1 Peter.

My contention is that nothing in 1 Peter, including its discussion of household duties, indicates an interest in promoting social assimilation. It was

precisely a temptation to assimilate so as to avoid further suffering that the
letter intended to counteract. To be sure, there were patterns of behavior that
the sectarian minority and the secular society commonly valued. Both Christians and non-Christians placed a premium on *agathopoiia* and avoiding vices,
as well as social order, domestic harmony, and the "gentle and quiet spirit"
of wives. On the other hand, according to 1 Peter, Christians hold that this
same "gentleness" should characterize *all* believers, males and females alike
(3:4, 15). Humility, moreover, is not only appropriate for slaves but typifies
all believers, superordinates and subordinates alike. Therefore servants/slaves
and wives provide the model for all Christians to emulate just as Jesus Christ
the suffering servant of God has established the ultimate model and rationale
for the reversal of values within the Christian brotherhood. First Peter makes
reference to both similar and dissimilar sets of values and establishes for all
such values a distinctively Christian configuration of motivations and legit-
imations; namely, obedience to God's will, solidarity with the rejected and
yet exalted and vindicated Lord, and membership in a new community created by God's mercy and marked by his holiness.

Where there is no conflict of interest between conformity to God's will
and subordination to human authorities established by God (2:13), submission is recommended "on account of the Lord" (2:13, 21:24). The avoidance
of evil and the doing of good is behavior consonant with both societal and
divine norms (2:1, 12, 14-16; 3:10-12, 13-17; 4:12-19).

But where Christian adherence to pagan values, customs, and moral stan-
dards would violate the will of God, and obscure the distinction between the
respect due the emperor and the fear reserved for God alone (2:17); where
retaliation sanctioned in society would betray the solidarity Christians have
with their nonretaliating Lord (2:18-25; 3:9, 15-16); where exploitation of role
and rank would deny the humility, love, and mutual service owed by all believers to one another (1:22, 2:17, 4:8-11, 5:2-5) as "good household stewards of god's varied grace" (4:10-11); where continued association with
nonbelievers and their sinful desires and futile ways (1:18; 2:11; 4:2-4) would
contradict the reality of their conversion, their holy union with God and Jesus
Christ and their incorporation into a new family united by a distinctive faith
and hope (1:3-2:10); then in such instances when the distinctive identity,
cohesion, and commitments of the brotherhood are at stake, the household of
God is to manifest its distinctiveness through behavior consonant with the will
of God and through social disengagement, nonconformity, and resistance
(1:13-21, 2:11, 4:2-4; 5:8-9). Though the price for such nonconformity be
societal abuse and Christian suffering, such suffering should be experienced
as a divine test of faith, solidarity with the suffering Christ and the suffering
brotherhood, and an occasion for glorifying God (1:6; 2:12, 18-25; 3:13-22;
4:12-19; 5:1, 8-9). Ultimate judgment and vindication of the righteous is in

the hands of a faithful creator, the God of grace by whom the believers are called, sustained, and blessed (1:14-17, 2:9-10, 23; 4:5-6, 17-19; 5:5-11).

In comparison with my colleague's analysis, this interpretation has several advantages. First, it takes into account the content of the entire letter. Secondly, it requires no assumption of discrepancy between the aim of the letter and that of the instruction on household duties in particular. Thus a coherent line of argument is brought to light. Third, this analysis reveals how 1 Peter grappled with *both* aspects of the social dilemma described in terms of linkage and boundaries. Fourth, it makes more comprehensible and consistent use of the sociological concepts of linkage and boundary maintenance than does Balch's partial treatment. Although he introduced these concepts as ''an alternative to the 'conversionist sect' model'' that I used in *Home* (Paper, 12), they have provided him little means for proving his assumption regarding assimilation. In point of fact, these concepts identify issues with which any conversionist sect must be concerned. My analysis has shown how the recommendations in 1 Peter were designed to urge an effective balance between intergroup communication and preserving lines of demarcation. I maintain that, were he to follow through on the implications of these concepts, he would arrive at conclusions closer to those of my own.

This is an appropriate point at which to respond to a question raised earlier in the paper (5-7) concerning sociological theory. The study of early Christianity as a social phenomenon and of its literature as media of social interaction requires the use of the theories, models, and methods of the social science. All reconstructions of the social world of early Christianity or of particular situations such as that implied in 1 Peter are based not only on sets of data but also on conceptions of how the data are related. Some investigators make their conceptual models explicit, most exegetes leave theirs implicit, and thus unavailable for evaluation.[15] In *Home* I have proposed that similarities between the Petrine community and the ideal type of a conversionist sect enable the latter to serve as a useful model for conceptualizing the social conditions and dynamics at work in the former. It is important to recognize, of course, that ideal types in general are heuristic devices and not historiographic descriptions. They are models that help organize data so as to form generalizations at a useful level of abstraction.

> First, a model can help us gain insight into the essential nature of a real phenomenon, by emphasizing significant features and ignoring nonessential ones. Second, use of a model facilitates scientific analysis because the ab-

---

[15]On the use and explication of models in historical and exegetical research see the important studies of Thomas F. Carney, *The Shape of the Past: Models and Antiquity* (Lawrence KS: Coronado Press, 1975), and Bruce J. Malina, *The New Testament World. Insights from Cultural Anthropology* (Atlanta: John Knox, 1981).

stract concepts and symbols that comprise it are easier to manipulate than is
the phenomenon they represent, and also because a model is usually more
internally consistent than our observations of reality. Finally, a model can
alert us to similarities existing among several seemingly different phenom-
ena.[16]

One of the essential tests of a good model is that it fit all the data in the
text under examination. "If the data have to be forced or prove insufficient,
then the model has to be questioned, adapted, or rejected."[17] In the case of
my interpretation of 1 Peter, Balch claims that I have forced the data onto a
"Procrustean bed" (Paper, 7). The data, he states, fail to fit the model of a
conversionist sect. If this criticism is to carry weight, however, it must be
demonstrated by a thorough reexamination of the entire text and the model
used for its interpretation. This Balch has not done. Nor has he provided us
with a more adequate model to replace it. In fact it is not at all clear that there
is any coherent model underlying his interpretation of the Petrine situation
since he fails to take into account all the evidence. His concepts of linkage
and boundary maintenance are a welcome contribution to the discussion. But
at this point in Balch's reflections they remain isolated concepts in search of
an integrating model. On the other hand, in this essay I have attempted to
show that issues of linkage and boundary maintenance are concerns of a conversionist sect like the Petrine community and that this sectarian model serves
as a valuable analytical tool for discerning the letter's overall situation and
strategy.

The final section of Balch's paper raises some questions concerning the
basis of the ecclesial model of Christian community in 1 Peter and the connection between the ethos advocated through this familial model and the
christological kerygma. The Petrine concept of the believing community
constituting a household of God is based upon the everyday experience of
family, household, and home as a paramount and enduring source of personal, social, and religious identity. It is a symbol of collective identity rooted
in, yet transcending the limits of, mundane reality. In questioning the central
importance of this symbol in 1 Peter, Balch makes a curious statement (Paper, 16):

> The Roman household was merely a political expediency for early Chris-
> tianity, and a temporary expediency at that. The domestic code is dropped
> by later authors. Prof. Elliott has mistaken a mere expediency for an identity
> symbol.

---

[16]Olsen, *The Process of Social Organization*, 21.

[17]Bruce J. Malina, "Why Interpret the Bible with the Social Sciences," *American Baptist
Quarterly* 2:2 (1983): 119-33, 130.

In my earlier study (*Home,* 165-266) I have shown the importance and enduring significance of the household in the ancient world as a fundamental basis and model of human community. As the Christian literature amply attests, the household constituted the focus of the Christian mission, the locus of its worship, the basis of its material support, a model for its organization, and a potent symbol of its evangelical message. It is incomprehensible to me on what grounds Balch would dismiss the household as a mere "temporary expediency." That "the domestic code is dropped by later Christian authors" is hardly proof that households and house churches themselves evaporated or were replaced by some other form of Christian organization.[18] In 1 Peter we see how a concrete physical and social form of human organization, the household, provided a model for conceptualizing a community embracing God the father and his reborn children. The power of this communal symbol derives from the actual experience of household and home as the most basic and intimate sphere of identity and belonging, personal and collective origin and destiny. Balch perhaps is led to criticize my view as "utopian" (Paper, 11) because he fails to distinguish what I have said about the domestic conditions within the divided households of slaves and wives, on the one hand, from what I said about the ecclesial household of faith, on the other. The latter is indeed a utopian concept in that it embodies a vision of an *ideal* community, a vision designed to inspire filial trust in God, fraternal love within the brotherhood, and familial solidarity in the face of social estrangement.

It is also not clear why and on what grounds Balch would divorce Christian ethos from Christian mythos. I certainly concur that "the Christ story" figures prominently in the message of 1 Peter and have already shown the key role it plays in affirming the distinctive identity of the believers, in providing a christological rationale for their subordination and endurance of suffering, and in establishing a basis for their hope (*Home,* passim). In 1 Peter the kerygma of Christ's suffering, death, resurrection, and exaltation, his rejection by men and his favor with God, is used to stress the solidarity between suffering believers and their suffering yet vindicated Lord. Through faith in Christ believers are incorporated into the household of God; as he is elect and precious in God's sight, so are they (2:4-10). Through his resurrection and God's mercy they have been born anew to a living hope (1:3). As the blood of the holy one liberated them from the futile ways of the fathers (1:18-19), so believers as God's obedient children are to be holy "and not conformed to the passions of your former ignorance" because they are now subject to the Father's will (1:14-17). Moreover, in more extended passages such as 2:18-25,

---

[18]On the continuing importance of the household communities and house churches in the pre-Constantinian period see Hans-Josef Klauck, *Hausgemeinde und Hauskirche im frühen Christentum* (Stuttgarter Bibelstudien 103; Stuttgart: Katholisches Bibelwerk, 1981).

3:13-4:12-19 we see how a distinctive Christian ethos of patient suffering is founded on the suffering of the crucified and vindicated Christ.[19]

Throughout the letter familial terminology and metaphors (*oikos, oikodomein, oiketēs, synoikein, oikonomoi;* rebirth, God as Father, believers as children and brothers, brotherhood, brotherly love, household service) are employed to relate this christological kerygma to an encouragement and exhortation of the addressees as the household of God. To state that "the key identity symbol [for Christianity in 1 Peter] is a mythos not an ethos, a story not a political institution (Paper, 16), is to mistake a political institution for a Christian style of life described in familial terms. In 1 Peter this description of Christian life unites ethos with mythos. Here mythos and ethos are woven into a seamless whole. What the letter has joined together Balch would rent asunder.

Moreover he states with reference to Israel's past that its mythos alone "gave Israel identity, life" (Paper, 17). Quite apart from whatever version of that myth Balch has in mind—myths undergo limitless modifications in the hands of their transmitters and receivers!—what does Balch imagine the mere telling of a myth would accomplish? Myths become socially significant and effective only when they become embodied in corporate forms of social life. Judaism in Babylon resisted assimilation not by simply repeating its myth but by developing social institutions, norms of conduct, and patterns of behavior consonant with its Torah and effective for the maintenance of its corporate identity and distinctive style of life. For early Christianity it was no different. Balch's divorcing of mythos and ethos is an unfortunate return to the discredited idealist view of history that ideas alone, disconnected from material and social reality, have the power to transform individuals and society. It is best in this case to let sleeping dogs lie.

CONCLUSIONS

Our discussion has covered a broad range of questions concerning exegetical method, appropriate data bases, and use of sociological theory and models in the analysis of a biblical text in its social context. These issues have ramifications extending beyond an interpretation of 1 Peter, the immediate focus of our attention here. In regard to an examination of the situation and

---

[19]For a more extensive examination of the christological tradition in 1 Peter and of 2:18-25 in particular see John H. Elliott, "Backward and Forward 'In His Steps': Following Jesus from Rome to Raymond and Beyond. The Tradition, Redaction and Reception of 1 Peter 2:18-25," in *Discipleship in the New Testament,* ed. Fernando F. Segovia (Philadelphia: Fortress, 1985).

strategy of this text, however, I would offer the following summarizing remarks.

1. An analysis of the entirety of 1 Peter is required for a determination of
its social situation, its general strategy, and of the meaning and function of
any of its component parts.

2. Such an analysis reveals that instruction on domestic duties and relationships formed an essential ingredient in the letter's overall argument. A
modified household code provided a logical schema for encouraging behavior appropriate for a Christian community conceived as the family or household of God.

3. Intergroup linkages and boundary maintenance are interrelated concerns of any sectarian movement such as that of early Christianity.

4. These concepts, along with the more comprehensive model of sectarian formation, supply useful tools for the understanding and interpretation of
the situation and strategy of 1 Peter. In response to a situation of intergroup
conflict and a concern for missionary recruitment, the letter recommends tac-
tics for promoting effective intergroup communication and simultaneously
maintaining internal group identity, cohesion, and boundaries.

5. Reconstruction of social situations and conceptualization of social dynamics implied in ancient texts presumes the use of social models. In order
to serve as useful heuristic tools, these models should be valid social-scientific models assessed positively by social-scientific research, appropriate to
the data under examination, and made explicit so as to allow for evaluation
of conclusions reached through their employment.

6. Neither the household code in 1 Peter nor the letter as a whole advocates a program of Christian assimilation. To the contrary, the letter affirms
the distinctive communal identity and seeks to strengthen the solidarity of the
Christian brotherhood so that it might resist external pressures urging cultural
conformity and thereby make effective witness to the distinctive features of
its communal life, its allegiance and its hope of salvation.

7. In 1 Peter, as in the literature of early Christianity in general, its mythos and ethos are inseparably related. The christological mythos inspires and
shapes the Christian ethos; its ethos embodies its mythos.

8. The social basis of Christian mission, worship, and organization was
the household. The symbolization of the people of God constituting a
"household or family of God" derives its power from the personal, social,
and religious significance attached to family and home as a place of identity,
belonging, and unity. In a suspicious and hostile society, states 1 Peter,
Christians suffer the consequences of strangeness and alienation. But as believers who have found peace and union in Christ, they can endure such estrangement with fortitude and hope. For in the family of the faithful the
homeless of society have a home with God.

CHAPTER 5

HELLENIZATION/ ACCULTURATION IN 1 PETER

DAVID L. BALCH
BRITE DIVINITY SCHOOL
FORT WORTH, TEXAS 76129

In *How to Write History* Lucian describes the epidemic that struck the people of Abdera. Falling ill, they all went mad and began singing and writing, imagining themselves to be tragedians like Euripides. Thereafter the Abderans were proverbial simpletons. Lucian compares this with the fever of many in his day who were writing history. "They are all Thucydideses, Herodotuses and Xenophons. . . . " (*History* 2, trans. Kilburn in LCL).

Many NT scholars today are Durkheims, Parsonses, Simels, Geertzes, Douglases, and Wilsons. Lucian's task of criticizing this epidemic is relatively easy; the best scholars among us are having difficulty synthesizing disciplines in a way that helps interpret our texts. In this essay, I will criticize others' attempts to write social history, and I will try such history myself, hoping to avoid becoming another citizen of Abdera!

Three cautions are in order. Sociological theory should be "suggestive rather than generative."[1] It should suggest questions and possibilities, not determine what we do or do not see in our texts. Sociological theory should

---

[1]Wayne A. Meeks, *The First Urban Christians. The Social World of the Apostle Paul* (New Haven: Yale University, 1983) 5.

not generate early Christian movements and relationships on paper that never existed in history, which is the result when theory is utilized too rigidly. Second, theory should be employed "piecemeal, as needed, where it fits."[2] Neither one theorist nor even one basic orientation, for example, either functionalist or conflict analysis, will answer all our questions.[3] Jonathan Turner introduces his plea for the importance of sociological theory with a "blunt admission: From the perspective of ideal scientific theory, sociology has a long way to go."[4] A third caution: sociological theory will help us be more objective but not "disinterested." The historical-critical method is crucial as an objective check on our subjective opinions, but, happily, we all retain the latter. I am interested in whether, and if so how, we may reinterpret these sacred texts for contemporary Christian ethics;[5] Professor Elliott also asks a modern question and answers it on the basis of 1 Peter.[6] But given these cautions we can move beyond a reductionist focus on the abstractions of the history of ideas and attempt a social description of early Christianity.[7] This article is an effort to contribute to the social description of early Petrine Christianity.

First, I will summarize the historical theses which I proposed on the basis of a literary study of the domestic codes in 1 Peter.[8] Second, I will summarize John Elliott's quite different historical and sociological reconstruction.[9] After

---

[2]Ibid., 6.

[3]When John Elliott and I first discussed the sociological interpretation of 1 Peter at the annual AAR/SBL meeting in New York three years ago (Dec. 1982), I appealed to Gerd Theissen, *Sociology of Early Palestinian Christianity* (Philadelphia: Fortress, 1978) 114-15, who suggests that functionalist theory is the appropriate tool for interpreting Hellenistic Christianity. Now I think that aspects of the conflict functionalism of L. A. Coser also shed light on the social tensions experienced by early Petrine Christianity. But Professor Elliott and I still analyze those social tensions in fundamentally different ways.

[4]Jonathan H. Turner, *The Structure of Sociological Theory* 3d ed. (Homewood: Dorsey, 1982) 13. Cp. H. G. Barnett, "Culture Processes," *American Anthropologist* 42 (1940): 21-48, at p. 21. Hereafter this journal title will be abbreviated *AA*.

[5]David L. Balch, "Early Christian Criticism of Patriarchal Authority: 1 Peter 2:11-3:12," *USQR* 39:3 (1984): 161-73.

[6]John H. Elliott, "Everyone a priest? No!" *Lutheran Forum* 9:4 (1975): 40-42; also "Death of a Slogan: from Royal Priests to Celebrating Community," *Una Sancta* 25:3 (1968): 18-31. On the problems of perspective and selection of evidence in historical research, see Richard Palmer, *Hermeneutics: Interpretation Theory in Schleiermacher, Dilthey, Heidegger and Gadamer* (Evanston: Northwestern University, 1969); also Carl Becker, *Everyman His Own Historian* (El Paso: Texas Western College, 1959).

[7]Meeks, *The First Urban Christians*, 3-4.

[8]David L. Balch, *Let Wives be Submissive. The Domestic Code in 1 Peter* (SBLMS 26; Chico: Scholars, 1981). Hereafter cited as *Wives*.

[9]John H. Elliott, *A Home for the Homeless. A Sociological Exegesis of 1 Peter, Its Situation and Strategy* (Philadelphia: Fortress, 1981). Hereafter cited as *Home*.

a critique of the way Elliott utilizes the sociology of religion and conflict analysis, I will argue that sociological and anthropological theories of acculturation throw considerable light on the social situation reflected in 1 Peter, which stresses "doing good" as praised by Roman governors and living harmoniously *in* Greco-Roman households. My suggestions about acculturation in 1 Peter are based on a) theoretical statements analyzing this social process (see n. 42), b) on numerous field reports abstracted by Siegel (see n. 41), c) on a comparison of the social situation reflected in 1 Peter with the social tendencies of hellenistic diaspora Judaism, especially as analyzed recently by Collins, d) and on 1 Peter 3:6, 8, 11, texts which summarize the meaning of the domestic code in this letter by urging Christians to seek "peace" and "harmony" with their unjust Roman masters, their pagan husbands, and others. Such acculturation means that Petrine Christianity accepted hellenistic social values in tension with important values in Jewish tradition (in the Torah) and even in tension with the early Jesus movement, changes that raise questions about continuity and identity in early Christianity.

First, the domestic or household code found in 1 Peter 2:11-3:12 has its historical and social source in the dominant Greco-Roman culture, as described specifically by the Greek social and political scientist Aristotle,[10] who asserts (in his *Politics* I 1253b 1-14) that masters rule slaves, husbands have authority over wives, and fathers over children; Aristotle outlines the form which appears later in the domestic codes of Colossians and Ephesians and is modified in 1 Peter. This, Aristotle argues, would result in a hierarchical harmony in the many households that compose cities, which domestic order would further produce stability, harmony, and order in the city-state.

Second, influential Roman philosophers, governors, and emperors (for example, Cicero, Seneca, and Augustus Caesar) found this ethic useful in their attempt to bring order to an aggressively expanding Roman empire. As ruling conquerors, it fit their value system to argue that some persons are intellectually and politically superior, others intellectually and politically inferior. Power, they argued, is gained by those who are intellectually superior and morally better; conquered nations and ethnic groups are intellectually inferior to and morally worse than Romans (Polybius, *History* 6.2.9-10; Dionysius of Halicarnassus, *Roman Antiquities* 2.3.5). This means that foreign religions which criticize Roman social and religious values are perceived as a threat to Roman rule. The "corruption" of Roman manners would lead, they

---

[10]See Stephen G. Salkever, "Aristotle's Social Science," *Political Theory* 9:4 (November 1981): 479-508, who says that the subject matter of his *Politics* belongs to the social sciences, although his method is not a modern one. However, Aristotle did send his students to *observe* the "constitutions" or "cultures" of many cities (see Balch, *Wives* 37 on Heraclides Lembus' excerpts of Aristotle's *Constitutions*).

thought, to a decline in Roman power; therefore, when Octavian (later Augustus) got into a civil war with Antony and Cleopatra, there was religious propaganda on both sides. The Roman Octavian accused Antony of having "abandoned all his ancestors' habits of life," and he exhorted his soldiers to "allow no woman (Cleopatra) to make herself equal to a man" (Dio Cassius, *Roman History* 50.25.3 and 38.3). Democratic equality between husband and wife in Cleopatra's Egypt, if allowed to influence Roman households, would cause the government to degenerate into a democracy, and they perceived this changed form of government to be morally worse than the aristocracy or monarchy which had brought them to power. Cleopatra's goddess, Isis, who "gave women the same power as men," was perceived as a threat to continued Roman rule.[11]

Since foreign cults were perceived by the Romans as a threat to their social order, apologists for these religions responded by insisting that devotees of Isis, Yahweh or Jesus were obedient. The Jewish apologist Josephus in his work *Against Apion* repeatedly insists that Jews are obedient persons in the Roman Empire.[12] The domestic codes in the New Testament emphasize the obedience of certain classes. First Peter 3:15 exhorts Christians to be prepared to give a defense (an *apologia*) of their behavior to shame pagan critics, and this defense would include a description of their properly submissive domestic relationships.[13]

Professor Elliott's second book on 1 Peter makes several significant contributions to the understanding of the social-legal status of "resident aliens and visiting strangers" (1 Pet. 2:11).[14] His discussion of the date of the letter is the best available.[15] He clearly emphasizes the significant differences between 1 Peter and the correspondence of Paul.[16] He gives a stimulating discussion of the ideology of the Petrine group in Rome.[17] He attempts to interpret

---

[11]*Wives,* 65-80, with quotations from pp. 70-71.

[12]Ibid., 54-55, 76.

[13]Ibid., 73, 75-76, 81-86, 90-95, 106-109. For a discussion of the earliest non-Christian references to Christians, over against which the need of an apologetic response can be seen, see Henry J. Cadbury, *The Book of Acts in History* (London: Adam and Charles Black, 1955) 115-19, who discusses e.g. Suetonius, *Claudius,* 25.5.

Elliott, *Home* 111 understands me to be saying that the entire letter fosters an attitude of conformity and shows no interest in Gentile mission. Actually, I am suggesting that the *domestic code* (not the whole letter) involves acculturation. I see that 1 Peter as a whole (see 1:12, 23-25; 2:2, 25) is written in the context of an active Christian mission.

[14]*Home,* 24, 30, 36, 42, 68, 187.

[15]Ibid., 60, 64, 84-87.

[16]Ibid., 64, 271, 277.

[17]Ibid., ch. 5.

this letter in light of contemporary sociological theory, but these theoretical hypotheses are problematic.

The social conflict, according to Elliott's analysis, involves a simple apocalyptic dualism.[18] There is the rural house of God over against the evil city,[19] the poor and the rich,[20] insiders and outsiders,[21] God and the devil,[22] positive and negative reference groups,[23] social separation versus accommodation and conformity,[24] the proletariat versus the bourgeoisie.[25] Congruent with this simple social dualism, Elliott emphasizes the "numerous contrasts or antitheses which fill the letter": (ancient) prophets/you, disbelievers/faithful, disobedient/obedient, sinners/righteous, evildoers/Christians.[26]

Given this understanding of the letter in terms of a simple apocalyptic and social dualism, it follows for Professor Elliott that the letter focuses on encouraging the "termination of previous associations"[27] with the Gentiles, termination of "past familial, social and religious ties,"[28] to become "a

---

[18]Ibid., 71. While Elliott overemphasizes future-oriented apocalyptic, E. G. Selwyn, "Eschatology in 1 Peter," in *The Background of the NT and its Eschatology,* In Honour of C. H. Dodd, ed. W. D. Davies and D. Daube, 394-401 (Cambridge: Cambridge University, 1956) probably overemphasizes its "realized eschatology."

[19]*Home,* 63, 65, 69, 121, 128, 193-95.

[20]Ibid., 70-72.

[21]Ibid., 79, 211, 230.

[22]Ibid., 81, 115, 120, 226. Elliott writes of the "thorough stereotypification of the one common diabolical 'enemy' who opposed both the Christians and their God" (*Home* 226). And: "For ideological purposes all inimical outsiders were reduced to one common social ("Gentiles," 2:12; 4:3) and demonic (5:8-9) denominator" (*Home* 81).

[23]*Home,* 115.

[24]Ibid., 128.

[25]Ibid., 193-94. This *reverses* the evaluation of the domestic code by Martin Dibelius, *An die Kolosser, Epheser, an Philemon* (Tübingen: Mohr, 1913) 48-49: "sittlich-buergerlichen Pflichten." Compare E. A. Judge, *The Social Pattern of the Christian Groups in the First Century* (London: Tyndale, 1960) 60: "Far from being a socially depressed group, then if the Corinthians are at all typical, the Christians were dominated by a socially pretentious section of the population of the big cities." This is expanded by Abraham Malherbe, *Social Aspects of Early Christianity,* 2nd ed. (Philadelphia: Fortress, 1983) ch. 2.

First Peter with its Aristotelian domestic code is also addressed primarily to *urban* Christians. For example, "slaves were little used in agriculture" (*Home* 69, quoting Broughton), a historical observation confirmed by a sociological one. See Gideon Sjoberg, *The Preindustrial City. Past and Present* (New York: Free, 1960) 134: slavery is "historically more a part of the urban than of the rural scene." And most importantly, the domestic code itself assumes and is a model for the *polis* (city).

[26]*Home,* 119-20, 226.

[27]Ibid., 66.

[28]Ibid., 75, 69, 78-80, 83, 105, 107-109, 128-29, 142, 199, 210-11, 225.

community set apart and disengaged from the routine affairs of civic and social life."[29] "The predominant danger to the sect is the attraction of social
conformity,"[30] to which the author responds by encouraging social distinctiveness (1 Pet. 1:3, 14-16, 18-19, 2:11; 3:9, 13-17; 4:2-4, 12-19; 5:8-8).[31]
"From *all* Gentile modes of behavior and sin this household is to distance
itself."[32]

One of the difficulties of understanding Professor Elliott's sociological
description of the Petrine community is that he gives few extra-Biblical examples of what these separated sectarians look like.[33] When Professor Elliott
repeatedly refers to "social separation," how much alienation is involved?
The specific examples he gives[34] are the postexilic priests who formed the
Holiness Code of Leviticus, 1 Enoch,[35] and Qumran, all of whom withdrew
into spatially secluded communities, which remind me of the Old Order
Amish, of Hasidic Jews, and of the "Old Believers" among the Russian Or-
thodox, not of the Christian slaves and wives in 1 Peter who are being exhorted to continue to be subordinate *in* Greco-Roman households. It is no
accident that the Old Order Amish, Hasidic Jews and Old Believers are not
missionary groups. If the boundaries of Petrine Christianity were as closed as
Elliott suggests, the missionary interest reflected in 1 Peter as a whole would
be inexplicable.

This description of the social situation reflected in the letter is oversim-
plified, and the source of Elliott's misunderstanding is an overemphasis on
conflict theory and a rigid application of Bryan Wilson's early sociological
theories. He quotes Wilson's article on sect development:

> If the sect is to persist as an organization it *must* not only separate its mem-
> bers from the world, but *must* also maintain the dissimilarity of its own val-
> ues from those of the secular society. Its members *must* not normally be
> allowed to accept the values of the status system of the external world. The
> sect *must* see itself as marginal to the wider society . . . Status *must* be sta-

---

[29]Ibid., 79.

[30]Ibid., 98, n. 76.

[31]Ibid., 69, 75.

[32]Ibid., 231 (my emphasis). Elliott (*Home* 108-10) modifies this primarily when discussing Theophil Spörri, *Der Gemeindegedanke im ersten Petrusbrief: Ein Beitrag zur Struktur
des urchristlichen Kirchenbegriffs* (Neutestamentliche Forschungen 2.2; Gütersloh: C. Bertelsmann, 1925).

[33]He does refer to one study of a Chinese family (*Home* 245, n. 45).

[34]*Home*, 123-24, 126, 142.

[35]Theissen, *Sociology,* 29 refers to "exclusive conventicles" in relation to the Simili-
tudes of Ethiopic Enoch, a *contrast* to the Palestinian Christian communities which were "more
open to the world around" (p. 22).

tus within the sect, and this should be the only group to which the status-conscious individual makes reference.[36]

Wilson's "must," which here occurs five times, or the term "required," reappears in Elliott's book,[37] and it has kept him from seeing some significant social tendencies reflected in the text of 1 Peter. Elliott here quotes one of Wilson's early articles, but Wilson has revised his views several times. It is stimulating to see Wilson's creative mind adjusting his theories to the empirical data, but it is a mistake to utilize the theories too rigidly at one stage in their development. Elliott argues that the Petrine communities in Rome and Asia Minor are best understood as a "conversionist sect"[38] as that is defined by Wilson. Presently, the most popular sociological study and analysis of a conversionist sect is one by John Lofland and Rodney Stark,[39] a study of the early development of the followers of Rev. Moon in the Bay area. Recently Lofland has published an article in which he "revisited" his own earlier theory. At the conclusion he writes,

> I fear some investigators get hung up in trying to determine if the world-saver model is "right" as regards the group they have studied. In my view,

---

[36]*Home,* 103 (my emphases). Bryan R. Wilson, "An Analysis of Sect Development," *American Sociological Review* 24 (1959): 3-15, at pp. 12-13. Wilson himself does not seem prescriptive. Note his cautions in *Magic and the Millennium* (London: Heinemann, 1973) 10, 12, 18 (with n. 11), 19, 26. The warnings are even stronger in *Religion in Sociological Perspective* (Oxford: Oxford University, 1982) ch. 4, "The Sociology of Sects." "The ideal type is constructed in the full knowledge that actual cases diverge from it . . . " (*Religion* 95) Even over against his own typology of seven types of sect, he says: "The ideal-type construct of the sect proved, in practice, to lack the generality that might have been expected of it" (Ibid., 101). These types "are essentially tools, and their purpose is not one of classification . . . Ideal types are not empty boxes into which the sociologist drops appropriate cases . . . " (Ibid., 105). For an alternative schematization, see Michael Hill, *A Sociology of Religion* (London: Heinemann, 1973) ch. 4.

[37]*Home,* 73, 101-104, 127, 159, 230.

[38]Wilson, *Magic,* 22, 28, 38 says this involves a highly emotional, individual, crisis conversion. We know that some of the recipients of 1 Peter were recent converts, but we do not know the specifics of their experience of it. When entire households were converted, how individual and emotional was the slaves' conversion, whose religious sentiments typically followed the inclinations of the patriarch?

Elliott also quotes (*Home* 74) Robin Scroggs's list of seven sectarian characteristics of early Christianity, one of which involves egalitarianism. Then he repeatedly uses phrases describing this "community of equals" (*Home* 101, 105, 134, 136, 139, 122, 148-49). There is no textual evidence for this. This mistaken characterization of Petrine Christianity results from the misapplication of sociological theory and from a questionable methodological principle: "In regard to the admonitions of 1 Peter we may assume that what is *proscribed* in the letter was possibly current practice in the audience . . . " (*Home* 83).

[39]"Becoming a World-Saver: A Theory of Conversion to a Deviant Perspective," *American Sociological Review* 30 (1956): 862-75. I owe this reference to Lewis R. Rambo, "Current Research on Religious Conversion," *Religious Studies Review* 8 (1982): 146-59.

such investigators would advance us better by looking at the conversion process directly and reporting what they saw . . . I would urge now that people
ought not so compulsively wear the tinted spectacles wrought by Lofland
and Stark when they go to look at conversion.[40]

ACCULTURATION

Those aspects of 1 Peter which are obscured by the particular way Elliott
utilizes Bryon Wilson's theories of sectarian development can be described
in terms of sociological theories of acculturation.[41] Instead of the assumption
that "all Gentile modes of behavior" are sinful, anthropologists studying acculturation emphasize that there is a "selection"[42] by the receiving culture
among cultural traits of the donor culture. Some foreign traits are accepted
and/or adapted; others are rejected.[43] For understanding early Petrine Christianity as expressed in our epistle, the following dynamics of "intercultural
transmission" are crucial:

> One of the obvious invariant processes of acculturation . . . is the trans-
> mission of cultural materials (objects, traits, or ideas) between the two sys-
> tems. . . . In the most general terms we can make two statements about
> intercultural transmission: (1) that the patterns and values of the receiving
> culture seem to function as selective screens in a manner that results in the
> enthusiastic acceptance of some elements, the firm rejection of other ele-
> ments; and (2) that the elements which are transmitted undergo transfor-
> mations in the receiving cultural systems.[44]

---

[40]John Lofland, " 'Becoming a World-Saver' Revisited," *American Behavioral Scientist*
20 (1977): 805-18 at pp. 816-17.

[41]There were many studies of acculturation between the 1930s and the 1950s, many of
which focused either on the peoples of the South Pacific or on the ethnic groups of North
America, especially American Indians. For a survey of the latter see Bernard J. Siegel, ed.,
Acculturation. Critical Abstracts, North America (Stanford Anthropological Series 2; Stanford: Stanford University, 1955).

[42]R. Redfield, R. Linton, and M. J. Herskovits, "Memorandum for the Study of Acculturation," *AA* 38 (1936): 149-52, at pp. 151, 152. Also B. J. Siegel et al., "Acculturation: An Exploratory Formulation," *AA* 56 (1954): 973-1002; acculturation involves "the selective adaptation
of value systems," (p. 981; cp. 983, 985). See B. J. Siegel, "Introduction," *Acculturation: Critical Abstracts, North America,* 13 and Fred W. Voget, "The American Indian in Transition: Reformation and Accommodation," *AA* 58 (1956): 249-63, at pp. 250, 252, 256.

[43]Redfield et al., "Memorandum," 152.

[44]Siegel et al., "Exploratory Formulation," 985. As Elliott asserted in his 1982 response
to my critique, these two are "diametrically opposed" and "in contradiction" to each other.
But overemphasis on *rational* consistency blocks our ability to perceive different emphases in
social movements and in our texts. For several years I taught a course on Amish and Mennonite culture. My students would laugh when they saw that Amish refuse to drive (modern

Further, "a model of its family life" may be one of the cultural values communicated from the dominant to the receiving culture, but "the family configuration is certain to be refracted" by the "filter of traditional and idiosyncratic perception."[45] These processes are important in understanding the social dynamics and tensions reflected in 1 Peter. There is "firm rejection" of patterns that the author of 1 Peter perceives as common in pagan society (1 Pet. 1:18; 4:3-4), as Elliott emphasizes. But on the other hand, 1 Pet. 2:12-14 "enthusiastically accepts" ethical ideas and patterns of conduct that the Roman emperor and his governors praise as "good."[46] Contrary to a simple dualistic view, *both* Christians and pagans recognize good behavior (1 Pet. 2:12-15; 3:13-16). W. C. van Unnik, on a point that Elliott never stresses, says:

> The interesting thing is that human authorities are supposed to recognize what is 'well-doing', and that a general rule of a state towards its citizens is meant, which must be—according to the will of God—an incitement for the Christians to live up to this standard of first-class citizens in order to stop slander against Christianity.[47]

American) motorized cars and tractors, but would use motorized farm machinery like thrashers *drawn by horses*. The students' rational criteria and values often blocked further questions about the social function of contradictory actions. However ridiculous to us, the Amish neither buy new tractors nor simply use the traditional horses. They climb (or descend) a "ladder of acculturation." However inconsistent, horse-drawn motorized machinery maintains social difference and distance from the dominant culture; they help maintain some Amish values. Some Amish, usually a minority and often younger folk, notice the inconsistency and either acculturate further or react toward the "old order." Some social conformity/acculturation *and* boundary maintenance are possible simultaneously; Siegel calls it an "invariant" process. Rational either/ors are irrelevant in studying Amish Americans or hellenistic Jewish Christians.

[45]Siegel et al., "Exploratory Formulation," 983. I discuss the "refraction" and "transformation" of the Greco/Roman domestic code in Petrine Christianity in "Early Christian Criticism of Patriarchal Authority: 1 Peter 2:11-3:12."

[46]W. C. van Unnik, "The Teaching of Good Works in 1 Peter," *NTS* 1 (1954-1955): 92-110, at p. 93, now in his *Sparsa Collecta. The Collected Essays of W. C. van Unnik* (NovTSup 30; Leiden: Brill, 1980), part 2, 83-105, at pp. 84-85. Both pagans and Christians do good, but the Christian "foundation is quite different from the Greek: God's calling and not human goodness; and its aim is different: not to earn glory for oneself, but to make the way free for the Gospel towards the disobedient." (Ibid., 108-109). I add that Romans' motivation was influenced by their thinking that the most virtuous *rule* in the world (see n. 68 below). They wanted to "do good" and be powerful.

[47]van Unnik, "The Teaching of Good Works in 1 Peter," 99. Judge, *The Social Pattern*, 73 refers to the early Christians' "acute sensitivity to public opinion" and notes their feeling that "any abnormal behavior would only feed the willing rumours that circulated to their discredit. It is from this preoccupation that much of their social teaching starts; . . . it was formulated primarily for defense rather than attack." Writing specifically about 1 Peter, he says, "Drunkenness, brawling and bad domestic relations were all likely to attract unwelcome attention. In spite of the provocative attitude of their opponents, nothing must be done that would upset the government" (p. 74).

> In every respect the relation with fellow-men is central, not a retreat
> from the world, but a life in the given conditions . . . Good works are also
> extended to outsiders: in subjection to the state authorities, to masters in
> performing one's duty, to husbands even if they are unbelieving . . . No
> special 'Christian', but truly human ethics are demanded.[48]

One should not read the domestic code and conclude that the letter encourages the termination of past familial ties. I conclude that Elliott has mis-
interpreted the nature of the social conflict and change that occurred in early
Petrine Christianity by simple dualistic contrasts like rural house of God/evil
city, God/devil, insiders/outsiders.

Anthropological studies of the acculturation process provide several
analogies to the early Jewish Christian adaptation of foreign (Greco-Roman),
domestic ethics. On the one hand, the dominant culture's household patterns
can be rejected, as they were by some American Indians. The Plains tribes,
unlike the Woodland tribes, generally "did not foster an inflation of the father image or tend to the development of submissive attitudes toward authority," so they were "crushed into submission" and experienced
"catastrophic change."[49] On the other hand, some immigrant groups did adapt
American family patterns. The following two examples give a feel for the way
social dynamics operated in early Petrine (and Pauline) Christianity. In all
these cases, the family dynamic in the immigrants' culture differs from those

---

[48]van Unnik, "The Teaching of Good Works in 1 Peter," 107. Elliott never cites van
Unnik's article which deals with early Christians' attention to pagans' response as an ethical
theme: "Die Rücksicht auf die Reaktion der Nicht-Christen als Motiv in der altchristlichen
Paraenese," in *Judentum, Urchristentum, Kirche,* Festschrift J. Jeremias, ed. W. Eltester
(Berlin: Alfred Toepelmann, 1960) 221-34, now in his *Sparsa Collecta,* part 2, 307-22. Eduard Schweizer, "Traditional ethical patterns in the Pauline and post-Pauline letters and their
development (lists of vices and house-tables)," in *Text and Interpretation. Studies in the NT
Presented to Matthew Black,* ed. E. Best and R. Mcl. Wilson (Cambridge: Cambridge University, 1979) 195-209, at p. 207 says:

> House-tables even originated in Colossians, probably in defense *against* a move-
> ment which *tried to abandon this world* . . . They call the church back to its divine
> service in marriage, parentage and everyday work . . . They no longer distinguish
> an outstanding group of high moral standards from the abominable immorality of the
> world . . . House-tables describe what Jewish or heathen authors would equally rec-
> ommend and what could actually also be found in their culture. (My emphases)

Schweizer says the domestic codes oppose sectarian withdrawal; Elliott says they encourage
it. Schweizer and I have independently come to the same conclusion. Further, Elliott's claim
that L. Goppelt, *Der Erste Petrusbrief* (MeyerK; Göttingen: Vendenhoeck and Ruprecht, 1978)
interprets this letter as he does is wrong. True, Christian refusal to conform is the basis of conflict (1 Pet. 4:3-4), but one should not emigrate out of one's social station; Christians are placed
in the institutions of society (*Erste Petrusbrief* 59, 176).

[49]Victor Barnouw, *Acculturation and Personality among the Wisconsin Chippewa*
(American Anthropological Association Memoirs 72; American Anthropological Association,
1950) 11, 64, 74-75 as abstracted by Siegel, *Acculturation,* 25.

in the dominant culture, and the immigrants acculturate in the direction of patterns in the dominant society.

Japanese immigrants to America seek to reconstruct the family life of Japan, which involves a high degree of dominance and control of parents over children. Certain deferential attitudes are one of the most important significant factors in these Japanese families. But when American institutions (churches, schools, movie theaters) introduce new ideas, the status of Japanese men and women in the family changes as does the relationship between generations. Younger Japanese come into conflict with their parents over the "submission and recognition of authority and prestige" expected by the latter. Japanese and American families are so different that "what one does and says in this situation reveals in part the extent to which one is Americanized."[50]

Humphreys's hypothesis, similarly, is "that the changes in the structure of the (Detroit Mexican) family, under the impact of a new social and cultural environment, constitute a highly sensitive index of the process of acculturation."[51] The status of the Mexican father in Detroit declines. His "moral protection over the wife and female children" is not reinforced in Detroit in the same way as in Mexico, so that the wife may effect a reversal from subordination to superordination in family roles. In Mexico the status hierarchy in the family runs father, mother, son, daughter, in that order. But in Detroit, the son assumes a position about equal with the father, and the daughter climbs to the same level as the mother. Humphreys argues: "since we regard the family as the social structure in which the self-conceptions of those who occupy roles are most intimately related to one another, we believe it will reflect most truly the changing meanings generated by the larger culture."[52]

These sociological studies suggest that Jews in different cultures in Capernaum, Ephesus and Rome, probably experienced significantly different household relationships.[53] First Peter, written by a hellenistic Jewish Chris-

---

[50]Forrest E. LaViolette, *Americans of Japanese Ancestry: A Study of Assimilation in the American Community* (Toronto: Canadian Institute of International Affairs, 1946) 109 as abstracted by Siegel, *Acculturation,* 87-91.

[51]Norman D. Humphreys, "The Changing Structure of the Detroit Mexican Family: An Index of Acculturation," *American Sociological Review* 9 (1944): 622-26, at p. 622, as abstracted in Siegel, *Acculturation,* 192-94.

[52]Ibid. Compare the studies of the household structure of blacks in the South, Chinese in Philadelphia, Pawnee, and Sioux abstracted by Siegel, *Acculturation,* 33, 98-99, 101, 107-108, 128, 131. Cp. H. G. Barnett, "Culture Processes," *AA* 42 (1940): 21-48, at pp. 26, 32, 46.

[53]Dionysius, *Rom. Ant.* II.26-27 observes differences between Greek and Roman household relationships. Several Greek and Roman authors criticize Jewish family life (see Balch, "Two Apologetic Encomia: Dionysius on Rome and Josephus on the Jews," *Journal for the Study of Judaism* 13:1-2 (1982): 102-22, 118, n.43.

A. Irving Hallowell, "Ojibwa Personality and Acculturation," *International Congress of Americanists,* 29th Proceedings (1952): 105-12 outlines the four "levels of acculturation" found

tian author from Rome "to the exiles of the Dispersion" in Asia Minor (1 Pet. 1:1), continues the acculturation process in the hellenistic Jewish diaspora. The social situation in Diaspora Judaism is more likely to give us valid clues about hellenized Jewish Christianity than are the Palestinian conventicles that produced 1 Enoch, the Qumran scrolls, and the levitical Holiness code.

Hellenized Diaspora Jews tried to maintain their tradition in an environment dominated by gentiles. Collins concludes:

> . . . the dominant tendency of Diaspora Jewry was to live as loyal subjects of their gentile masters and participate in the culture and society as fully as possible within the constraints of their religious tradition.[54]

Diaspora Jews reduced the dissonance between their culture and Hellenism in various ways, by modifying either their own or pagans' ideas.[55] Those Mosaic laws that would be understood by gentiles were emphasized, while some distinctive symbols of Judaism (circumcision and kosher food laws) that caused offense were played down.[56] This distinction between Jewish tradition and Hellenized Judaism is problematic. Palestine was Hellenized. Still, Collins's summary of the different emphases is very helpful:

> We should not, of course conclude that there were no differences at all between Palestine and the Diaspora. Palestinian Judaism produced no philosopher analogous to Philo. The Diaspora has nothing to compare with the rabbinic corpus. . . . While even such reclusive areas as Qumran show Hellenistic influence, attempts to express the Jewish tradition in explicitly Hellenistic forms are relatively few in Palestinian Judaism while they predominate in the Diaspora.[57]

Collins's book gives many examples of Hellenistic forms in the diaspora, and

---

in this tribe; the article is abstracted by Siegel, *Acculturation,* 183-86. There are thirteen rungs on the "ladder" of acculturation among the German Amish and Mennonites; see John A. Hostetler, *Amish Society,* 3d ed. (Baltimore: Johns Hopkins, 1980) 285, 290-91. Elliott's simple contrasts ignore this social process in relation to hellenistic Jewish Christians.

[54]John J. Collins, *Between Athens and Jerusalem. Jewish Identity in the Hellenistic Diaspora* (New York: Crossroad, 1983) 129.

Collins's book is a significant advance in the understanding of Hellenistic Judaism, but his basic distinction between "politics" and "ethics" in hellenistic Judaism is not a good one. Shalom M. Paul, *Studies in the Book of the Covenant in the Light of Cuneiform and Biblical Law* (SVT 38; Leiden: Brill, 1970) 8, 34 observes that this Biblical code blends legal, moral and cultic prescriptions, as do the Holiness Code and Deuteronomy. In Aristotle, too, politics and ethics are not separate. Philo, the hellenistic jew, in *On Joseph,* repeats Plato's politics and ethics (see Balch, *Wives,* 52-53).

[55]Collins, *Hellenistic Diaspora,* 9.

[56]Ibid., 137-43, 161-68, 244-46.

[57]Ibid., 11.

I add another: diaspora Jews modified their ideas about the structured roles involved in living together in households in the direction of Hellenistic patterns.[58] In outlining the ''common ethic'' of diaspora Judaism, Collins[59] emphasizes Philo, *Hypothetica,* Josephus, *Against Apion* 2:190-219 and Pseudo-Phocylides, *Maxims,* exactly those texts to which students of domestic ethics in the New Testament have appealed since Dibelius and Weidinger early in this century![60] These two works of Philo and Josephus turn out to be rhetorical ''apologetic encomia,'' a form common in Greek oratory, also utilized, for example, by Dionysius of Halicarnassus, Aristides and Libanius, a form with very little traditional, distinctively Jewish content.[61] The form as employed by Josephus is apologetic in that it responds to prior, common criticisms of the Jewish people, including Jewish customs in the structure of household relationships.[62] Consistent with Collins's observations, this hellenistic form and the domestic ethic it includes are stressed by Jews in diaspora, not in Palestine.[63]

The ethic in these two works by Philo and Josephus, the ''common ethic'' of diaspora Judaism, is explicitly labeled ''apologetic'' by both Eusebius, (*Preparation for the Gospel* 8.10, which preserves extracts of Philo, *Hypothetica*) and Josephus (*Against Apion* 2.147), as is the same ethic in 1 Peter (3:15, ''Always be prepared to make an *apologia* to anyone who calls you to account for the hope that is in you. . . . ''). Again, this sort of ''apology'' is not traditionally Jewish. Some typical short examples, in addition to those cited in my article on ''Two Apologetic Encomia,'' illustrate this point.

According to Xenophon in his short work *Socrates' Defense (apologia) to the Jury*[64] there were three charges against the philosopher, one of which

---

[58]Balch, *Wives,* 52-56, 65-67, 73-76, 82-86, 90-93, 108 and especially Balch, ''Two Apologetic Encomia,'' 112-13, 118.

[59]Collins, *Hellenistic Diaspora,* 143.

[60]Balch, *Wives,* 2, 54.

[61]Balch, ''Two Apologetic Encomia,'' although Josephus does object to making piety merely a subheading under the virtue of justice (Ibid., 117).

[62]Ibid., 118, n. 43 which cites critics like Hecataeus of Abdera (in Diodorus of Sicily 40.3.8), whose opinions on Jewish marriage well qualify him as a citizen of Abdera!

[63]*Pace* David Daube, *The New Testament and Rabbinic Judaism* (London: Athlone, 1956) 90-105 and W. D. Davies, *Paul and Rabbinic Judaism* (London: SPCK, 1956) 121-36. Josephus was Palestinian, but he wrote in Rome as a client of the Flavians. OT and Palestinian sources do not contain the form of the NT domestic codes, a form that includes a) pairs of social classes reciprocally related to each other b) in super- and subordinate social roles. M. Kiddushin 1.1-7 does not conform to this pattern. For a recent comment on the problem of imperatival participles, see Blass-Debrunner-Rehkopf, §417, n.1.

[64]I quote the Loeb edition edited by Todd. I owe this reference to Prof. John Leopold of U.C. Berkeley, who observes that while Xenophon does not accurately represent the historical Socrates, his work is an appeal to popular values.

was the corruption of the young (*Defense* 10). These charges might be summed up as "wrong-doing" (*adikon; Defense* 3 and 22). Socrates' apology was that he had lived his whole life piously and righteously (*dikaios; Defense* 5). But his accuser refers to "those whom you have persuaded to obey you rather than their parents" (*Defense* 20). Socrates admits this, and tries to explain it. Finally, he is executed "unjustly" (*adikos; Defense* 26). I conclude that obedience in certain social relationships, the kind of obedience recommended in the Petrine domestic code, was crucial for Greek values, rhetoric (apologetic!) and courts.

A second influential rhetorical example in which praise is given for obedience (cp. 1 Pet. 2:14) is Pericles' Funeral Oration, as reported by Thucydides 2.37.3. At this funeral, Pericles praises the city of Athens, for whom the soldiers who fought against Sparta had died. He first praises the form of Athens' government, a democracy; and he praises Athenians as follows:

> We give our obedience to those whom we put in positions of authority, and we obey the laws themselves, especially those which are for the protection of the oppressed, and those unwritten laws which it is an acknowledged shame to break.[65]

Although these speeches (not exactly as reported) were made in 399 and 430 BC, similar rhetorical examples occur centuries later. Christians would have to "apologize" if they were perceived as "doing wrong," that is, perceived as teaching certain classes to be insubordinate (see 1 Pet. 3:15), and centuries later, governors and rhetoricians still praised citizens for obedience or criticized them for disobedience.[66] One aspect of "doing good" involves maintaining these social relationships *in* Greco-Roman *households,* not terminating them and withdrawing into sectarian isolation.

What this means in Roman society is clarified by a striking passage in Dionysius. A man who had been honored with two consulships was expelled from the Senate because he was "extravagant" in supplying himself with silver goblets. Dionysius, a rhetorician and a historian who trained governors for Roman provinces,[67] explains why:

> for what took place in the homes (*kat oikian*) they (the Lacedaemonians)

---

[65]This speech is translated and rhetorically analyzed by Edward P. J. Corbett, *Classical Rhetoric for the Modern Student* (New York: Oxford University, 1971) 229-39. The praise of justice and democratic government is a "special topic."

[66]Balch, "Two Apologetic Encomia." Elliott, *Home,* 216 argues that Josephus' apologetic in *Against Apion* is later than 1 Peter so is not relevant to the discussion. However, the point is that Josephus' work is a *typical* apologetic encomium, a rhetorical form used over several centuries, e.g., by Dionysius of Halicarnassus in the first century *BC*. See also Stanley F. Bonner, *Education in Ancient Rome* (Berkeley: University of California, 1977) 263-67.

[67]Balch, *Wives,* 74.

took no thought or precaution, holding that each man's house-door marked the boundary within which he was free to live as he pleased. But the Romans, throwing open every house (*oikia*) and extending the authority of the censors even to the bedchamber, made that office the overseer and guardian of everything that took place in the homes; for they believed that neither a master should be cruel in the punishments meted out to his slaves, nor a father unduly harsh or lenient in the training of his children, nor a husband unjust in his partnership with his lawfully-wedded wife, nor children disobedient toward their aged parents, . . . nor any other of the things that are done contrary to propriety (*para to kathakon*) and the advantage of the state (*sumpheron te polei;* Dionysius, *Roman Antiquities* 20.13.2-3, trans. Cary in LCL)

Most modern Westerners share the view of the Lacedaemonians and would find these opinions potentially tyrannical! But Romans included these values among those that "caused" their military and political success (see Dionysius, *Rom. Ant.* 2.3.6).[68] Any devotees of foreign cults who threatened these values would have to "apologize," to explain themselves, to the Roman governor.[69] Thus it is not surprising to find the Roman domestic ethics outlined by Dionysius (*Rom. Ant.* 2.25-27 and 20.13.2-3) in those texts that Collins refers to as containing the "common ethic" of diaspora Judaism as well as in the Petrine epistle to the Christian diaspora. What Wilson says in his revised estimate of sects applies:

In the matter of moral values, however, sectarian teaching is by no means always fundamentally different in kind from the traditional moral orientations . . . But the sects are more intense, more scrupulous, and more demanding about their moral requirements.[70]

The Petrine apologetic means that these Christians lived simultaneously in two cultures, two "houses." There was the "spiritual house" (1 Pet. 2:5), the "house of God" (4:17), the "brotherhood" (1:22; 2:17; 3:8; 5:9, 14), to which they converted and with which they suffered. But they also lived in a second "house" (*oikos, oikia*). Although the Greek words themselves are not used in 1 Pet. 2:11-3:12, the hellenistic form of the domestic code found there does describe a (second) "house" in other Greek authors, for example, in Aristotle and Arius Didymus.[71] However, Elliott's impression of the (one?) house in 1 Peter is as follows:

---

[68]Balch, "Two Apologetic Encomia," 110, 112, 116. On the Roman's "cultural imperialism," see J. P. V. D. Balsdon, "Romans: The God's Own People," ch. 1 in *Romans and Aliens* (Chapel Hill: University of North Carolina, 1979), a reference I owe to John Schütz.

[69]Balch, *Wives,* ch. 5.

[70]Wilson, *Religion,* 94.

[71]See Balch, *Wives,* 34, 42 for quotation of the texts.

As *oikos* symbolizes the bonds which unite, it also implies the factors which divide. . . . *Outside* the home the Christian sectarians lived a threatened and vulnerable existence in hostile Gentile territory. There they were strangers and aliens, suspected, accused, maligned, misunderstood, grieved and caused to suffer . . . There the Gentiles were in league with the ancient adversary of God, the devil himself (1 Peter 5:8) . . . Salvation, community, acceptance and love were available only within the household of God . . . Here alone was a community shaped and motivated by fraternal love, mutual respect and humble service.[72]

First Peter does use such language, but there is other language in the letter that suggests the alternative possibility that Christians might be able to live in "peace" and "harmony" in this (second) household. In 1 Pet. 3:6, Sarah is the example of submissiveness recalled for Christian wives, for she was "calling him (Abraham) lord," a quotation of Gen. 18:12. The rabbis had played with this story:

R. Hananja, the captain of the priests, [shortly before 70] said, "and give you peace" [Num. 6:26] in your house . . . " Great is peace, for (on account of it, God) changed the remark of Sarah. For it says, "for I am old." (Gen. 18:13).[73]

The rabbis' playfulness is clarified by *Midrash Rabbah to Lev* 9:9 (111 b):

Bar Kappara said: Great is peace, for the Scriptures reported in the Torah a prevarication which was used in order to maintain peace between Abraham and Sarah. "And Sarah laughed within herself, saying . . . and my master is old" (Gen. 18:12); but (when God repeated this) to Abraham, He said: (Sarah said:) "and I am old" (Gen. 18:13).

Sarah, the mother of women proselytes,[74] is presented as the model for these Christian women whose husbands are still pagan (1 Pet. 3:1; see 1 Cor. 7:13, 15-16). Genesis 18:12-13 is associated with the important priestly blessing in Num. 6:26, which is interpreted to mean "peace in your *house*."

Elsewhere,[75] I make five observations that suggest that 1 Pet. 3:8-12 is a summary of the preceding domestic code, and again, a key exhortation in this summary of 1 Pet. 2:11-3:12 is "seek peace" (1 Pet. 3:11 quoting Ps.

---

[72]*Home,* 230-31 (Elliott's emphasis).

[73]*Sifre* to Num. 6:26, 42(121b). See Balch, *Wives,* 103-104, where it is noted that this is a saying from the school of Ishmael; he was concerned with *derekh erez,* which is not legal Torah, but rather human custom, social habit, patterns of daily life. See W. Bacher, *Die Exegetische Terminologie der jüdischen Traditions Literatur* (Hildesheim: Georg Olms, 1965) 2, p. 25.

[74]Balch, *Wives,* 105.

[75]Ibid., 88.

34:15b).[76] Hebrews 12:14 quotes the same phrase in a persecution context, and it also appears in 1 Clement 22, just following another household code. The author of 1 Peter hopes that exhortations to obedience directed to Christian wives with pagan husbands and to Christian slaves whose masters were treating them "unjustly" will result in "peace" in the Greco-Roman household.

A third text points in the same direction. First Pet. 3:8 exhorts to "harmony (*homophrones*)," a very important topos in hellenistic ethics.[77] I quote only one text:

> Again, take our households (*oikoi*)—although their safety depends not only on the like-mindedness (*homophrosune*) of master and mistress but also on the obedience of the servants, yet both the bickering of master and mistress and the wickedness of the servants have wrecked many households. . . . The good marriage, what else is it save concord between man and wife? And the bad marriage, what is it save their discord? (Dio Chrysostom, *Or.* 38.15-16, trans. Crosby in LCL)

However difficult certain sociological theories make it to see, the author hoped for peace and harmony, not only in the "spiritual house" (1 Pet. 2:5) but also in the Greco-Roman houses where these slaves and wives lived and related to others in society. Much of the ethical parenesis of the letter, which Elliott and I agree has been modified to address the situation of the recipients,[78] is directed to slaves and wives who live in religiously *divided,* pagan *households*. The author of 1 Peter was concerned about Christians' experience *inside* households. He wrote to encourage Christian slaves who were being beaten by harsh masters and were suffering unjustly (1 Pet. 2:18-20, 23) in real households, many of them ruled by pagan masters, who are not addressed by the author.[79] Some Christians, including the educated author of this letter, certainly owned slaves. These masters are not addressed because the author is primarily concerned to address the social-political problem created when the masters did not convert. The author's modification of the three pairs of the Aristotelian domestic code and the emphasis on slaves and wives

---

[76]Ibid., 103-104.

[77]Ibid., 88-89. As would be expected, Josephus in his apology also emphasized harmony (see *Against Apion* 2:171 and Balch, "Two Apologetic Encomia," 117).

[78]Elliott, *Home,* 208-209; Balch, *Wives,* 106.

[79]See the stimulating article by E. Schweizer, "Die Weltlichkeit des Neuen Testaments: die Haustafeln," in *Beiträge zur alttestamentliche Theologie.* Festschrift für Walther Zimmerli, ed. H. Donner et al. (Göttingen: Vandenhoeck and Ruprecht, 1977) 397-413, at pp. 401-10. Elliott's suggestions (*Home* 70) that the omission of an exhortation to owners is due to the poverty of the community, or alternatively (p. 207), that this omission is due to the focus on the slaves as paradigmatic of the vulnerability of all the Christian sojourners, are inadequate.

demonstrates that one essential purpose in 2:11-3:12 is to "exhort and encourage" Christian slaves and wives to maintain defensible behavior in religiously divided households; the author's parenesis is directed to the problematic situation.[80] He/she also wrote to encourage wives who might be terrified *in* their *house* by pagan husbands (1 Pet. 3:1, 6). The Christian experience of the house reflected here is multivalent. For some Christian slaves and wives who lived in pagan houses, working and living together everyday in the same house with Christian masters and husbands was *not* available as a means of building community, of building affective commitment and relationships,[81] and the author of our letter chose to address much of his ethical advice to Christians in divided households. Again, reality was more complex than the dualism of Wilson's earlier sociological theory of sects as imposed on 1 Peter by Elliott.[82]

DISCONTINUITY WITH TRADITION

The movement toward peace and harmony with Greco-Roman society meant a movement away from important values in the Torah. The Jewish-Christian author of 1 Peter is exhorting these sectarians to accept and maintain a norm of behavior that differs radically from the way of life legislated and encouraged in Scripture.[83] Professor Elliott discusses *oikos/oikia* in the

---

[80]See Lohse, "Paraenesis and Kerygma in 1 Peter" (trans. above).

[81]R. M. Kante, "Commitment and the Internal Organization of Millennial Movements," *American Behavioral Scientist* 16 (1972): 219-43 at pp. 232-33. She then notes (pp. 234-35): "Communion is also developed through shared persecution . . . emotional enthusiasm is heightened through a deliberate break with convention. This welds the devotees together in a new faternity of people who have deliberately flouted the most sacred rules of the old society."

[82]When discussing Colossians, Ephesians, and 1 Peter, Dieter Lührmann, "Neutestamentliche Haustafeln und antike Ökonomie" *NTS* 27 (1980): 83-97 at p. 94, n. 60 refers to the religiously divided household at this stage of development within Christianity as the usual situation (*Normalfall*).

Where does Elliott's idea of the house *opposed* to the city come from (*Home* 192-93)? In classical thought, which our author has utilized, the house was the model, the paradigm, the source of the city. I see no indication that the Roman author of 1 Peter has reversed this idea; the slightly later Roman author of 1 Clement develops it. Martin Dibelius, *Rom und die Christen im ersten Jahrhundert,* Sitzungsberichte der Heidelberger Akademie der Wissenschaften, Philosophisch-historische Klasse 42:2 (1941) (Heidelberg: Carl Winter, 1942) 3-54, at p. 25 says all of 1 Clement was written to exhort the Corinthians to "learn to be submissive" (57.2). Note that an emphasis on submission to rulers concludes the long prayer in 1 Clement 59-61.

[83]Elliott repeatedly (*Home* 128, 130, 134, 180, 189, 194, 211-12, 214, 218, 233) says that the Christian emphasis on the house is new, unique, superior, distinctive. Certainly the affective bonds formed by these Christians in their sectarian communities were unique for them, but the ideas and the structure of a Greco-Roman house were not new. Pagan authors wrote books in which the idea of the "house" is more central than it is in 1 Peter, e.g. Aristotle (*Politics* I), Bryson, Callicratides, Philodemus, Stobaeus (IV. 28), and Xenophon.

Torah and the NT primarily from the point of view of their similarity.[84] However, the same word, *oikos,* does not refer to the same institution in the Torah and the NT. The central event of salvation in the OT was the freeing of *slaves* from Egypt, and this *mythos* produced an *ethos.* The *first* law in the Book of the Covenant legislated that Israelites free their Hebrew slaves after six years (Exod. 21:1-6). Shalom Paul says that "all laws in the Covenant Code pertaining to slaves are concerned with furthering his protection and preserving his human dignity."[85] This law is reformulated centuries later in Deut. 15:12-18, which then includes the demand that *female* slaves be freed too, and that they be given material gifts on the occasion.[86] Pointedly phrased, whereas the commands in the Torah protect slaves, the NT exhortations are repressive, and this reflects the cultural change from the Mosaic story of salvation to Greek politics.[87] Furthermore, the OT does not emphasize the subordination of wives. Genesis 3:16 refers to the idea, but in pre-exilic literature there is not a single reference to this story![88] The household values in Israelite society were radically different from the structure of the Greco-Roman house, and the Jewish author of 1 Peter is acculturating.[89]

Eduard Schweizer phrases this more provocatively.[90] He argues that the domestic code, already in its Petrine form, is the *paganization* of Christianity because it eventually leads, in 1 Clement 20, to the idealization of a divine, cosmic, Roman hierarchical order.[91] It was (and remains) socially and politically dangerous that 1 Pet. 2:18-25, 1 Tim. 6:1-2 and Titus 2:9-10 exhort slaves without exhorting masters also. This tendency dangerously reinforced Roman hierarchical society.

---

[84]*Home,* 182-86, 211.

[85]Shalom M. Paul, *Studies in the Book of Covenant,* 40; see pp. 43, 64.

[86]See Calum M. Carmichael, *The Laws of Deuteronomy* (Ithica: Cornell University, 1974) 53-61.

[87]On the other hand, against Elliott (*Home* 159, n. 110; 220), these sectarians did not swallow Roman politics whole. Against the Aristotelian tradition (see NE V 1134b 9-18), they assumed that masters' treatment of slaves could be "unjust" (1 Pet. 2:19, 23; Col. 4:1). Second, over against Graeco-Roman values (see Plutarch, *Advice to Bride and Groom* 140D), they insisted that wives had the right to choose their own God, a religious choice with social and political consequences. See the article cited in n. 5.

[88]See James P. Pritchard, "Man's Predicament in Eden," *The Review of Religion* 13:1 (1948): 5-23 at p. 6. The story is not used in theological circles until the second century BC.

[89]Elliott's argument (*Home* 139, 190) that the author is not stressing *sub*ordination but only order is incorrect.

[90]Schweizer, "Weltlichkeit," 407, 410.

[91]See J. J. Thierry, "Note sur 'TA ELACHISTA TON ZOON' au chapitre XX de la I^a Clementis," *Vigiliae Christianae* 14 (1960): 235-44 on Dio Chrysostom *Or.* 40.32-41 and 48.16.

The domestic code emphasizes values that differ not only from the To-rah, but also with some values of the early Jesus movement in Palestine.[92] Women wandered around Galilee with Jesus, supporting him and his follow-ers financially (Mark 15:40-41; Luke 8:1-3; 24:10). Their wealth suggests that they were not simply uneducated rural peasants. Jeremias has evaluated this as ''an unprecedented happening in the history of that time.''[93] Elisabeth Schüssler Fiorenza notices that two Markan texts (3:31-35; 10:28-30) prom-ise the new convert other brothers, sisters, and mothers, but omit (Roman pa-triarchal) fathers. Matthew (23:9) develops this as a critique of leadership in the congregation: ''Call no man on earth your father.''[94] With a different em-phasis from the later domestic codes, Jesus taught that ''whoever does not receive the kingdom of God like a child (slave) shall not enter it'' (Mark 10:15).[95] These texts suggest a significant shift in values from the early rural Palestinian Jesus movement to urban, hellenistic, ''diaspora,'' Petrine, Jew-ish Christianity,[96] a string of adjectives that points to the complexity of the acculturation process. The domestic code is one aspect of early Christian accul-turation in Hellenistic society over against the Jesus tradition itself! Later Chris-tian authors, after the mid-second century AD, no longer utilize the code.[97] These radical changes illustrate a certain flexibility in early Christian life-style; James Sanders refers to this phenomenon in the canon as ''adaptable for life.''[98]

THE CHRIST STORY

A final question: If this ethical material on the household involves ac-culturation, how is the *boundary* maintained in 1 Peter, over against the ten-dency to paganization that Schweizer perceives in the developing Christian

---

[92]Three years ago when Prof. Elliott and I began these discussions, I quoted Theissen's view of the social contrasts between rural Palestinian and urban Hellenistic Christianity. The views expressed above are a result of conclusions which developed while I did research for ch. 4, ''Society in Palestine'' in John Stambaugh and David L. Balch, *The New Testament in its Social Environment* (Library of Early Christianity: Resources for NT Study, ed. Wayne A. Meeks; Philadelphia: Westminster, 1986).

[93]J. Jeremias, *Jerusalem in the Time of Jesus* (Philadelphia: Fortress Press, 1949) 374.

[94]Elisabeth Schüssler Fiorenza, *In Memory of Her. A Feminist Theological Reconstruc-tion of Christian Origins* (New York: Crossroad, 1984) 147.

[95]Ibid., 148. See R. Bultmann, *The History of the Synoptic Tradition* (New York: Harper and Row, 1968) 105.

[96]Contrast L. Goppelt, ''Jesus und die 'Haustafel'-Tradition,'' in *Orientierung an Jesus. Zur Theologie der Synoptiker,* für Josef Schmid, hrsg. Paul Hoffmann et al. (Frieburg: Herder, 1973) 93-106, who stresses the continuity between Jesus and the *Haustafel* tradition.

[97]The exception is Pseudo-Ignatius (see Balch, *Wives* 80, n. 58).

[98]James A. Sanders, ''Adaptable for Life: The Nature and Function of Canon,'' in *Mag-nalia Dei. The Mighty Acts of God.* Essays on the Bible and Archaeology in Memory of G. Ernest Wright (Garden City: Doubleday, 1976) 531-60.

use of the household code?[99] Elliott's answer is clear. The idea of the community as the *oikos tou theou* (house of God) functioned as the chief integrative concept of 1 Peter."[100] He refers to "the compelling force of *oikos* as a symbol of communal identity . . . ."[101] "The central term, however, in the Petrine response to *paroikia* was *oikos*."[102] He explains the success of Christianity as reflected in 1 Peter first by its focus on the family, along with Christianity's distinctiveness, its solidarity in suffering, and its social cohesion.[103] This emphasis on the *oikos* is puzzling from the point of view of "sociological exegesis." The author of 1 Peter does envision such peaceful, harmonious households as possible, but present *experience* was of *divided* households, unjust masters, and many pagan husbands. Given the discontinuities just outlined between a) Torah plus the early Jesus movement, b) "domesticated" Petrine Christianity, and c) later hellenistic Christianity which, however, does not employ the form of the domestic code, it is an exaggeration to label the *oikos* an identity symbol. The Roman household was a political expediency for early Petrine Christianity, and a temporary expediency at that. *Every* household code found in early Christian texts occurs in documents which reflect high tension with Roman society.[104] Several of these texts are explicitly "apologetic," for example, Col. 4:6,[105] 1 Pet. 3:15, Titus 2:3-5, 1 Tim. 5:14,[106] that is, they appeal to Greco-Roman cultural values and

---

[99]For a statement of this problem in a contemporary sect see J. Howard Kauffman, "Boundary Maintenance and Cultural Assimilation of Contemporary Mennonites," *Mennonite Quarterly Review* 51 (1977): 227-40. In the 1982 discussion with Prof. Elliott, I based my remarks on acculturation largely on Kauffman's observations, but a) this is only one field study, as important as it is, and b) the analogy of modern Mennonites with early Petrine Christianity is open to several objections which the present use of general theory of of acculturation and diverse field studies is not.

[100]*Home,* 270.

[101]Ibid., 230.

[102]Ibid., 232-33.

[103]Ibid., 288; cp. 224.

[104]Balch, *Wives,* 80, n. 58.

[105]Ibid., 112, n. 37.

[106]Hans-Josef Klauck, *Hausgemeinde und Hauskirche im frühen Christentum* (Stuttgarter Bibelstudien 103; Stuttgart: Katholisches Bibelwerk, 1981) 101 observes that "the house church did not survive the first centuries" (my trans.). Again, "In 312 AD Eusebius consecrated a church in Tyre for the first time as bishop (*Hist. Eccl.* 10.3-4). . . .The transition from private house to cult building has many parallels in this historical period, from dinner and family table, about which the house church assembled for the Lord's Supper, to sacred sacrificial altar reserved for a priest. . . . The Synod of Laodicea, between 360 and 370 AD, legislated a decisive termination of the domestic celebration of the eucharist: 'Bishops and Presbyters may no longer celebrate the offering in houses' (Canon 58)." (My trans. of Klauck, *Hausgemeinde* 77). The Christian "house" is a pre-Constantinian institution.

they belong to a limited period of church history,[107] to the post-Pauline, late first-century and early second-century church. A focus on the house and on domestic ethics did not provide identity and continuity for early Christians.

In 1 Peter itself, the final and characteristic basis for the ethical exhortations is Christological.[108] Beyond adding "for the Lord's sake" (1 Pet. 2:13) or "mindful of God" (2:19), the author quotes traditional Christological confessions and hymns. Bultmann characterizes 1 Pet. 1:20 plus 3:18-19, 22 as a confession and 2:21-24 as a hymn.[109] Christian slaves and wives who face a contest with the unbelieving world have confessed Christ, the new Enoch, who has won the decisive victory by his passion, resurrection, and ascension over the angelic powers of evil.[110] The hymn sung (1 Pet. 2:21-24) strengthens the slaves with the image of the suffering Christ. This Christological story was the identity symbol and remained so for Christians, unlike the Roman household *ethos*. I am not emphasizing a mental *idea*. The key identity symbol was a *mythos* not an *ethos,* a sacred story, not a domestic political institution, Christology not codified ethics.[111]

Similarly, James Sanders notes that in the greatest crisis situation in ancient Israel, the destruction of Jerusalem and the exile, the cultic and royal institutions and practices did not survive; priestly and Davidic social structures died. They were not essential to Israel's identity.[112] An old, sacred story

---

[107]Ibid.

[108]Eduard Lohse, "Paraenese und Kerygma im 1. Petrusbrief," *ZNTW* 45 (1954): 86, trans. above.

[109]R. Bultmann, "Bekenntnis- und Liedfragmente im ersten Petrusbrief," *Coniectanea Neotestamentica* 9 (1947): 1-14.

[110]W. J. Dalton, *Christ's Proclamation to the Spirits. A Study of 1 Peter 3:18-4:6* (AnBib 23; Rome: Pontifical Biblical Institute, 1965) 200.

[111]Larry Shinn, *Two Sacred Worlds. Experience and Structure in the World's Religions* (Nashville: Abingdon, 1977) chs. 3-4 makes a similar point about the relationship of myth to imperative and ethic. Cp. Stanley Hauerwas, *A Community of Character* (Notre Dame: Notre Dame, 1981) 53-71.

I assume that the "core values" of Roman culture (the *politeia*) are presented by Dionysius, *Roman Antiquities* 1.9-2.29. See Balch, "Two Apologetic Encomia," 107-14. (For the translation of *politeia* as "culture," see Leo Strauss, *Natural Right and History* (Chicago: University of Chicago, 1953) 135-38. If so, one of the theses of L. A. Coser's conflict functionalism becomes relevant: "The more a conflict group can appeal to the core values of a system, the less likely is the conflict to create dissensus over these values and the more likely is it to promote integration into the system." (Lewis A. Coser, "The Functions of Dissent," in *The Dynamics of Dissent,* ed. Jules H. Masserman [Science and Psychoanalysis 13; New York: Grune and Stratton, 1968]158-68, as reformulated by Turner, *The Structure of Sociological Theory,* 170.) The appeal in 1 Peter to Roman household values promoted integration into Roman society.

[112]Sanders, "Adaptable for Life," 549-50.

which was repeated in the crisis gave Israel life and identity. Although they were forced to relate to very different social and political institutions, they survived in Babylon (cp. 1 Pet. 5:13) because they did not assimilate another culture's different identifying *mythos*. As Israel learned to live without priests and kings, the church has learned to live without emperors and slaves (1 Pet. 2:13, 18) and can learn to live without the Roman form of marriage, wives subordinate to husbands (1 Pet. 3:1), while still maintaining its identity through retelling the story of Jesus' death and resurrection.

CHAPTER 6

THE LITERARY AND THEOLOGICAL FUNCTION OF 1 PETER 1:3-12

DAVID W. KENDALL
THE FREE METHODIST CHURCH
CHARLOTTE, MICHIGAN 48813

In 1976 John H. Elliott described the status of 1 Peter in the estimation of modern New Testament exegetes as second class and as that of a stepchild of the New Testament canon.[1] In recent years this status has been elevated somewhat by a renewed scholarly interest in 1 Peter. As a result, there is a growing consensus that 1 Peter should be viewed as a genuine epistle which makes an important theological statement in its own right. Despite this consensus, however, several issues continue to be debated in the scholarly community.

Three of these issues are of particular concern for this article. First, while there is a general consensus that the evidence of 1 Peter indicates its coherence, there is no agreement on the literary structure of 1 Peter.[2] Second, past

---

[1]J. H. Elliott, "The Rehabilitation of an Exegetical Stepchild: 1 Peter in Recent Research," *JBL* 95 (1976): 243.

[2]The following survey articles indicate both the general consensus and the lack of agreement on the literary structure of 1 Peter: R. P. Martin, "The composition of 1 Peter in Recent Study," *Vox Evangelica: Biblical and Historical Essays by Members of the Faculty of the London Bible College,* ed. R. P. Martin (London: Epworth, 1962): 29-42; Elliott, "Exegetical Stepchild," 243-54; D. Sylva, "1 Peter Studies: The State of the Discipline," *BTB* 10 (1980): 153-63; E. Cothenet, *"Les Orientations actuelles de l'Exegese de la Premiere Lettre de Pierre," Etudes sur la Premiere Lettre de Pierre,* ed. C. Perrot (Paris: *Les Editions du Cerf,* 1980) 13-42; F. Neugebauer, *"Zur Deutung und Bedeutung des 1. Petrusbrief,"* NTS 26 (1979-1980): 61-86.

proposals for the structure of 1 Peter and past accounts of its theology have been undecided as to the literary and theological relationship between various sections and divisions of the epistle: this includes the relationship between 1:3-12 and 1:13-5:11. Third, there is still no consensus on the major theme of 1 Peter or on how its different motifs relate to each other.

In what follows we hope to shed some light on each of these issues by observing the literary and theological relationship between 1 Peter 1:3-12 and 1:13-5:11. In order to accomplish this goal we shall first sketch the logic of 1 Peter and draw several conclusions regarding its overall structure and the function of 1:3-12 within that structure. We will then seek to illustrate and substantiate our understanding of the literary function of 1:3-12 by examining how this passage relates to each of the succeeding sections of 1 Peter. Further, we shall suggest that the literary function of 1:3-12 within 1 Peter has important consequences for discovering the theological message of 1 Peter. Finally, we conclude the essay by drawing out exegetical and interpretive implications of our study that have a bearing on several of the major issues confronting Petrine scholars.

THE STRUCTURE OF 1 PETER

The introductory pericope of 1 Peter (1:3-12) constitutes the first main division of the letter. In this section the author declares that God has granted Christians an entirely new existence (1:3-5). This existence is described as a life of hope and joy (vv. 3, 6, 8) but also as a life subject to various afflictions (vv. 6-7).[3] The fact that Christian life involves both hope and affliction is clarified by the author's assertion that affliction serves the redemptive purposes of God and that the Christians' faithfulness in affliction will bring them to glory at the revelation of Jesus Christ (vv. 6-7). The author bases these assertions on the Christ event itself, which he summarizes as an experience of sufferings and subsequent glories and which is the basis of the readers' present Christian life (vv. 10-12).

The author's introductory declarations concerning the nature of Christian existence serve as the foundation for the exhortations that comprise the bulk of the epistle (1:13-5:11). These exhortations divide themselves into three main segments. The first segment is to be found in 1:13-2:10, where the author draws out the general implications of Christian existence as he has described it in 1:3-12. Thus, on the basis of God's saving initiatives, Christians are to be true to their calling as God's people. What it means to be God's people is

---

[3]With nearly all recent commentators we understand the "trials and afflictions" of vv. 6-7 as indicative of the present experience of the readers.

described in the three subsections of 1:13-2:10: to be God's people means to be holy (1:14-21), to be loving (1:22-2:3), and to be elect in Christ (2:4-10).

These general implications of Christian existence are specified in the next segment of the parenesis, 2:11-4:11. That is, the author indicates the precise ways in which the Christians' holiness, love, and election are to be expressed in the circumstances faced by the readers. The principles that govern the life of Christians in their particular situations are stated in 2:11-12. Negatively, they must repudiate fleshly desires; positively, they must maintain good conduct among the pagans. These principles are then applied to several situations: Christians in society (2:13-17); servants under cruel masters (2:18-25); wives who face non-Christian husbands (3:1-6); husbands in relation to their Christian wives (3:7); and the whole community in its situation of conflict with hostile non-Christians (3:8-4:11). In all of these concrete situations, the good conduct of Christians is expressed primarily by means of submission and humility, characteristics that are preeminently illustrated in the sufferings of Jesus who serves as a model for appropriate Christian response to all forms of conflict.

The author concludes his epistle with a climactic summary of his main concerns (4:12-5:11). In this section, the main themes of the letter are synthesized and the author's instructions are reiterated from three perspectives: with respect to Christians as they face a hostile nonbelieving world (4:12-19); with respect to Christian conduct within the community (from leaders to members) in light of the situation of hostility (5:1-7); and with respect to God's eternal designs in the cosmic struggle which underlies the Christians' situation of conflict (5:8-11). From each of these perspectives the author urges his readers to base their conduct upon the future that God has given them in their calling and rebirth.

On the basis of this sketch of the logic and flow of thought in 1 Peter it seems that the structure of the epistle involves the following. In general terms the epistle may be divided into two distinct blocks of material. First, there is the opening pericope (1:3-12) which is characterized by a series of declarations on the nature of the believers' life in grace. Second, these declarations are followed by an extended parenesis (1:13-5:11) that explicates the nature of the believers' responsibilities as God's people in a hostile world. These two blocks of material are related to each other in that 1:3-12 provides an introduction to 1:13-5:11. The precise ways in which the former introduces the latter will be clarified as we proceed.

It should also be observed that the parenesis (1:13-5:11) is structured in two important ways. First, there is a movement from the general to the particular. That is, in 1:13-2:10 the author sets forth general exhortations to be God's people and in 2:11-4:11 these general exhortations are given particular application to the various situations faced by the readers who are urged to act as God's people. Second, the author's parenesis concludes with a climactic summary of his most important concerns in 4:12-5:11.[4]

What distinguishes this proposal for the structure of 1 Peter from others is the unique role that it assigns to the introductory pericope, 1:3-12. In fact, we would argue that 1 Peter 1:3-12 serves as an introduction to the epistle as a whole. That the author's remarks in 1:3-12 introduces *some* of his exhortations is acknowledged by nearly all commentators. The claim of this proposal, however, is that 1:3-12 provides the foundation for *all* of the author's subsequent remarks.

THE INTRODUCTORY CHARACTER OF 1 PETER 1:3-12

In order to substantiate and to clarify the introductory character of 1 Peter 1:3-12 it is necessary to examine briefly how this passage relates to the epistle as a whole. Our examination will proceed in three parts: the main themes and overall message of 1:3-12; the ways in which 1:3-12 relates to the three main divisions of the parenesis—1:13-2:10; 2:11-4:11; and 4:12-5:11; how an appreciation of 1:3-12 as introductory to the whole epistle helps us discern the primary theological motifs of 1 Peter and the way in which varied themes relate to each other.

---

[4]This sketch of the structure of 1 Peter is summarized in the following annotated outline.
I. *1:3-12* DECLARATIONS ON THE NATURE OF SAVING GRACE
    Regeneration to a new way of life.
    (This is the true grace of God, 5:12)
II. *1:13-5:11* IMPLICATIONS OF SAVING GRACE
    Living out the implications of the new way of life.
    (Stand in this grace, 5:12)
    A. *1:13-2:10* Hope upon grace and be true to your calling as God's people.
        The believers' new way of life is described as one determined by their hope (1:13, 21), obedience (1:14), nonconformity and holiness (1:14-16), exile status (1:17), love within the Christian community (1:22ff.), and incorporation into the destiny of Christ (2:4-10).
    B. *2:11-4:11* Act as God's people.
        The believers' new way of life involves situations of conflict or suffering in which they are called to live out the implications of saving grace (to "do good"). In such situations the believers' sufferings are related to those of Christ.
    C. *4:12-5:11* Depend upon God's future.
        The believers' new way of life involves a present participation in the suffering of Christ and a future of exultation and glory at the revelation of Christ. This pattern of present suffering and future glory is the basis for the believers' hope and confidence as they face God's eschatological judgment. Furthermore, this pattern also provides a model for Christian life (both for leaders and for all members of the community), a model which corresponds to God's calling and which assures believers of their final vindication (5:10).

The Main Themes and Overall Message of 1:3-12

First Peter begins with an ascription of blessing to God who has mercifully regenerated believers to an entirely new life.[5] This new existence is grounded in the resurrection of Jesus and is oriented to a future goal expressed in terms of a living hope, an eternal inheritance, and final salvation. The life of believers is thus determined by an active hope and a steadfast faith that impels them toward their future and preserves them along the way (vv. 3-5).

Moreover, certain paradoxical consequences flow directly from the nature of Christian life. Those who have been reborn are caused to rejoice as they anticipate and are in the process of realizing their final salvation.[6] Such exultation is not mitigated by the fact that they must face affliction without the security of ''seeing'' the Lord in whom they have placed their hope, faith, and love (vv. 8-9). Because of their future destiny, Christians recognize their present sufferings as instruments of purging through which God will bring them to glory (vv. 6-7). Similarly, they do not place confidence in past or present ''sight.'' Rather, their faith is grounded in the resurrection of Jesus which signals the decisive intrusion of God's future into human history and guarantees this future for his own. Finally, the author underscores the fulfillment that has come to Christians by contrasting the present age of salvation with all prior epochs (vv. 10-12). In the sufferings and glories of Jesus, saving grace has now become a reality for Christians who stand on the threshold of the new age. In short, on the basis of God's deed in Christ, believers are positioned at the apex not only of salvation history but also of the cosmic drama of redemption, for even angels are attracted by the wonder of saving grace (v. 12).

From these remarks several conclusions may be drawn regarding the believers' life in saving grace. First, the expression of salvation as a climax to

---

[5]For the exegesis of 1:3-12 see, in addition to the commentators, M. A. Chevallier, ''*1 Pierre 1:1-2:10: structure litteraire et consequences exegetiques,*'' *RHPR* 55 (1971): 129-42; G. Delling, ''*Der Bezug der Christlichen Existenz auf das Heilshandeln Gottes nach dem ersten Petrusbrief,*'' *Neues Testament und Christliche Existenz: Festschrift für Herbert Braun zu 70. Geburtstag am 4. mai 1973,* ed. H. D. Betz and L. Schottroff (Tübingen: J. C. B. Mohr, 1973) 95-113; D. E. Hiebert, ''Peter's Thanksgiving for Our Salvation,'' *Studia Missionalia* 29 (1980): 85-103; M. H. Scharlemann, ''An Apostolic Descant (An exegetical study of 1 Peter 1:3-12),'' *Concordia Journal* 2 (1976): 9-17; P. G. Dautzenberg, ''Sōtēria Psychōn (1 Pt. 1:9),'' *BZ* 8 (1964): 262-76; D. W. Kendall, *The Introductory Character of 1 Peter 1:3-12* (Ann Arbor MI: Xerox University Microfilms, 1984) 79-174.

[6]Discussions of the difficult phrase *en hō* as it is used in 1 Peter may be found in Kendall, 109-12; B. Reicke, *The Disobedient Spirits and Christian Baptism: A Study of 1 Peter 3:19 and its Context* (Copenhagen: Eina Mjunksgaard, 1946) 103-13; W. J. Dalton, *Christ's Proclamation to the Spirits: A Study of 1 Peter 3:18–4:6* (Rome: Pontifical Biblical Institute, 1965) 133-43; P. R. Fink, ''The Use and Significance of *en hō* in 1 Peter,'' *Grace Journal* 8:2 (1967): 33-39.

Christian life in each of the units of our passage (see vv. 10-12 with reference to whole passage; v. 5 with reference to vv. 3-5; v. 9 with reference to vv. 6-9) suggests that Christian life is dynamic and eschatological. It involves a way of life definitively shaped by its future goal that has already broken into present reality. "Salvation," therefore, embraces past, present, and future. Though salvation is the goal of Christian life, it has been manifested historically in the sufferings and glories of Jesus Christ and constitutes a present reality for those who have received grace in the proclamation of the gospel.[7]

Second, the way leading to salvation also involves various kinds of sufferings. Such sufferings, however, stand in a new light for they are interpreted from the perspective of the eschatological goal to which Christians are drawn. From this perspective it becomes clear that sufferings are the temporary but necessary destiny of believers and are placed in the service of their future glorification. This pattern of sufferings and glories is given further significance by its use as a summary for the vocation of Christ. In this way, the author implies that the afflictions of these believers come about because of their faithfulness to the new way of life granted by God and that such suffering places them in the succession of their Lord. Therefore they may be sure of glory since their hope is grounded in the fact that "God raised *him* and gave *him* glory" (1:21).

Finally, God's saving initiatives result in a life of exultation which anticipates the coming consummation. Such joy is already suffused with glory and is thus incomprehensible in natural terms. For this reason, neither affliction nor insecurity can quench it. In fact, when suffering is seen in its proper light it becomes an incentive for continued rejoicing.

1:3-12 and Exhortations to Be God's People (1:13-2:10)

In this first section of the author's parenesis he exhorts his readers to become God's people. What it means to be God's people is intimately connected with the author's explication of saving grace in 1:3-12. In general terms, God's people must place their hope in the grace that will be consummated at the revelation of Christ (1:13). This grace, however, is none other than the saving grace that the author has described in his introduction. Thus, the author indicates that the most fundamental exhortation of his epistle calls believers to base their lives upon saving grace. If this is so, then the author's description of saving grace in 1:3-12 is foundational for the parenetic concerns of 1 Peter.

In more specific terms, to be God's people and to hope on saving grace is to lead a distinctive life (*anastrophē*), which the author describes from a

---

[7]The discussions of Dautzenberg ("*Sōtēria Psychōn*") and Hiebert ("Peter's Thanksgiving") are especially illuminating on this point.

threefold perspective (1:14-2:10).[8] First, with respect to the world, the *anastrophē* of believers is characterized by nonconformity and by holiness (1:14-21).[9] Such a life proceeds from a reverential fear of God and leads to various forms of conflict with a nonbelieving society.[10] Moreover, in relation to other Christians, the believers' *anastrophē* is distinguished by a sincere brotherly love that supports the community as it faces conflict and as it grows toward final salvation (1:22-2:3).[11] Finally, the author concludes this section by declaring that the believers' way of life as God's people reflects the destiny of Christ (2:4-10).[12] As the readers approach the living Lord who has been re-

[8]For instructive treatments of *anastrophē* and *anastrephō* see especially G. Bertram, "*strephō*," *TDNT* 7, 714-29; G. Schückler, "*Wandel im Glauben als Missionarisches Zeugnis*," *Zeitschrift für Missionswissenschaft und Religionswissenschaft* 4 (1967): 289-99.

[9]For the exegesis of 1:14-21 see especially M. H. Scharlemann, "Exodus Ethics," *Concordia Journal* 2 (1976): 165-70; C. Blendinger, "*Kirche als Fremdlingschaft*," *Communio Viatorum* 10 (1967): 123-34; W. Brandt, "*Wandel als Zeugnis nach dem 1. Petrusbrief*," *Verbum Dei manet in aeternum. Eine Festschrift für Otto Schmitz zu seinem siebzigsten Geburtstag am 16. Juni 1952*, ed. W. Foerster (Witten: Luther, 1953) 10-25; Schückler, "*Wandel in Glauben;*" W. C. Van Unnik, "The Redemption of 1 Peter 1:18-19 and the Problem of the First Epistle of Peter," *Sparsa Collecta: The Collected Essays of W. C. Van Unnik* (*NovTSupp* 30, London: E. J. Brill, 1980) 3-82; W. C. Van Unnik, "The Critique of Paganism in 1 Peter 1:18," *Neotestamentica et Semetica: Studies in Honour of Matthew Black*, ed. E. E. Ellis and M. Wilcox (Edinburgh: T. & T. Clark, 1969) 129-42.

[10]The conflict generated by the believer's life-style is not stated explicitly in 1:14-21. It is, however, implied in the notion of redemption from ancestral ways (1:19, see Van Unnik, "Critique of Paganism"), especially as this notion is interpreted in light of the explicit reason for the believer's suffering that is given in 4:2-4. This conflict is also implied by the author's use of "exile-language" to describe the believer's life. For excellent treatments of the exile-motif see Blendinger, "*Kirche als Fremdlingschaft*," N. Brox, "*Situation und Sprache der Minderheit im ersten Petrusbrief*," *Kairos* 19 (1977): 1-13; V. P. Furnish, "Elect Sojourners in Christ: An Approach to the Theology of 1 Peter," *PSTJ* 28 (1975): 1-11, C. Wolff, "*Christ und Welt im 1. Petrusbrief*" *TLZ* 100 (1975): 333-42. The most comprehensive treatment of the *paroikos/oikos* theme is given by J. H. Elliott, *A Home For The Homeless: A Sociological Exegesis of 1 Peter, Its Situation and Strategy* (Philadelphia: Fortress, 1981).

[11]For the exegesis of 1:22-2:3 see especially W. Grundmann, "*Die Nēpioi in der urchristlichen Paränese*," *NTS* 5 (1958-1959): 188-205; H. Goldstein, *Paulinische Gemeinde im ersten Petrusbrief* (*SBS* 80, Stuttgart: K. B. W., 1975); E. Cothenet, "*Le Realisme de l'Esperance chretienne Selon 1 Pierre*," *NTS* 27 (1981): 564-72; F. W. Danker, "1 Peter 1:24-2:17—A Consolatory Pericope," *ZNW* 58 (1967): 93-102; T. Spörri, *Der Gemeindegedanke im ersten Petrusbrief* (Gütersloh: Bertelsmann, 1925).

[12]This passage has generated an enormous body of literature. See especially J. H. Elliott, *The Elect and the Holy: An Exegetical Examination of 1 Peter 2:4-10 and the Phrase Basileion Ierateuma* (*NovTSup* 12; Leiden: E. J. Brill, 1966); E. Best, "1 Peter 2:4-10—A Reconsideration," *NovT* 11 (1969): 270-93; Danker, "1 Peter 1:24-2:17;" Spörri, *Gemeindegedanke*, 19-20; C. F. D. Moule, "Sanctuary and Sacrifice in the Church of the New Testament," *JTS* (n.s.) 1 (1950): 29-41; K. R. Snodgrass, "1 Peter 2:1-10: Its Literary Formation and Literary Affinities," *NTS* 24 (1977): 97-106; B. Gärtner, *The Temple and the Community in Qumran and in the New Testament* (Cambridge: University Press, 1965) 72-88; Goldstein, *Paulinische Gemeinde*, 27-32.

jected by humanity but is chosen and honored by God they understand their own sufferings as the consequence of their faith and are encouraged to remain faithful as they await God's vindication.[13]

Thus, the author's exhortations to be God's people are rooted in his introductory declarations on the nature of saving grace. The fact that saving grace results in a distinctive way of life becomes the basis for the author's description of the reader's responsibility and provides a rationale both for their situation of conflict and for their perseverance in joy and hope. That is, even though saving grace requires believers to lead a distinctive life (holiness and love), which inevitably leads to suffering, it also provides them with the power and incentive to remain hopeful and faithful. Through their union with Christ they recognize their suffering as a validation of their faithfulness and as an indication that such suffering will ultimately lead to glory. In the meantime, since believers have been reborn they now belong to a loving community that supports them in their suffering.

1:3-12 and Exhortations to Act as God's People (2:11-4:11)

If the author's first hortatory section (1:13-2:10) draws out the general implications of saving grace (1:3-12) the second section (2:11-4:11) applies these general principles to the concrete situations of the readers. This movement from the general to the particular implies that the exhortations of 2:11-4:11 are closely related to the declarations of 1:3-12.

To be more precise, 1:3-12 stands in an introductory relationship to 2:11-4:11. This relationship is indicated by the presence of three important motifs in 2:11-4:11. First, a situation of conflict and suffering is acknowledged as the context in which believers must act as God's people. Thus, believers are called to maintain their distinctive *anastrophē* so that unbelievers who slander them may glorify God on the day of visitation (2:12).[14] Moreover, the author's parenesis on Christians in society (2:13-17)[15] clearly indicates that

---

[13]That 2:4-10 affirms the incorporation of the believer into the destiny of Christ is emphasized especially by Norbert Brox, *Der erste Petrusbrief* (*EKKNT*, Zürich: Benziger, 1979) 95-97, 107-108. See also Goldstein (*Paulinische Gemeinde*, 27-29) and Spörri (*Gemeindegedanke*, 22).

[14]Helpful treatments of 2:11-12 may be found in Spörri, *Gemeindegedanke*, 89; H. W. Beyer "*episkeptomai*," *TDNT* 2, 599-622; W. C. Van Unnik, "*Die Rücksicht auf die Reaktion der Nicht-christen als motiv in der altchristlichen Paränese*," *Judentum, Urchristentum, Kirche: Festschrift für Joachim Jeremias* (*BZNW* 26, ed. W. Eltester, Berlin: Töpelmann) 221-34; W. C. Van Unnik, "The Teaching of Good Works in 1 Peter," *NTS* 1 (1954-1955): 92-110; Schückler, "*Wandel im Glauben*."

[15]On 1 Peter's social parenesis see H. Goldstein, "*Die politischen Paränesen in 1 Petr 2 und Rom 13*," *BibLeb* 14 (1973): 88-104; K. Philipps, *Kirche in der Gesellschaft nach dem 1. Petrusbrief* (Gütersloh: Gütersloh-Gerd Mohn, 1971) 29-35; B. Schwank, "*Wie freie—aber als Sklaven Gottes (1. Petr 2:16)*," *Erbe und Auftrag* 36 (1960): 5-12; H. Teichert, "*1 Peter 2:13—eine crux interpretum?*" *TLZ* 74 (1949): 303-304.

even though believers must submit to those in authority, their obligation to submit is transcended by a higher allegiance to God and the Christian community (2:17).[16] This higher allegiance is the precondition for conflict in society (2:15, in fact, implies conflict). Further, each of the specific situations the author addresses reveals this element of conflict and suffering. Slaves are called to endure unjust suffering under cruel masters (2:18-25)[17] and wives whose husbands are nonbelievers live in a potentially frightening situation (3:6).[18] Even husbands find that their new life in grace requires them to treat their wives in a way that conflicts with the expectations of society (3:7).[19] Finally, when the entire community is addressed it becomes clear that all of the readers are subject to suffering and abuse (3:9, 16; 4:1-6). That life in grace leads to affliction was first announced in 1:3-12. Therefore, the prominence of this motif in 2:11-4:11 supports the claim that 1:3-12 functions as an introduction to this section.

The second motif is that believers must respond to their conflict situation by living out the implications of saving grace as it is described in 1:3-12. In 1:13-2:10 the author clearly indicates that saving grace demands a distinctive *anastrophē,* a life determined by their experience of grace and by their expectation that this grace will soon be consummated (1:13). This life expresses itself in nonconformity and holiness in the world (1:14-21) and in fervent love within the community (1:22-2:3). In 2:11-4:11 the distinctive *anastrophē* that saving grace requires is expressed primarily by the concept of doing good.[20] The believers' call to do good in 2:11-12 is given concrete application in the

---

[16]This higher allegiance is seen clearly in 2:17; the readers are called to *honor* the emperor and all people but to *fear* God and *love* the brotherhood.

[17]On 2:18-25 see Goldstein, *Paulinische Gemeinde,* 28-29; Horst Goldstein, *"Die Kirche als Schar derer, die ihrem leidenden Herrn mit dem Zeil der Gottesgemeinschaft nachfolgen,"* BibLeb 15 (1974): 38-54; J. W. Thompson, "Be Submissive to your Masters—A Study of 1 Peter 2:18-25," *Restoration Quarterly* 9 (1966): 66-78; Theo Sorg, *"In spannungen Leben 1. Petrus 2:21-25,"* *Theologische Beiträge* 4 (1973): 145-50; H. Millauer, *Leiden als Gnade, Eine Traditionsgeschichtliche Untersuchung zur Leidens-theologie des ersten Petrusbrief* (*Europäische Hochschulschriften* 56, Bern: H. Lang, 1976) 65-84, 90-101; H. Schlier, *"Eine Adhortatio aus Rom. Die Botschaft des ersten Petrusbrief," Strukturen Christlicher Existenz: Festgabe für F. Wulf,* ed. H. Schlier (Würzburg: Echter, 1968) 63-65; D. E. Hiebert, "Following Christ's Example: An Exposition of 1 Peter 2:21-25," *BSac* 139 (1982): 32-45; Elliott, *Home for Homeless,* 205-207.

[18]For the exegesis of 3:1-6 see D. L. Balch, *Let Wives Be Submissive. The Domestic Code in 1 Peter,* SBLDS 26 (Ann Arbor: Edwards Bros., 1981).

[19]See B. Reicke, *"Die Gnosis der männer nach 1 Ptr. 3:7"* Neotestamanentliche Studien *für Rudolf Bultmann zu seinem 70. Geburtstag am 20. August 1954* (Berlin: Töpelmann, 1954) 296-304.

[20]On this concept see Van Unnik, "Teaching of Good Works;" Schückler, *"Wandel im Glauben;"* W. Grundmann, *"agathos,"* TDNT 1, 10-18.

several units of 2:13-4:11. Hence, to do good is to be submissive and to show honor to all persons (2:13-17; 3:1-2, 7, 8), to shape one's conduct on the basis of one's commitment to God (2:19; 3:16; 3:21), to suffer unjustly (2:18-19; 3:9-14; 4:1-6), to repudiate vengeance (2:19-23; 3:9, 15-16; 4:1), to rely upon God's ultimate vindication (2:12; implied in 2:23 and 3:9; 3:10-17; 4:5-6), and to love fellow believers (3:8; 4:7-11). All of these expressions of doing good are concrete ways in which believers actualize the implications of saving grace. When believers "do good" they prepare themselves for the consummation at the revelation of Christ and, in the process, their lives bear witness to God's grace before nonbelievers (2:12; 3:1-2).

Finally, in 1:3-12 the author related the readers' experience of affliction and their expectation of glory to the sufferings and glories of Christ (1:6-7, 10-11). This relationship was clarified in 2:4-8 where the author declares that believers share the destiny of Christ, the One rejected by humanity but honored and chosen by God. On this basis, believers may face their own rejection with the confidence that they also are honored and chosen by God. In the present section (2:11-4:11) the association between the readers' suffering and that of Christ is given special prominence. Both servants and the entire Christian community are called to suffer as Christ suffered (2:21-23; 3:9, 10-17, 18; 4:1). In addition, that Christ's sufferings were answered by God's vindication and that he is now recognized as Lord of all assures the readers that their unjust suffering will also lead to vindication (implied in 2:24-25; 3:10-17 in connection with 3:18-22; 4:5-6).

1:3-12 and the Final Exhortations to Depend Upon God's Future

In 4:12-5:11 the author summarizes and reformulates the exhortations that have concerned him throughout his epistle.[21] In doing so, he draws heavily upon the declarations of 1:3-12. This fact is discerned most clearly in his treatment of the readers' suffering. Even if the author uses different terms to describe their afflictions ("in the name of Christ," v. 14; "as a Christian," v. 16) the context reveals that, as in earlier portions of the epistle, they are various forms of unjust suffering that result from the readers' life in grace.[22] Moreover, these sufferings are a sign that the readers are participants in the destiny of Christ and, as such, are destined for future glory. Furthermore, even

[21]Of particular interest for this section of 1 Peter are Millauer, *Leiden als,* 84-90; Goldstein, *Paulinische Gemeinde,* 18-22, Spörri, *Gemeindegedanke,* 111-18; W. Marxen, *"Der Mitälteste und Zeuge der Leiden Christi. Eine martyrologische Begründung des 'Rom-primats' im 1. Petrusbrief?" Theologia crucis—signum crucis: Festschrift für Erich Dinkler zum 70. Geburtstag,* ed. C. Andresen and G. Klein (Tübingen: J. C. B. Mohr, 1979) 377-93; J. H. Elliott, "Ministry and Church Order in the New Testament: A Traditio-Historical Analysis (1 Pt. 5:1-5 and plls)," *CBQ* 32 (1970): 367-91.

[22]See Brox, *Petrusbrief,* 212-24.

though this glory awaits its final *denouement* at the revelation of Christ it has already become a reality in the believers' lives and causes them to rejoice with eschatological joy. Finally, the author once again stresses that unjust suffering ultimately serves God's redemptive purposes by purging and testing the faith of his people.

Again, the close relationship between 4:12-5:11 and 1:3-12 may be discerned in the strong eschatological mood that characterizes both of these sections. The similarity in eschatological mood is clearly indicated by the recurrence of key terms (for example, *peirasmos, pathein, oligon*) and motifs (for example, the imminence of final salvation). In addition, it is important to observe that this mood, so striking in 1:3-12 and 4:12-5:11, is less prominent in the parenesis that comprises the middle section of the epistle. In other words, the author frames his exhortations to become God's people (1:13-2:10) and to act as God's people (2:11-4:11) with sections that emphasize the hope and confidence believers may have as they fulfill their responsibilities in a hostile world. This fact reveals not only the literary and theological strategy of the author but also the close relationship between 1:3-12 and 4:12-5:11.

Finally, in both 1:3-12 and 4:12-5:11 the author stresses the initiative and sovereignty of God in order to bolster the readers' hope. Thus, in the introduction the final destiny of believers is assured by the fact that God's power protects them until they take possession of their inheritance, an inheritance described as incorruptible, undefiled, unfading, and reserved in heaven (1:3-5). In the conclusion the readers are once again assured of their final salvation. This time, however, the assurance comes through the author's assertion that, in contrast to believers who are receiving salvation as the end (*telos*) of their faith (1:9), unbelievers will soon receive condemnation as the end (*telos*) of their disobedience (1:17-18). In the final analysis both the introduction and the conclusion affirm that God is absolutely sovereign. His mighty hand is poised over the readers' situation (5:6). In the beginning it was God who brought new life to the readers (1:3), a life characterized by temporary suffering but also destined for eternal glory (1:5, 6-7; 5:10). Likewise, at the end, it is God who has called them to glory and who will strengthen, restore, and establish them after their temporary sufferings (5:10).

Conclusion

The predominant motifs and concerns of 1 Peter 1:13-5:11 indicate that the author's opening remarks in 1:3-12 function as an introduction to his entire epistle. The present examination has underscored important evidence to support this conclusion in each of the units that comprise 1 Peter. By way of summary we would suggest two ways in which 1:3-12 serves as an introduction to the author's parenetic concerns (1:13-5:11).

hope

First, the terminology and motifs of 1:3-12 often anticipate those of succeeding sections of the letter. Several examples will illustrate this anticipation. In 1:3 the author describes the readers as reborn to a living hope. This description of regenerate life suggests that the concept of hope plays an important role in the author's understanding of life in grace. Hence, we are not surprised to find that his first exhortation involves hoping (1:13) and that Christians must always be prepared to explain their hope to outsiders (3:15; cf. 1:21; 3:5). A second example may be found in a comparison between 1:6-7 and the motifs and terminology of the author's conclusion (4:12-5:11). In both passages we find suffering described as a trial by fire that ultimately serves God's redemptive purposes (1:7; 4:12); as an occasion for present exultation (1:6; 4:13); and as a temporary but inevitable component of Christian existence (1:6; 5:10). A final example of the way in which 1:3-12 anticipates the themes of 1:13-5:11 is seen in the relationship between the readers' sufferings and those of Christ. In the introduction the author implies that his readers' life in grace is parallel to the destiny of Christ, both of which may be summarized in terms of present suffering and future glory (1:6-7, 10-11). As we have noted, this implication anticipates the author's more explicit, recurring assertion that believers are called to share the destiny of their Lord (2:4-8; 2:18-23; 3:9-22; 4:1, 12; 5:10).

The second way 1:3-12 introduces the parenesis of 1:13-5:11 is that the former serves as the presupposition for the latter. That is, 1:3-12 provides the foundation upon which the author bases his exhortations. Saving grace, as it is described in 1:3-12, requires a distinctive way of life (*anastrophē*) and the author's concern in 1:13-5:11 is to encourage his readers in this way. Thus, if 1:13-2:10 draws out the general implications of the believers' life in saving grace, then 2:11-4:11 applies these general implications to the readers' specific situations. Finally, 4:12-5:11 brings the epistle to a climactic conclusion by summarizing the implications of saving grace that have been explicated in earlier portions of the parenesis.

If, in fact, 1 Peter 1:3-12 functions as an introduction to the epistle then a recognition of this fact should help us interpret the theology of 1 Peter. Therefore, we now turn to a consideration of the overall message of 1 Peter and to a demonstration of how an appreciation of the introductory character of 1:3-12 contributes to an understanding of that message.

THE IMPLICATIONS
OF THE INTRODUCTORY CHARACTER OF 1 PETER 1:3-12
FOR DISCERNING THE THEOLOGICAL MESSAGE OF 1 PETER

An appreciation of the introductory character of 1 Peter 1:3-12 provides an important clue to the theological message of the epistle as a whole. We shall first summarize the overall message of 1 Peter and then indicate how

1:3-12 underscores that message when its introductory character is acknowledged.[23]

The overall message of 1 Peter may be summarized in the following way: saving grace demands both a movement from present suffering to future glory and a fellowship of love. The author of 1 Peter addresses a number of Christian communities in Asia Minor, communities that have found that their life as God's people has brought them alienation, conflict, and suffering.[24] The author writes his letter in order to bear witness to the genuine grace of God and to admonish his readers to remain in that grace (5:12). In order to accomplish this purpose, the author begins the epistle with a panoramic description of the nature of the readers' life in grace (1:3-12). Believers have been reborn to an entirely new life that is characterized by hope and joy and that is destined for glory and final salvation. This destiny is certain even though Christian life requires believers to experience present suffering as they are on their way to future glory, a requirement that is endemic to saving grace and that finds its archetypical expression in the vocation of Christ. Thus, the movement from present suffering to future glory not only depicts the vocation of Christ but also becomes paradigmatic for the believers' life in grace.

This conclusion is confirmed repeatedly throughout the succeeding sections of 1 Peter. As we have seen, nearly every pericope within 1:13-5:11 presupposes a situation in which the readers are faced with conflict and suffering in a non-Christian world. In each case the author affirms the fact of suffering as a necessary consequence of the believers' life in grace and as a reflection of the vocation of Christ. Hence, because the readers have encountered saving grace (1:3-12) they must live a distinctive life (*anastrophē*) by not conforming to pagan society, by living as resident aliens in the fear of God, and by their incorporation into the destiny of Christ—the One rejected by humanity but honored by God (1:13-21; 2:4-10). In short, saving grace demands a life-style that leads believers to experience present suffering (cf. 4:1-4) but that also assures them of future glory, since their destiny is bound up with the destiny of Christ.

Moreover, the author exhorts his readers to remain faithful to the implications of saving grace as they face their varied situations of conflict and suffering

---

[23]On the general theology of 1 Peter see, in addition to the commentaries, F. W. Beare, "The Teaching of First Peter," *ATR* 27 (1945): 284-96; Brox, "*Situation und Sprache;*" M. A. Chevallier, "*Condition et Vocation des Chretiens en Diaspora,*" *RevScRel* 48 (1974): 387-98; Goldstein, "*Die Kirche als Schar;*" D. M. Miller, "Deliverance and Destiny: Salvation in First Peter," *Int.* 9 (1955): 413-25; Schlier, "*Adhortatio;*" Spörri, *Gemeindegedanke;* W. C. Van Unnik, "Christianity According to 1 Peter," *ExpTim* 68 (1956-1957): 79-83.

[24]Throughout the epistle this conflict is presupposed. See 1:6-7; 2:4-8; 2:12; 2:18-20; 3:1-2; 3:9, 14, 15, 17; 4:1-2; 4:12-19; 5:8-9, 10.

(2:11-4:11). In every situation the readers must "do good" and express concretely the distinctive life-style that is to characterize God's people (2:11-12). While this life-style *may* attract unbelievers and lead ultimately to their conversion (2:12, 15; 3:1-2) it more often provokes unbelievers and causes them to abuse believers. In such situations believers must recognize that their lives are ultimately in God's hands and that they, like their Lord, must remain faithful. As the readers bear their suffering innocently they may be sure that final victory and glory will be theirs, since their lives are grounded in the redemptive work of Christ whose own suffering was met by glory (2:21-25; 3:18-22).

Finally, when the author brings his epistle to a climactic summary (4:12-5:11) he states explicitly that the believers' life in grace involves a participation in the suffering and glory of Christ (4:12-13; 5:1, 10). This fact provides both an explanation for the readers' suffering and a rationale for their continued hope and joy. That is, believers suffer because they are bound to their Lord whose vocation was to suffer. On this basis, the readers should not be surprised by their suffering but should view it as a verification that they share the vocation of Christ (4:12-13). This vocation, however, involves more than present suffering; it also involves future glory. To share Christ's vocation, therefore, is to move from present suffering to future glory. On this basis, the readers can exult even in the worst of situations, for they know that suffering is only temporary and that the God of all grace has called them to eternal glory (5:10).

This theme—that saving grace involves the movement from present suffering to future glory—more than any other, characterizes the author's understanding of Christian life in a hostile nonbelieving world. The author's opening declarations (1:3-12), when viewed as introductory, underscore the significance of this theme for the whole of 1 Peter and it does so in a twofold way. First, as we have seen, this theme is anticipated in 1:3-12. The author describes saving grace as a way of life that leads to suffering (v. 6) but that also culminates in final salvation (vv. 5, 9) and in the reception of praise, glory, and honor (v. 7). In addition, the author declares that this pattern of present suffering and future glory is endemic to grace as it was expressed historically in the sufferings and glories of Christ (vv. 10-11) and as it is now proclaimed in the Christian gospel (v. 12). In this way, 1:3-12 anticipates and, thus, underscores this motif which plays such a dominant role throughout the epistle.

The second way in which 1:3-12, when viewed as an introduction, underscores the significance of this theme is that it provides the basis for the author's exhortations. That is, the author's declarations in 1:3-12 issue in his call to a distinctive way of life (1:13-5:11), a way that leads the readers into conflict and suffering but that also leads to glory since it is the way of Christ himself. When we appreciate this causal relationship between the declarations in 1:3-12 and the exhortations in 1:13-5:11 we find additional support

love

not only for the presence but also for the prominence of this theme throughout 1 Peter.[25]

Saving grace, however, involves more than a life that moves from present suffering in a hostile world to future glory. It also involves a life in a community that is characterized primarily by fraternal love. Because believers have encountered saving grace they must love each other fervently and repudiate everything that would impede the full expression of love within the community (1:22-2:3). Believers express their love for one another concretely when they relate to each other in a spirit of humility, compassion, and like-mindedness (3:8). Above all, it is *love* that distinguishes the Christian community from other groups as believers prepare for God's eschatological judgment by fostering a spirit of forgiveness, by offering hospitality to the stranger, and by using their grace-gifts to serve each other to the glory of God (4:7-11). In short, saving grace creates a loving community in which believers find support and encouragement as they face conflict in a nonbelieving world.

This second aspect of saving grace, like the first, is also underscored when we recognize the introductory character of 1 Peter 1:3-12. If the author declares that the readers have been reborn to a new way of life he explicates the implications of that declaration for the community in terms of fraternal love. Since believers have been regenerated they must love each other fervently (1:22-23). This relationship between regeneration and love suggests that all expressions of community life are to be shaped decisively by the believers' experience of saving grace. Therefore, the author's demand that the readers love each other, as it occurs throughout the epistle in various forms, is ultimately rooted in his declarations on the nature of saving grace in 1:3-12. For this reason, an appreciation of the introductory character of 1:3-12 underscores the significance of fraternal love as a primary consequence of the believers' new life in grace.

From these considerations, we offer two conclusions in regard to the message of 1 Peter. First, the author's primary concerns may be summarized in our description of saving grace as a movement from present suffering to future glory in the nonbelieving world and as a fellowship of love in the believing community. Second, a recognition that 1:3-12 functions as an introduction to the letter underscores the predominance of these concerns in all of the author's remarks. That is, when we interpret 1:3-12 as an introduction to the whole epistle we see that the author places *primary* emphasis upon the

---

[25]Most interpreters of 1 Peter note the importance of this theme. Few, however, understand this theme to be as central to the message of the whole book as we do. See the helpful discussions by Goldstein ("*Die Kirche als Schar*"), Filson ("Partakers with Christ: Suffering in First Peter," *Int.* 9 [1955]: 400-12), and Millauer (*Leiden als,* 15-63).

nature and implications of saving grace.[26] Therefore, he accomplishes his stated aim (5:12) by urging his readers to understand their suffering as the inevitable consequence of grace. This grace, however, will lead ultimately to glory and, in the meantime, supports the readers by creating a fellowship of love within the Christian community.

EXEGETICAL AND INTERPRETIVE IMPLICATIONS

If 1 Peter 1:3-12 functions as an introduction to the whole of 1 Peter then the literary function of this passage has important implications for several of the exegetical and interpretive issues that confront Petrine scholars. First, if each section of 1 Peter finds an introduction in 1:3-12, as we have sought to demonstrate, then we have found additional evidence in support of the recent scholarly consensus on the unity of the epistle.[27] Additionally, this evidence, in turn, also implies that baptismal themes or a baptismal occasion cannot have the prominence that some have sought to give them. To be sure, baptism as the occasion for and the main theme of 1 Peter still remains as one of the major proposals for understanding the epistle.[28] As we have observed, however, the main themes of 1:3-12 and their relationship to those of 1:13-5:11 suggest that 1 Peter addresses the whole community of believers, not simply new converts, and elaborates the nature of saving grace for those believers as they live in a hostile world.

 household codes

Our discussion of the introductory character of 1:3-12 also sheds some light on 1 Peter's use of the traditional *Haustafel* (house-code). First, that the author addresses almost exclusively those in subordinate roles has been the basis for much discussion and disagreement.[29] This phenomenon has been

---

[26]The operative word here is *primary*. The author of 1 Peter uses a wide variety of images and themes and we are not suggesting that this account does full justice to this variety. We are suggesting, however, that our summary of 1 Peter's message in terms of saving grace and its implications constitutes a thematic complex that coordinates the author's varied themes. The motifs that are often cited as the main theme of 1 Peter (e.g., hope, suffering, holiness, good conduct, submission) relate to each other in that they are all expressions of the nature and consequence of saving grace.

[27]We are not suggesting that this essay has really demonstrated 1 Peter's coherence. This has been demonstrated convincingly, to our mind, by others. We would insist, however, that the literary function of 1:3-12, as we have described it, is an important indication of 1 Peter's coherence.

[28]E.g., B. Reicke, *The Epistles of James, Peter, and Jude, AB* 37 (Garden City NY: Doubleday, 1980) 74.

[29]In general it is accurate to say only subordinates are addressed though we should note the exception in 3:7. In this respect the Petrine *Haustafel* contrasts with that of other New Testament writers. The use of the *Haustafel* in early Christianity is analyzed in very helpful ways by Elliott (*Home for Homeless*) and Balch (*Let Wives Be Submissive*).

explained in a variety of ways. Scholars who view baptismal themes as primary often argue that the addressees in the *Haustafel* are the baptizands. Others have argued that the *Haustafel* indicates the sociological status of the readers, namely, they belong to the lower rungs of society.[30] In contrast to these explanations, others have suggested that the author of 1 Peter addresses those in subordinate roles in order to make a theological point. Thus believers who daily live in subordinate roles, with their ambiguities and possibilities for conflict, provide the best model for the author's understanding of life in grace, a life that inevitably involves conflict and suffering in the hostile nonbelieving world.[31] When the introductory character of 1:3-12 is recognized this latter explanation for the author's near exclusive attention to those in subordinate roles finds strong confirmation. If, as we have argued, in these opening verses the author sketches a view of Christian life that involves present suffering but future glory, and if in the verses that follow the author attempts to work out the implications of that view, then it becomes clear why the *Haustafel* focuses especially upon persons who exemplify that view.

In recent years 1 Peter has been subject to careful sociological and historical analysis. Out of such analysis has come the question of whether the author of 1 Peter uses the *Haustafel* parenesis to promote cultural assimilation or social distance between the readers and their nonbelieving society. In other words, does the author stress primarily the similarity between Christian conduct and the social expectations of his day or does he place primary emphasis upon the distinctive quality of Christian behavior as opposed to non-Christian behavior?[32]

In our view, the latter alternative makes the best sense of the data when the introductory character of 1:3-12 is appreciated fully. The themes of 1:3-12, which anticipate those of 1:13-5:11, clearly lift before the readers an understanding of life in grace that underscores the sharp contrast between Christian and non-Christian life. Moreover, if the exhortations to Christian *anastrophē* in 1:13-5:11 set forth the implications of saving grace as described in 1:3-12, then there is a fundamental difference between Christian

---

[30]Recently Balch (*Let Wives Be Submissive*) has implied this by arguing that the House-code is used apologetically to counter the charge of critics that Christianity is socially disruptive. Accordingly, in Balch's view, the author of 1 Peter addresses his remarks *primarily* to those whose role in society is one of subordination. The groups specified in the *Haustafel*, therefore, indicate the reader's social situation.

[31]This point is demonstrated by the fact that nearly all the exhortations to house-servants (2:18-25) are later repeated to the whole community (see Elliott, *Home for Homeless*, 205-207).

[32]The primary advocates of these views are Balch and Elliott. Balch (*Let Wives Be Submissive*) argues that the *Haustafel* is used in 1 Peter apologetically to demonstrate that Christian conduct is not necessarily socially disruptive. Elliott (*Home for Homeless*, 208-20) concludes that the *Haustafel* underscores the distinctive identity and behavior of Christians.

and non-Christian life-style. Even if on some occasions Christians behave in the same way as non-Christians (for example, submission) the author of 1 Peter still insists that Christian behavior is motivated and actualized in distinctive ways. Finally, if 1:3-12 introduces the whole epistle then it is clear that Christian life-style will lead to conflict and suffering precisely because it is so different from non-Christian life-style.[33] It seems apparent, then, that the literary and theological function of 1:3-12 indicates the author's primary concern to clarify and reinforce the distinctive character of Christian life-style.

Finally, one reason scholars in the past have rejected the coherence and theological integrity of 1 Peter is the wide variety of traditions and motifs used by its author. As we have seen, however, an appreciation of the introductory function of 1:3-12 suggests a way of integrating these diverse traditions and motifs. From the opening blessing until the closing doxology the author of 1 Peter sketches an understanding of saving grace that inspires his readers with hope and solidifies their sense of communion even though they are called upon to face temporary suffering. Saving grace demands a movement from present suffering to future glory and a fellowship of love.

---

[33]E.g., Christian life involves a rebirth to a living hope (1:3) and a life of hoping (1:13). In 3:15 the readers, in their situation of conflict, are urged to explain their hope to anyone who asks. That is, their hope distinguishes them from non-Christians and must be explained. The author of 1 Peter both identifies "hope" as the believers' mark of distinction and insists that believers confirm and clarify the distinction before nonbelievers.

CHAPTER 7

THE FUNCTIONAL CHRISTOLOGY OF FIRST PETER

EARL RICHARD
LOYOLA UNIVERSITY
NEW ORLEANS, LOUISIANA 70118

In the light of recent studies on the social setting and literary character of First Peter,[1] it has become all the clearer that the author employs a well-defined and particular Christology in his effort to foster perseverance among the Christians of Asia Minor. It will be the goal of this study to examine the author's use of the Jesus tradition (early hymnic fragments) and of Christology (soteriological and typological elements) in his parenetic composition. To achieve this objective I propose to divide my study into three parts. The first will consist of a review of some basic issues in the light of current scholarship on First Peter; the second will examine the author's use of the Christological hymn tradition; and the third, the principal part of the study, will discuss the function of the author's Christology, particularly its soteriological, paradigmatic, ethical, and eschatological dimensions.

---

[1]See particularly J. H. Elliott, *A Home for the Homeless: A Sociological Exegesis of 1 Peter, Its Situation and Strategy* (Philadelphia: Fortress, 1981), and D. L. Balch, *Let Wives Be Submissive: The Domestic Code in 1 Peter* (Chico: Scholars, 1981).

CURRENT SCHOLARSHIP AND BASIC ISSUES

One would probably have to agree that 1 Peter, once called an "exegetical step-child," is now seriously being rehabilitated in contemporary scholarship. The literature has increased considerably over the last twenty-five years, and as a result "research since 1958 generally has tended to challenge old assumptions while simultaneously raising new questions."[2] The letter, once considered a pious fabrication of second-century Catholicism or "Early Catholicism," has, as a result, emerged as an important document for understanding the early Christian community's historical and theological evolution.[3]

The Christian movement began to spread throughout the Roman empire long before the writing of 1 Peter. Already in the 40s and 50s, during Paul's ministry, Christian communities are attested throughout Syria, Asia Minor, Greece, and even Rome. Our letter, scholars are agreed, states that it is being written from Rome (that is, Babylon—5:13) to the provinces of Asia Minor: Pontus, Galatia, Cappadocia, Asia, and Bithynia (1:1). The Jesus movement has undergone important transformations since the time of Paul and so the author calls it a "brotherhood" (*adelphotēs:* 2:17; 5:9), acknowledges that its leadership is in the hands of "elders" (5:1), takes seriously the believers' relation to the state (2:13 f.), and intimates that suffering as a Christian is now a common phenomenon (4:16; 5:9).

Scholars are generally agreed that the letter is pseudonymous.[4] The author has adopted the strategy of invoking the name and authority of Peter (the same is true, though to a greater degree, for 2 Peter) to add weight to his exhortations and to insure a positive response from his audience. We need not review the numerous indications of non-Petrine authorship nor consider it necessary to examine once-popular amanuensis theories.[5] Instead, it is best to appeal to the author's relation to and use of a Petrine legend to give added authority to his composition. There are many hints in the New Testament

[2]J. H. Elliott, "The Rehabilitation of an Exegetical Step-Child: 1 Peter in Recent Research," *JBL* 95 (1976): 243-54, citation 254.

[3]There exist the following convenient bibliographical tools and surveys of the research: Elliott, "Rehabilitation;" D. Sylva, "1 Peter Studies: The State of the Discipline," *BTB* 10 (1980): 155-63; idem, "A 1 Peter Bibliography," *JETS* 25 (1982): 75-89; E. Cothenet, "Les orientations actuelles de l'exégèse de la première lettre de Pierre" and "Bibliographie sélective sur la première lettre de Pierre" in *Etudes sur la première lettre de Pierre*, ed. C. Perrot (Paris: Editions du Cerf, 1980) 13-42 and 269-74 respectively.

[4]See W. G. Kümmel, *Introduction to the New Testament* (Nashville: Abingdon, 1975) 421-24.

[5]Sylva, "1 Peter Studies," 155-56 and Cothenet, "Orientations actuelles," 37-40.

(Paul, Acts, 1 Peter) and early post NT writers (especially Clement of Rome and Papias) that lend credence to the hypothesis of a Petrine group at Rome to which our author—and that of the much later writer of 2 Peter—belonged. He appeals to the venerable figures of this group (Peter, Silvanus, and Mark) to authenticate his message to the churches of Asia Minor. From these facts, therefore, we are probably to conclude that the church of Rome and the Petrine tradition, even at this early stage, are emerging as a source of unity for the general church and as a center of theological activity.[6]

Though the addressees are called "exiles of the diaspora" (1:1—see also James 1:1) and though there are frequent allusions to the Greek scriptures as well as repeated use of Jewish images, there are strong indications that they are Gentile Christians ("passions of your former ignorance" 1:14; "futile ways inherited from your fathers" 1:18, etc.). Such texts seem to eliminate Jewish converts. Furthermore, there is no concern for typically Jewish issues such as kosher food laws, circumcision, and the Law generally. The term, "diaspora," must therefore be used to represent Christians living in the midst of non-Christians, who are in fact called Gentiles (2:12; 4:3). Lastly, it must be pointed out that the extensive use of the Old Testament and its images in the letter[7] points both to a church that is in close contact with its Jewish heritage, of a limited scope, of course, and to an author who may very well be a Hellenistic Jewish Christian.

We now turn to the literary character of 1 Peter. While in some post-Pauline texts the epistolary characteristics have disappeared totally or in part, this is not the case for 1 Peter.[8] The letter begins and ends in typical epistolary fashion with a standard opening (sender, addressee, greeting) and closing (greeting, doxology, benediction). Though it starts with a thanksgiving (similar to that of 2 Corinthians and Ephesians) and doctrinal statement (1:3f.—the two coincide), it soon adopts the form and tone of the later parenetic epistles (1:13f.).[9] From that point on, the letter without fail consists of alternation

---

[6]L. Goppelt, *Der erste Petrusbrief* (Göttingen: Vandenhoeck & Ruprecht, 1978) 30-37; Elliott, "Rehabilitation," 248, idem, *Home for the Homeless,* 270-82; G. Krodel, "The First Letter of Peter" in *Hebrews, James, 1 and 2 Peter, Jude, Revelation,* ed. G. Krodel (Philadelphia: Fortress, 1977) 58-59, though hesitantly; *Peter in the New Testament,* ed. R. E. Brown, et al. (NY: Paulist, 1973) 149-56; D. Senior, *1 & 2 Peter* (Wilmington: Glazier, 1980) xii-xvi.

[7]J. Schlosser, "Ancien testament et Christologie dans la *prima petri*" in Perrot, *Etudes,* 65-96; F. W. Danker, "1 Peter 1, 24-3, 17—A Consolatory Pericope," *ZNW* 58 (1967): 93-102; and T. P. Osborne, "Guide Lines for Christian Suffering: A Source-Critical and Theological Study of 1 Peter 2, 21-25," *Biblica* 64 (1983): 381-408.

[8]W. G. Doty, *Letters in Primitive Christianity* (Philadelphia: Fortress, 1973); see also Elliott, "Rehabilitation," 248-49.

[9]E. Lohse, "Paränese und Kerygma im 1. Petrusbrief," *ZNW* 54 (1954): 68-89 (see English version in the present volume); see also Cothenet, "Orientations actuelles," 26-27.

between imperative and indicative, that is, advice followed by examples or statements of theological justification. As one might expect in epistolary literature, the author, besides employing the ubiquitous imperative (and participle as imperative),[10] frequently addresses his audience directly (1:1; 2:11; 4:12 and often in parenetic sections).[11]

Earlier composite theories, a liturgical tract or baptismal homily followed by a later parenetic text about persecution, once common in introductions and the preoccupation of 1960s studies[12] are now rejected or greatly undermined by redaction and structural analyses. Recent studies are convincing that see 1 Peter as a unitary composition whose epistolary features are integral to the document. Vocabulary and stylistic studies as well as structural and theological examination[13] show that there exist no notable differences between the two sections of the letter, but, on the contrary that, there exist numerous links between the two. Further, the break at 4:11-12 is real but no greater than that which exists at 2:11. In short, scholars now more readily admit that between the opening (1:1-2) and closing (5:12-14), the author has inserted three major sections: 1) 1:3-2:10 on God's chosen people (birth, baptism); 2) 2:11-4:11 on ethics for exiles or interim ethics; and 3) 4:12-5:11 consisting of renewed exhortation. We therefore offer the following outline:

A. 1:1-2	Opening	"exiles" "chosen"	
B. 1:3-2:10	Through mercy, chosen to be God's people	1:1, 3 *vs* 2:9-10	inner community ransom-baptism
(1) 1:3-12	New birth through resurrection of Jesus	"born anew"	
(2) 1:13-25	Birth: all to obedience and holiness	"obedient children"	
(3) 2:1-10	Growth: babes, spiritual house, chosen race, God's people, note of judgment and decision	"newborn babes"	

---

[10]F. Blass, A. Debrunner, R. W. Funk, *A Greek Grammar of the New Testament and Other Early Christian Literature* (Chicago: University of Chicago, 1961) 245-46 (# 468).

[11]On the genre of 1 Peter see W. J. Dalton, *Christ's Proclamation to the Spirits: A Study of 1 Peter 3:18-4:6* (Rome: PBI, 1965) 62-71.

[12]For example, N. Perrin, *The New Testament: An Introduction* (NY: Harcourt Brace Jovanovich, 1974) 253-75; see Kümmel, *Introduction,* 419-20, for a list of scholars proposing composite theories; see also Sylva, "1 Peter Studies," 159-61; and Cothenet, "Orientations actuelles," 21-25.

[13]Balch, *Let Wives Be Submissive,* 123-31; Elliott, *Home for the Homeless,* 234-36; Goppelt, *Erste Petrusbrief,* 37-47; Dalton, *Christ's Proclamation,* 76-82; see also N. Turner, *Grammar of New Testament Greek,* vol. 4: *Style* (Edinburgh: Clark, 1976-1980) 121. For a somewhat different analysis, see M.-A. Chevallier, "1 Pierre 1/1 à 2/10: structure littéraire et conséquences exégétiques," *RHPR* 51 (1971): 129-42.

C. 2:11-4:11	Exhortation for aliens and exiles:	"beloved/exhort"	
	Interim Ethics		
(1) 2:11-3:12	Domestic Code (*Haustafeln*)	"aliens and exiles"	
2:11-12	Introduction	"submission"	
2:13-17	Duty to Human Institutions	"speak ag. you as	
2:18-25	Duty of Servants/Slaves	*evil*-doers"	
3:1-6	Duty of Wives		
3:7	Duty of Husbands		
3:8-12	Conclusion		
(2) 3:13-4:6	Christ as Lord, Baptism, Living in Spirit	"to do you *evil*"	
(3) 4:7-11	Eschatological Exhortation	"end at hand"	
D. 4:12-5:11	Renewed Exhortation	"beloved"	
(1) 4:12-19	Maltreatment as Christians		
(2) 5:1-5	Exhortation to Old and Young	"exhort"	
(3) 5:6-11	Eschatological Exhortation	"devil"	
E. 5:12-14	Closing	"likewise chosen"	

social adaptability — imitation (bracketed alongside rows C through E)

The above schema, among other things, attempts to illustrate the numerous and convincing literary and theological links that exist between various parts of the composition. The thanksgiving section, much as in Paul, announces the major themes of the early part of the letter; the ending of the letter renews many of the themes found at the beginning; and various motifs are strategically situated throughout the letter. The last point mentioned leads N. Turner, somewhat severely, to qualify the frequent repetition of terms as "this author's monotonous habit of often failing to find any synonym at all."[14]

As complement to the above discussion on unity of composition, several observations should be made concerning the peculiarities of the principal sections of the letter. In effect, not all the factors noted in support of a composite theory need be discarded. That the theme of baptism appears only prior to 4:12 need not indicate a separate text but rather the reworking by the author of his own homiletic notes to fit the occasion. Besides, the first part of the letter (1:3-2:10) establishes the foundation for the author's exhortation—that is, the first part deals with the new life (baptism), which the Christ-event has made possible. Further, the differences that some allege exist concerning the theme of suffering/persecution between the two blocks of the letter (before and after 4:11) are more apparent than real since the use of the optative mood in the earlier references need not indicate mere possibility but rather could convey the writer's delicate, indirect approach to the reality of suffering.[15]

This brings us to a final introductory consideration, the occasion for the writing of 1 Peter and the related issue of the date of composition, both of which revolve around the theme of suffering. From the very beginning the

---

[14]*Style*, 127; see also D. C. Arichea and E. A. Nida, *A Translator's Handbook on the First Letter from Peter* (NY: UBS, 1980) 2-3.

[15]Balch, *Let Wives Be Submissive*, 127.

author is concerned with this theme. Reference is made to ''the sprinkling of
(Christ's) blood'' in 1:2 (see also 1:19), to the ''various trials'' that the audience ''may have to suffer for a little while'' in 1:6, and a repetition of this
last statement at the end of the letter (5:9-10). Further, the allusion in 1:7 to
purification by fire immediately calls 4:12 to mind: ''the fiery ordeal which
comes upon you to prove you.'' First Peter then is interested in a theology of
suffering.[16] What is at issue, however, is the nature of the suffering alluded
to in the text, for 4:14-16 clearly indicates that Christians are being persecuted or harassed because they are Christians (''for the name of Christ'').

Earlier scholars interpreted these data as referring to persecution and proposed three possible dates for 1 Peter: the time of the Trajan-Pliny correspondence (c. A.D. 122), that of Domitian's reign (81-96), or that of Nero's
administration (54-68). Of course there are serious objections to all three—
Nero's persecution is entirely too early and was limited to Rome; further, there
is no reference to the emperor cult in 1 Peter as there is in the Book of Revelation (on the contrary see 1 Pet. 2:17); lastly, the late, ''official'' persecution of Trajan's reign is ruled out. Besides, if the letter were dated to the
second century one would expect a more developed structure for the Christian
communities (as in Ignatius of Antioch), some indication of the delay of the
parousia (the contrary obtains in the eschatological sections), and a different
reaction vis-à-vis Roman society (for example, a persecution mentality, a
ghetto or withdrawal attitude, an otherworldly spirituality, for example).[17]

Since First Peter exhibits a decidedly positive attitude toward Roman culture
and society, we conclude that it would be earlier than Revelation (negative reference to Babylon and the theme of emperor cult), also probably earlier than Hebrews (where persecution is an accepted fact of Christian existence—see 10:32-
34), and about the time of Luke-Acts (c. 80-90).[18] Indeed, the correlation of 1
Peter to Luke-Acts is multifaceted: similar positive attitudes toward Roman culture, optimism vis-à-vis secular culture, many common motifs (for example,
judgment of the living and the dead, cornerstone and stumbling block themes,

---

[16]T. P. Osborne, ''Guide Lines,'' *Biblica* 64 (1983): 381-82, lists 15 recent studies on
the theme of Christian suffering in First Peter.

[17]One should note, most recently, Elliott's claim that 1 Peter aims at cultural segregation,
Home for the Homeless, 101-64 (see also essay in present volume) or Brox, ''Situation und
Sprache der Minderheit im ersten Petrusbrief,'' *Kairos* 19 (1977): 1-13, that the author is pre-
paring his audience for martyrdom.

[18]In general agreement with Goppelt, *Erste Petrusbrief,* 60-66 and Balch, *Let Wives Be
Submissive,* 137-38, though in disagreement with their estimate of the relation of 1 Peter as
being prior in time to Luke-Acts. For a more general discussion of the situation and dating of
the letter, see C. Lepelley, ''Le contexte historique de la Première Lettre de Pierre,'' 43-64 in
Perrot, *Etudes;* Brox, ''Situation,'' 1-13; A. Puig Tàrrech, ''Le milieu de la Première Epître
de Pierre,'' *RCT* 5 (1980): 95-129, 331-402.

and so forth), fondness for the Greek Old Testament, and appeal to the Jesus tradition as an "imitatio Christi." The years of persecution have arrived for neither Luke nor 1 Peter who both believe that some *modus vivendi* can be worked out with the Roman populace. The two authors opt for different solutions to or strategies in the face of the problems that their communities or audiences face.[19] We are left to conclude that 1 Peter focuses upon Christian suffering, not as a result of persecution but as the result of hostility, harassment, and social, unofficial ostracism on the part of the general populace.[20]

FIRST PETER
AND THE CHRISTOLOGICAL HYMN TRADITION

a. *Hymnic Material in 1 Peter.* Careful reading of this letter reveals that our author knew and employed early hymnic material in composing his document. While various attempts have been made in the past to isolate these data, the classic proposals being those of Bo Reicke (1946), R. Bultmann (1949), and J. Jeremias (1949), the tendency has been to limit the investigation to 1 Peter 3:18-22.[21] The notable exception, of course, was Bultmann who also suggested 1:20 and 2:21-24 as likely candidates. Indeed his analysis, if not his conclusion for reconstructing a primitive Christological hymn or hymns,

---

[19]Recent sociological study, particularly the work of Elliott in *Home for the Homeless* (see also the publications of Balch, Brox, and Puig Tàrrech referred to in notes 1, 17, and 18 above), force us to take even more seriously than in the past the author's strategy in dealing with the Christian reality as that of a minority culture within the Greco-Roman world; note D. J. Harrington's interesting essay "The Church as a Minority Group" in *God's People in Christ: New Testament Perspective on the Church and Judaism* (Philadelphia: Fortress, 1980) 81-94, which treats 1 Peter, Hebrew, and Revelation from such a vantage point.

[20]Lohse, "Paränese und Kerygma," 73-85; Elliott, "Rehabilitation," 251-53; idem, *Home for the Homeless,* 84-87; Balch, *Let Wives Be Submissive,* 10-15, 125-27; Cothenet, "Orientations actuelles," 21; C. Wolff, "Christ und Welt in 1. Petrusbrief," *TLZ* 100 (1975): 333-42; Arichea and Nida, *Translator's Handbook,* 1-2; and more favorably inclined toward persecution, Brox, "Situation," 1-13.

[21]B. Reicke, *The Disobedient Spirits and Christian Baptism; A Study of 1 Peter 3:19 and Its Context* (Copenhagen: Munksgaard, 1946); R. Bultmann, "Bekenntnis-und Lied-fragmente im ersten Petrusbrief" in *Exegetica; Aufsatze zur Erforschung des Neuen Testaments,* ed. E. Dinkler (Tübingen: Mohr, 1967) 285-97 (originally published in *Coniectanea Neotestamentica* 11 [1947] 1-14); and J. Jeremias, "Zwischen Karfreitag und Osten," *ZNW* 42 (1949): 194-201. Among the more significant studies and commentaries we might mention: Lohse, "Paränese und Kerygma;" Dalton, *Christ's Proclamation;* F. W. Beare, *The First Epistle of Peter* (Oxford: Blackwell, 1970); J. T. Sanders, *The New Testament Christological Hymns: Their Historical Religious Background* (Cambridge: University Press, 1971); Goppelt, *Erste Petrusbrief;* N. Brox, *Der erste Petrusbrief* (Zurich: Benziger, 1979).

continues to be seminal for recent analyses, including the present one.[22] In the case of 2:21-24, however, few scholars have been willing to follow his suggestions, finding the data too ambiguous or altogether denying the existence of an early hymn. Perhaps the consensus of recent scholarship can best be expressed in the words of T. P. Osborne who concludes his study of this hypothesis by saying:

> it seems difficult to maintain as proven the assertion that an early Christological hymn is at the basis of 1 Pet 2, 21-25. While this remains a possibility, the more obvious solution is the reference to Isa 53 in the context of the author's treatment of unjust suffering, addressed to the community of former pagans now converted to Christianity but living within an unfriendly pagan society.[23]

This leaves us with the consideration of 3:18-22 (+ 1:20), a theory for which there has been considerably more enthusiasm. Relying primarily upon literary criteria and being conscious of hymnic motifs, we are able to discern fairly clearly hymnic fragments in 1:20 and 3:18—in each case the verses immediately following these two passages present hymn-like material and will require some attention.

The hymnic elements of 1:20 are clearly indicated by their anaphoric style, that is, two participial phrases that have Jesus as antecedent:

> destined from the foundation of the world
> manifested at the end of the times. (1:20)

Verse 21 breaks the pattern, however. While we find there two participial phrases, they no longer modify Christ but God as agent:

> God who raised him from the dead
> and who gave him glory. (1:21)

Since the pattern of this fragment (that is, abc c'b'a': "he raised him from the dead/glory to him he gave") seems independent of verse 20, we must probably disagree with Bultmann that v. 21 originally formed one hymn with verse

---

[22]See particularly M.-E. Boismard, *Quatre hymnes baptismales dans la Première Epître de Pierre* (Paris: Edition du Cerf, 1961); R. Deichgräber, *Gotteshymnus und Christushymnus in der frühen Christenheit; Untersuchungen zu Form, Sprache und Stil der fruhchristlichen Hymnen* (Göttingen: Vandenhoeck and Ruprecht, 1967); and H. Wengst, *Christologische Formeln und Lieder des Urchristentums* (Gütersloh: Mohn, 1972). Confer, however, the critiques of Bultmann's analysis by Lohse, "Paränese und Kerygma," 86-89; Dalton, *Christ's Proclamation,* 92-95; Goppelt, *Erste Petrusbrief,* 204-207, 239-42; R. P. Martin, "The composition of 1 Peter in Recent Study," 31-34 in *Vox Evangelica* (London: Epworth, 1962); and Osborne, "Guide Lines," 383-89.

[23]"Guide Lines," 38-39; see also J. Schlosser, "Ancien testament," 83-85; and M. Carrez, "L'esclavage dans la première épître de Pierre," 214-15 in C. Perrot, *Etudes;* for a different conclusion see G. Krodel, "The First Letter of Peter," 71.

20. If the themes of 1:21 seem to belong to the hymnic tradition, the structure and form of the fragment point to the early binary credal formula as *Sitz im Leben*.

Indeed a later passage in the letter presents not only themes similar to those found in 1:21 but also a continuation of the anaphoric style of 1:20. The text reads as follows:

> put to death in the flesh
> make alive in the spirit. (3:18)

As was the case in 1:20, the two members of the fragment open with two participial constructions redactionally connected by *men . . . de*. The following verse breaks this pattern, though not so radically as had been the case in 1:21, and one again encounters the author's stylistic tendency of constructing links by the use of relative clauses (*en hō kai*). Verse 3:19 contains a participial construction that might be reordered in the following way: "having gone to the spirits in prison." The author draws from the hermeneutical tradition of the period[24] and discusses further the theme of the imprisoned spirits, linking the Noah story to Christian baptism. However, in v. 22, as a commentary or extension of the phrase "through the resurrection of Jesus Christ," he dwells at length upon the post-resurrection activity of Christ. The entire verse merits being cited:

> who is at the right hand of God
> having gone to heaven
> where angels and authorities and powers are subject to him.

Once again the connecting link is a relative pronoun followed by straightforward prose although part b retains the original anaphoric style and the whole deals with the hymnic themes of enthronement, ascension to the heavenly realm, and domination or subjection of the cosmic powers.

In light of the above analysis, we conclude that there is a significant amount of hymnic material in 1 Peter but that owing to the author's extensive redaction we must accept the fact that there is little hope of reconstructing the original hymn(s).[25] The author's text reveals a variety of fragments that betray hymnic style and themes as well as credal formulae of diverse origins.

---

[24]See Dalton, *Christ's Proclamation*, 163-76, on the influence of the Enoch traditions and C. Perrot, "La descente aux enfers et la prédication aux morts," 231-46 in *Etudes;* see also the older essay of S. E. Johnson, "The Preaching to the Dead," *JBL* 79 (1960): 48-51.

[25]Recently, for example, Dalton, *Christ's Proclamation*, 97, has proposed that the hymn in part or whole consists of 3:18 and 22 and that vv. 19-21 are a "prose insertion" or "catechetical piece on Baptism"; G. Krodel, "The First Letter of Peter," 66-69, following Bultmann, offers 1:20; 3:18d-e and 22b-c as the limits of the original Christological hymn; while K. Shimada, "The Christological Credal Formula in 1 Peter 3, 18-22—Reconsidered," *Annual of the Japanese Biblical Institute* 5 (1979): 154-76, employing an array of form-critical

b. *Hymnic Pattern Presumed by 1 Peter*. Having isolated the liturgical fragments found in this document we might well inquire about the hymnic pattern
or mythic structure presumed by the author of 1 Peter, since he borrows from
this tradition both the pattern of his Christological vision and the basis of his
soteriological exposition. Six elements are easily discernible from the fragments discussed above: (1) destined, (2) manifested, (3) suffering/death, (4)
resurrection/alive in the spirit, (5) cosmic domination, and (6) glory/right
hand. While some of these components receive more emphasis, all six to
varying degrees contribute to the author's discussion.

(1) "Christ is destined/foreknown/chosen before the foundation of the world"
(1:20a). The Greek verb is *proginoskō*, a term that underscores prior knowledge,
plan, or choice rather than prior existence. If the author of 1 Peter is conversant
with the developing concept of preexistence (see #2 below), he shows no interest in it. Instead he employs this hymnic fragment to dwell upon the divine
plan: "foreknowledge" marks the beginning (pretemporal) and "manifesta-
tion" the final period of God's plan. The terms are clearly apocalyptic and are
to be related to the highly eschatological tone of the entire letter.

Not only is the Christ's mission situated within the divine plan, but also
the choice of believers (1:2—*prognosis*). Indeed, the author employs several
related concepts to underscore the importance of God's plan. The prophets
(1:10f.) prophesized, inquired about, and predicted various features of the
plan, not the least being the suffering and glory of Christ as well as the grace,
Good News, and salvation operative within that plan. It is God's mercy or
power that operates among believers to give new life (1:3; 2:10) or to guard
in adversity (1:5). Further, suffering for injustice—a major theme in the letter—is according to God's will (*thelema*: 2:15; 3:17; 4:2, 19). Finally and
most crucially, Jesus' attitude vis-à-vis the Father's plan is one of obedience,
the means by which he ransoms humanity and sets up the model for Christian
living.[26] Part one, then, concerns the divine plan and humanity's response.

(2) "Christ is manifested/revealed at the end of the times for you" (1:20b).
This member of the fragment is considerably more pregnant in meaning than

---

criteria, proposes that the hymn read as follows (using the RSV to translate Shimada's Greek
reconstruction):

> *Christ died for sins once for all*
> > *that he might bring us to God,*
> *and preached to the spirits in prison,*
>
> *who is at the right hand of God*
> > *having come into heaven*
> *with authorities and powers subject to him.*

[26]See F. H. Agnew, "1 Peter 1:2—An Alternative Translation," *CBQ* 45 (1983): 68-73;
his treatment of 1:2 is especially good regarding Christ's obedience as cause of election and
regarding humanity's obedience or disobedience—*hypakoē* and *apeitheō* respectively. See also
2:23: Jesus "trusted to him who judges justly."

the first; besides, its use in other Christological hymn passages (1 Tim. 3:16 and Heb. 9:26) suggests that a concept of preexistence is at least possible— Hebrews is certainly less vague. J. D. G. Dunn is probably right in seeing that such language probably evolved ''from the context of the predetermined purpose and mystery'' of God's plan and eventually was ''set more within the context of developing religious beliefs in pre-existent divine redeemers.''[27] Some scholars have proposed in the past that the pattern indicated by the six elements noted earlier and underscored by parts one and two would correspond to a preexistence Christology with ''destined'' and ''manifested'' signifying preexistence and incarnation respectively. It is more likely, however, that the author's hymnic material as well as his own thinking reflect a lower, exaltation Christology since he either is ignorant of or uninterested in the concept of preexistence.

> In 1 Peter 1:20 the key verb (''was made manifest'') is set in antithesis with ''predestined.'' That is to say, the contrast is not between pre-existence and incarnation, but between that which was predestined and that which was revealed. Christ was the one who was thus predestined and who was thus revealed or who appeared at the right time just as planned. In other words, Peter may well mean that what was ''made manifest'' was not so much Christ as what was pre-destined for Christ, God's eternal plan of salvation for Christ, believers (cf. 1.2) and the world.[28]

Confirmation of such a conclusion comes from the ending of Paul's letter to the Roman's, 16:25-27.

The first two elements, from what seems to be an independent hymnic fragment, are focused not upon the incarnational but upon the eschatological framework of the Christ-event, a framework that our author employs as the background of the Christian's life in the world. This plan is God's design from eternity and, while it has had some ''preexistence'' or reality prior to the coming of Jesus (time of the prophets 1:10f.; time of Abraham and Sarah, 2:5f., and of Noah, 3:20f.), it is the arrival of the Christ that ushers in the end-time. I would note also that the author hints at, though he does not always develop in a systematic way, the notion that the coming of Christ has made possible a long list of realities that have become traditional themes: the sending of the Spirit (1:12), the preaching of the Good News (1:12,23f.), the working of God's mercy (1:3), the formation of a house of God, the impor-

---

[27]*Christology in the Making: A New Testament Inquiry into the Origins of the Doctrine of the Incarnation* (Philadelphia: Westminster, 1980) 238.

[28]Ibid., 237; see also Goppelt, *Erste Petrusbrief*, 124-26.

tance of baptism, and so forth.[29] It was the coming of Jesus in the final age that put into motion the long-decided plan of God.

(3) "Jesus was put to death in the flesh" (3:18c). While 1 Peter insists upon the soteriological function of Jesus' death (ransomed by his blood, 1:18-19; death for the sins of all, 3:18a; on the cross/tree, 2:24; etc.) and therefore on numerous occasions underscores the death of Jesus, it is especially the terms that emphasize the passion or suffering not death that draw his attention. He is particularly fond of *paschō* (twelve times—applied to Jesus and to Christians) and the plural of *pathema* (sufferings—usually of Christ).[30] He stresses this theme because of his audience's situation, a theme that then becomes a central element of his soteriological schema and his parenetic concerns. We will have occasion to discuss at greater length the theme of suffering later.

(4) "Jesus was made alive in the spirit" (3:18d). Elements three and four can readily be seen as lifted right out of the early apostolic kerygma. Early Christian writers never fail to underscore the centrality of the dual concepts of death/resurrection. The author of 1 Peter is no exception; he insists that God raised Jesus from the dead, 1:21; and that he was made alive in the spirit, 3:18; and stresses the agency of the resurrection of Jesus Christ, 1:3 and 3:21. However, it is not the resurrection that holds his attention but the final stage of the Christological progression, namely the enthronement in glory (1:21). For him the resurrection is crucial (as it is for other New Testament writers) as a means (*dia*) or basis of new life, faith, and hope, but in the last analysis it is one stage in the process that is the Christ-event. Verses 1:3-4 are particularly instructive in this regard: God by his mercy has given new life and living hope through the resurrection of Jesus and the goal is the inheritance kept in heaven for us, that is, a sharing in the glory that Jesus now possesses (see below).

(5) Cosmic subjection or domination (3:22). First Peter is aware of early speculation concerning the Christ's post-resurrection cosmological activities. While there does not seem to be any trace of creation activity for the Christ (only 1:20 speaks of "before the foundation of the world" and 4:19 addresses God not the Christ as Creator), the author is aware of and interested

---

[29]See in particular: A. Vanhoye, "1 Pierre au carrefour des théologies du nouveau testament," 97-128; M.-A. Chevallier, "Comment lire aujourd'hui la Première Epître de Pierre," 129-52; J. Calloud, "Ce que parler vent dire," 175-206; and P. Sandevoir, "Un royaume de prêtres?" 219-29—all within C. Perrot, *Etudes;* D. Hill, "On Suffering and Baptism in 1 Peter," *NovTest* 18 (1976): 181-89; Dalton, *Christ's Proclamation,* 202-77; and J. Francis, " 'Like New-born Babes'—The Image of the Child in 1 Peter 2:2-3," *Studia Biblica* 3 (1978): 111-17.

[30]It is especially through his use of Isaiah 53 that the author is able to develop the salvific character of the suffering of Christ; see J. Schlosser, "Ancien testament," 90-93 and Osborne, "Guide Lines," 389-408.

in Christ's domination of all the powers (3:22c). His major concern is the efficacy of the Good News and its cosmic significance (spirits 3:22, angels 1:12, and the dead 4:6). The context of 3:22c is crucial; mention of the resurrection of Jesus immediately leads to the idea that he is in heaven at God's right hand and of course that all the powers encountered on "the way" have now come into subjection by Jesus' preaching.[31]

(6) Jesus Christ is in heaven at God's right hand (3:22) or put otherwise: "God . . . has given him glory" (1:21). This particular element, whether expressed as enthronement or related to the theme of "glory" (the noun and verb occur fourteen times in all), is very prominent in the author's letter. The former forms part of the Christological schema employed and the latter expresses the relationship of the author's Christology to other aspects of his thought. We will have occasion below to discuss this at greater length.

CHRISTOLOGY OF FIRST PETER

a. *Christological Schema and Functional Analysis.* The author of 1 Peter employs all six elements noted above during the composition of his letter, though some are more central than others. He knows the traditional binary kerygmatic pattern of death/resurrection (1:21; 3:18b), nonetheless, as the basis for the overall schema of his theological statement he chooses to emphasize two moments within that Christological progression: suffering/death and glory/right hand.

For our author Jesus is the image of suffering and glory. He obviously opts for the term "suffering" for the first part of the pattern because of the situation of his audience even though he associates several related concepts with that theme: blood of Christ, ransom, passion, death, and so forth. The Christ-event is being put at the service of the author's needs; he wishes to discuss suffering, not death or the life of Jesus and so he focuses, after the first part of the document,[32] upon that precise element of the Jesus tradition.

The second element of the pattern is also chosen with theological intent. The author could have stressed the theme of resurrection, as does Paul in 1 Cor. 15, to establish a foundation for Christian hope, but he, unlike Paul, is not interested in discussing the resurrection but in developing the theme of glory (*doxa*). A review of the texts where this term appears in 1 Peter shows that it refers either to the glory that God has given Jesus or that which the believer will share when Jesus returns at the *apocalypsis* or final revelation. The term "glory" then is chosen to emphasize the heavenly or post-resur-

---

[31]See n. 24 above.

[32]Lohse, "Paränese und Kerygma," 70, and Hill, "On Suffering and Baptism," 181-89.

rection life of Jesus and its bearing upon the Christian's life as an exile or sojourner.

We might therefore offer the following schema of the functional use which the author makes of his Christological traditions.

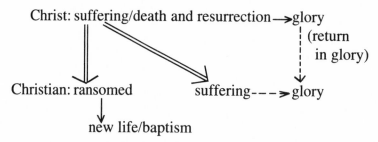

The themes of suffering and glory, representing the contours of the Christ-event, offer the framework for the author's understanding of the Christian's life in the world. The Christ has suffered, has gone to share in the Father's glory, and will return at the end-time to bestow glory upon those "chosen by the foreknowledge of God the Father" (1:1-2) and whose faith has been tested by the fire of suffering (1:5-7). At the same time, as the schema indicates, the author makes more extended use of the "suffering/death" theme. Not only does it express the Christian's situation in terms of suffering as parallel to that of the Christ, but it also underscores the soteriological function of that theme by insisting upon Jesus' death and its consequences for humanity.[33] We now pass on to a more extended discussion of the themes graphically exhibited in the schema.

b. *Christology and Its Soteriological Function.* From the early Christian community the author has inherited the notion of the atoning character of Jesus' death. Both references to the blood of Christ suggest a sacrificial context. Verse 1:2 ("sanctification . . . by . . . the sprinkling of the blood of Jesus Christ") seems to presuppose an Old Testament text such as Exod. 24:7-8[34] and 1:18-19 ("ransomed . . . with the precious blood of Christ") is obviously qualified by the phrase "like that of a lamb without blemish or spot." The latter, while probably related to Isaiah 52:3,[35] is drawn from the Jesus tradition, which itself underscored the soteriological character of the Christ-event through the image of "ransom," (see especially Mark 10:45).[36] In-

---

[33]In structuralist terms one would speak of syntagmic (soteriological) and paradigmatic (model) functions (parts 3. b and c); see J. Calloud and F. Genuyt, *La première épître de Pierre: analyse sémiotique* (Paris: Editions du Cerf, 1982) 152.

[34]Goppelt, *Erste Petrusbrief,* 87.

[35]Ibid., 122; F. Büchsel, "luo," *TDNT* 4:351.

[36]See the discussion of E. Best, "1 Peter and the Gospel Tradition," *NTS* 16 (1970): 99-100.

deed, it is the first part of the document that lays stress upon the soteriological—note also the use of *sōtēria* in 1:5, 9, 10; 2.2. Of course the author will return to this theme in the baptismal section of 3:13f. and in the paradigmatic passage of 2:18-25.

The first section of the letter with its emphasis upon the soteriological function of the Christ-event serves to establish the basis for the community's new life. Christians through God's mercy "have been born anew to a living hope through the resurrection of Jesus Christ from the dead" (1:3). Other passages underscore this new life (1:14; 2:2) or departure from the old (1:14, 18; 2:9, 10) though without explicit reference to this soteriological theme. Indeed, baptismal language permeates the first part of the letter and is related invariably to the themes of death and resurrection: 1:3, 21, 23; 2:4,10. The author in 3:20-22 while speaking of Noah's ark and water is once again led to associate baptism with the resurrection of Jesus.

From the outset the author puts the traditional Jesus material at the service of his ecclesiological task: by means of the death and resurrection of Jesus, whether employing the imagery of ransom, washing, conversion, or dying/rising of seeds, he is able to establish the basis for the community's unity, strength, and source of life. Though tested and in exile it is nonetheless a house built on living stones (like the rejected, chosen, and precious salvific stone),[37] a chosen race, a royal priesthood, a holy nation, and God's own people (2:4-5, 9). It is God's own people and so children of the Father whose task it is likewise to be holy (1:14-15). Through Jesus' salvific death God has given new life to humanity and has acquired a new people. Jesus bore the sins of humanity in his body for a purpose (2:24)—it is to this subject that we direct our attention in the next two sections of this presentation.

c. *Christology as the Pattern for Christian Life.* Once he has established the basis for Christian existence, the author proceeds to develop his major thesis: Jesus is the Christian's model of suffering and glory. Between these two polls of the Christological pattern, the suffering/death that has ransomed the Christian and bestowed new life (1:3, 18) and the establishment in glory, which is a future reality for the believer (1:4, 13), lies an interim period that concerns him and his audience (see the description of this situation at the end of part one above). The patient suffering of the Christian has God's approval, and he tells his audience, "for to this you have been called, because Christ also suffered for you leaving you an example (*hypogrammos*), that you might fol-

---

[37]On the stone imagery see Schlosser, "Ancien testament," 72-79; Goppelt, *Erste Petrusbrief,* 142-51; J. H. Elliott, *The Elect and the Holy: An Exegetical Examination of 1 Peter 2:4-10 and the Phrase 'Basileion Hierateuma'* (Leiden: Brill, 1966); E. Best, "1 Peter II, 4-10: A Reconsideration," *NovTest* 11 (1969): 270-93.

low in his steps'' (2:21).[38] Through Christ we have been ransomed (1:18); we are dead to sin and alive to righteousness (2:24a), healed by his wounds (2:24b), under his guardianship (2:25), have been constituted a house, priesthood, people of God, and so forth—all realities that have a direct bearing upon the present Christian situation.

The Christ's passage in time, however, has not simply achieved a series of given results (soteriological data) but has left or constituted a model or framework for the believer's vision of life: suffering that is teleologically conditioned by glory or salvation (more active still: Christ brings us to God—3:18). The author favors the term ''suffering'' rather than ''death'' as a concession to his audience's situation and his own rhetorical strategy. He has in mind the pain, abuse, and ostracization that Christians as a minority group suffer in a pagan society. These he relates to his Christological model, for imitation of Christ means obedience to the plan of God (1:2, 14, 22), the testing of one's faith (fire terminology), love of friend/brother and foe (1:22; 3:8 and 2:12; 3:6), responsible living within a society that must be subjected to God on the day of visitation (2:12),[39] and gentle, rational, and evangelistic confrontation with non-Christian neighbors (2:9; 3:15, 19, 22).

The pattern of suffering and glory (see the diagram given above) indicates the parameters of the Christian's concerns. On the one hand, the Christ suffered innocently (2:22) and as a result of his total trust in the just Judge now dwells in glory. The Christian, on the other, is experiencing similar suffering (as a Christian—2:12; 4:15) and, owing to the Christological pattern of Christian life, knows that glory is assured the one who lives a life of righteousness (1:21).[40] Even the prophets, the author insists, predicted this very model: ''the sufferings of Christ and the subsequent glory.''[41] In fact, their activity and service were directed to the Christian reality and in particular to the audience's plight (1:11-12). Like the Christ the Christian is not to revile or threaten even when provoked (2:23). Instead good conduct or behavior (2:12; 3:16) must be his or her weapon against maltreatment, for this has God's approval (2:15 & 20) and will ''put to silence the ignorance of foolish men'' (2:15).[42]

d. *Ethics and Eschatology in Relation to Christology.* The author gives fur-

---

[38]For an excellent, extended commentary on 1 Peter 2:21 see Osborne, ''Guide Lines,'' 389-93 and Calloud and Genuyt, *Première épître,* 152-63.

[39]See below for a discussion of the domestic codes: 2:11-3:12.

[40]Osborne, ''Guide Lines,'' 406-408.

[41]The author's use of the plural for both terms (''sufferings'' and ''glories'') underscores the very kind of model or the Christological paradigm established; see Arichea and Nida, *Translator's Handbook,* 30-31, and Calloud and Genuyt, *Première épître,* 66-67.

[42]Lohse, ''Paränese und Kerygma,'' 74.

ther direction to his theological statement in the way he views the interim period. In the first instance he shows great concern for the community's relations with fellow members as well as outsiders. Good behavior and patient suffering are frequently encouraged. In fact parenesis permeates the whole document, since the two last sections are devoted almost entirely to moral and social exhortation. It is particularly the domestic codes that dominate the center of the letter. These serve as moral guidance to encourage conduct figured to nullify pagan slanders, as a charter for confronting inquisitive outsiders,[43] and even as encouraging an outward missionizing thrust.[44]

It is significant of course that the author chooses the section on servants or slaves (2:18-25) to discourse upon the believer's model for Christian existence. Jesus, the servant, suffered unjustly and patiently and having been established in glory holds out hope and promise to the Christian sufferer. The codes then serve as a charter for proper Christian conduct among Gentile neighbors in order that all men might "live as servants of God" (2:16).[45]

A further ethical note needs to be made at this point. While the term *doxa* (glory) in the majority of cases refers to Christ's heavenly enthronement or the future participation in this by the believer, it is important to emphasize that for 1 Peter the future reality of glory is so crucial and dynamic that it impinges upon the interim period: for the spirit of glory rests now upon the believer (4:14) who in anticipation is to rejoice with unutterable and glorious joy (1:8) that God may be glorified now through Jesus Christ (4:11). This is the reason for the author's emphasis upon Christ's glory, for not only is it a goal that might give hope (the resurrection theme would have sufficed) but it is the goal of all beings to be glorified at the final revelation.[46] Indeed, he insists, "the God of all grace . . . has called you to his eternal glory in Christ" (5:10) that is, the "inheritance which is imperishable, undefiled and unfading, kept in heaven for you" (1:4)—it is in this light that the letter's "sojourner" terminology (*paroikos*) should be understood.

The ethics of the Christian in the world then is conditioned by teleological as well as eschatological and theological factors. The author hopes that husbands will be converted (3:1), that foolish neighbors might be silenced (2:15), that unbelieving compatriots might glorify God in the end (2:12), and that God's varied gifts might be shared ungrudgingly with others (4:7-10). The audience is told to live in the world as Christians not as Gentiles (4:1-6)

---

[43]Balch, *Let Wives Be Submissive*, 119; Cothenet, "Orientations actuelles," 30-32.

[44]Elliott, *Home for the Homeless*, 110-12 and 208-34 (though see Balch's discussion of Elliott's position in *Let Wives Be Submissive*, 132-36) and Wolff, "Christ und Welt," 33-42.

[45]Osborne, "Guide Lines," 389-408.

[46]Calloud calls this "installation du désir dans le désir," "Ce que parler vent dire," 203.

that by their good deeds and responsible living these same Gentiles might render glory and make society itself subject to God on the day of visitation (2:12). The Christian is "to live for the rest of the time in the flesh no longer by human passions but by the will of God" (4:2), that is, based upon the pattern that has God's approval (2:20).

In the second instance the author of 1 Peter reveals considerable interest in eschatology. The whole of God's plan as revealed in the Christ "was destined before the foundation of the world and made manifest at the end of the times" (1:20). The focus of the plan is upon the audience for he ends v. 20 with the phrase "for your sake." Equally, the prophets predicted the Christ's suffering and glory as being a model for the suffering audience of the provinces of Asia (1:12), a plan so marvelous that even angels long to see it. The "now" of God's plan is focused upon the new life bestowed upon the Christian by Jesus' death and resurrection, a time for following in Jesus' footsteps (2:21) and being under God's protection while awaiting the end-time (1:5) and the "not yet" envisions "an inheritance which is imperishable, undefiled, and unfading; kept in heaven for" the audience (1:3-4).

The author is convinced that the time is short for the sufferings to last (1:6; 5:10), for the time is at hand (4:7), and the apocalyptic enemy is on the prowl (5:8). The present time is one of testing (1:7; 4:12), one that looks to God's judgment (4:5-6) both upon unbeliever and the Christian household (4:17-19).

> Again and again in different ways (iii.12,16,17,iv.5,6,17f), Peter drives home his point that it is easier to endure the wrath of man than the wrath of God, and better to suffer in this age for doing right than in the day of visitation for doing wrong. It is, in fact, Peter's familiar and simple, but still pertinent, answer to the age-old biblical problem of the suffering righteous,[47]

made more pertinent by the example of the innocent sufferer par excellence, the Christ who "when he was reviled . . . did not revile in return; when he suffered . . . did not threaten; but . . . trusted to him who judges justly" (2:23). Christians, called by God to "eternal glory in Christ" (5:10), live in this world as exiles and aliens (1:1, 17; 2:11), all the while "tasting the kindness of the Lord" (2:3) and awaiting the final revelation of Jesus Christ (1:5, 7, 13; 4:13; 5:1—also 2:12) "when the chief Shepherd is manifested [and the audience] will obtain the unfading crown of glory" (5:4) and God "will himself restore, establish, and strengthen" his people (5:10b).

e. *A Final Note on Strategy and Rhetoric.* What Aristotle describes as the internal modes of demonstration: *ethos*/speaker, *pathos*/audience, and *logos*/

[47]J. R. Michaels, "Eschatology in 1 Peter III.17," *NTS* 13 (1967): 401.

arguments of the speech, are evident on every page of this New Testament document. I have dwelt upon the importance the writer lends to the audience's situation (*pathos:* suffering, social and cultural alienation). His logic and argument (*logos*) would require considerable analysis, but we might note the frequent use of examples, one of Aristotle's approved methods of argument (Sarah, Noah, prophets, and especially Christ) and particularly the ubiquitous use of *hos* (as) and related terms to convince and move his reader.

The element of *ethos* or reference to the speaker/writer deserves a longer note. A well-known Classical scholar, in his discussion of Judaeo-Christian rhetoric, interestingly notes that in this tradition "authority is analogous to ethos in classical rhetoric, but at a different metaphysical level" and further that "it is bolstered by something like pathos in the remembrance of the past suffering of a people and by their fears of future punishment or hopes of future reward."[48] Indeed the entire structure of 1 Peter is an appeal to authority, not on a rhetorical level (appeal to dominical injunctions) but on a metaphysical level: Christ's example, that is, his suffering and glory are the authority or model of Christian life in the world both as defense (3:15) and as life (2:21).

* * * * *

After stressing the soteriological role of Christ and its ecclesiological corollary, the author directs his attention to the particular elements of the Christological pattern, suffering and glory, which establishes for the Christian the model that God had seen as the fit instrument for the salvation of humanity, that is, patient suffering and subsequent glory (1:11). First Peter's Christology, therefore, functions as the paradigmatic and parenetic basis for Christian life in a pluralistic society, a rather successful strategy and, one might suggest, a timely and relevant one for the modern Christian community.

---

[48]G. Kennedy, *Classical Rhetoric and its Christian and Secular Tradition from Ancient to Modern Times* (Chapel Hill: University of North Carolina, 1980); idem, *The Art of Rhetoric in the Roman World, 300 B.C.-A.D. 300* (Princeton: University Press, 1972); also D. L. Clark, *Rhetoric in Greco-Roman Education* (NY: Columbia University, 1957).

CHAPTER 8

ONCE AGAIN:
THE PLAN OF 1 PETER

CHARLES H. TALBERT
WAKE FOREST UNIVERSITY
WINSTON-SALEM, NORTH CAROLINA 27109

In view of the absence of any widespread agreement today on the plan of 1 Peter,[1] the purpose of this essay is to offer yet another suggestion with the hope that it will be inclusive enough to reflect the various dimensions of this first-century text. In order to make such a proposal two issues must first be considered: (1) What are the criteria by which one arrives at a stated plan of the epistle? (2) What is the understanding of the letter presupposed in the plan? These questions will be addressed in this order, followed by the outline of 1 Peter that is the ultimate goal of this article.

---

[1]Many commentators echo the sentiments of C. Bigg, *Epistles of St. Peter and St. Jude* (ICC; Edinburgh: T. & T. Clark, 1902) 6: "There is no definite plan or logical evolution of a train of thought." Others, like F. W. Beare, *The First Epistle of Peter* (Oxford: Basil Blackwell, 1947), who think 1 Peter consists of a baptismal discourse (1:3-4:11) followed by the letter proper (4:15-5:14) offer an outline that reflects this point of view. It is interesting to note that even among those who affirm the unity of 1 Peter, there is great difficulty in seeing the outlines of the plan of the epistle. Note the differences in the proposals of Kendall and Richard in this volume, for example. Even if the unity of 1:3-2:10 is grasped, there are difficulties with how 2:11-5:11 fits together. This is so even for W. J. Dalton, *Christ's Proclamation to the Spirits* (AB, 23; Rome: Pontifical Biblical Institute, 1965) of whom David Balch, "Let Wives Be Submissive . . . " The Origin, Form and Apologetic Function of the Household Duty Code (Haustafel) in 1 Peter, Ph.D. Dissertation, Yale, 1974, p. 181, says: "The most successful attempt to analyze the plan of 1 Peter is that by Dalton."

What are the criteria by which one arrives at a stated plan of the epistle? The modern author who has addressed this issue most systematically is W. J. Dalton.[2] In Part Two, Examination of 1 Pet. 3:18-4:6, Chapter Two, The Plan of 1 Peter, Dalton focuses on the method of discovering the plan. He mentions inclusion (the binding together of units by the repetition, at the beginning and the end, of the same words or phrases); link-words (the indication of a new development in an author's thought by setting a significant word or phrase at the end of one section that is then taken up again at the beginning of the next, functioning as a spring-board for a new development); the announcement beforehand of important themes; the repetition of a key word to indicate the homogeneous nature of a section of a work; the change from statement to exhortation or vice versa to indicate division of one section from another; the arrangement of the whole and/ or its part in some form of symmetry (such as parallelism or chiasmus); the use of quotations from the OT as an end to an argument or development of thought. Using these criteria Dalton proposes an outline that correctly groups 1:3-2:10 together under the heading, "The Christian Vocation and Its Responsibilities," but misses the essential unity of 2:11-5:11, rather dividing this section into two: 2:11-3:12, "Obligations of Christian Life," and 3:13-5:11, "The Christian and Persecution."

The formal criteria employed by Dalton are legitimate but deficient when taken in isolation from certain conceptual and content criteria. On the one hand, it is necessary to distinguish conceptually between ground and warrants in an ethical discussion. A warrant is that which justifies or authorizes a norm or standard of behavior. For example, 1 Peter 2:18 ("Servants, be submissive to your masters with all respect, not only to the kind and gentle but also to the overbearing"—RSV) is a norm of behavior. Verses 21-25 ("For to this you have been called, because Christ also suffered for you, leaving you an example, that you should follow in his steps"—RSV) give the warrant for such behavior as is set forth in vs. 18. The warrant is christological, the example of Jesus. The ontological ground is the foundation for what is said or done. For Christians this is our new being in Christ. For example, 1 Peter 1:13 ("By his great mercy we have been born anew to a living hope through the resurrection of Jesus Christ from the dead"—RSV) states the ground of Christian existence, our new birth. Verse 13 ("Therefore gird up your minds, be sober, set your hope fully upon the grace that is coming to you at the revelation of Jesus Christ"—RSV) points to a ramification of the Christians' ground. Any adequate plan of 1 Peter must reflect the fact that 1:3-2:10 deals with the ground of Christian existence (conversion spoken of in terms of multiple metaphors like new birth, ransoming, tasting, election)

---

[2]W. J. Dalton, *Christ's Proclamation to the Spirits*, 72-86.

and its ramifications, while 2:11-5:11 treats the norms of Christian behavior together with their warrants. This conceptual distinction between the two main sections of the letter is absolutely crucial for understanding its message.

On the other hand, recognition of two simple distinctions in the content of 2:11-5:11 yields yet another clue to the plan of 1 Peter. There is first of all a variation in the groups addressed: (A) To all Christians (2:11-17; 3:8-4:6; 5:5b-11); (B) To specific Christian groups (2:18-3:7; 5:1-5a). If this is noted, then there is a pattern in the section (2:11-5:11) dealing with the norms of Christian living and their warrants. It runs: A (2:11-17), B (2:18-3:7), A' (3:8-4:6), B' (5:1-52), A'' (5:5b-11). There is secondly within the sections addressed to all the Christians a distinction between the parenesis dealing with (1) life in the Christian community (3:8-12; 4:7-11; 5:5b-6) and that focusing on (2) life in the world (3:13-4:6; 4:12-19; 5:7-10). Attention to this matter of content in the unit 3:8-4:19 (To all the Christians) yields a pattern: 1 (3:8-12), 2 (3:13-4:6), 1' (4:7-11), 2' (4:12-19). Such an analysis shows clearly that there should not be a break at 4:11 but that 4:12-19 belongs together with 3:8-4:11 in one large thought unit addressed to all Christians about both 1 (life in the Christian community) and 2 (life in the world). Having looked briefly at the matter of criteria by which one arrives at a stated plan of the epistle, it is now necessary to touch on the second matter.

What is the understanding of the epistle as a whole presupposed in the plan? The view of 1 Peter presupposed in the outline at the end of this article will be set forth as answers to several specific questions. (1) Of what does 1 Peter consist? 1 Peter 5:12 says: "By Silvanus, a faithful brother as I regard him, I have written briefly to you, exhorting (*parakalōn*) and declaring (*epimarturōn*) that this is the true grace of God; stand fast in it" (RSV). This is a fair description of the contents of 1 Peter.[3] (a) Exhortation refers to the admonition addressed to those already won to the faith which is designed to lead them to conduct worthy of the Gospel (for example, Rom. 12:1; 2 Cor. 10:1; Eph. 4:1; Phil. 2:1; 4:2; 1 Thess. 4:1; 1 Tim. 2:1; 1 Pet. 2:11; 5:1; cf. Heb. 13:22; 1 Pet. 5:12; Jude 3, where the three authors understand their whole documents as exhortation). Such admonition is usually connected with either its ground or its warrant (for example, Rom. 12:1—by the mercy of God; 2 Cor. 10:1—by the meekness and gentleness of Christ; 1 Thess. 4:1—in the Lord Jesus).[4] As used in 1 Peter 5:12, exhortation refers to "what to do," that is, to the norms of Christian behavior. (In the outline, these norms are given as "The Call" in I and as "Exhortations" in II.) (b) Declaration refers

---

[3]W. C. van Unnik, "I Peter," *IDB* III, 758-66.

[4]*TDNT* V, 795.

to an attestation of an accompanying assertion.[5] What is attested in 1 Peter 5:12 is stated in the following accusative with infinitive (*tautēn einai alēthē charin tou theou*—"this to be the true grace of God"). The expression, "this is the true grace of God," refers both to the ground of the readers described throughout the writing, namely, the new existence into which they have been introduced by Christ, and to the warrants for various specific actions offered in the document as a whole.[6] As used in 1 Peter 5:12, declaration refers to "why do it," that is, both to the ground and to the warrants for the Christian behavior asked for in the exhortations. (In the outline, the ground of Christian existence is given in I as "Therefore," "Since," "Because"; in II the warrants are given as motivations.) In the simplest terms, 1 Peter describes itself as consisting of what to do and why do it.

(2) For whom were the norms and their bases (both ground and warrants) given? (a) 1 Peter is addressed to resident aliens (*parepidēmois*—1:1-2 and 2:11); aliens (*paroikous*—2:11) who stay in a strange land (*paroikias*—1:17); people living beyond the limits of their homeland (*diasporas*—1:1). This, I think, is figurative language referring to people who, because they are Christians, do not belong to the present age but live as resident aliens in this world. They were outsiders, strangers both socially and religiously (cf. Epistle to Diognetus 5:5, 6, 10).[7] (b) These Christians were mainly Gentiles (1:14, 18; 4:3-4). (c) They lived in Pontus, Galatia, Cappadocia, Asia, and Bithynia (1:1b).

(3) What is the social context of such teaching for these people? (a) Church context—Is 1 Peter connected with the beginning of the Christian life? That is, is it catechetical, to prepare for baptism?[8] Or is it liturgical, a baptismal liturgy?[9] Or is it connected with later growth in the Christian life? That is, is it parenesis?[10] The latter seems to me more persuasive than the former. If one takes Leo G. Perdue's classification of occasions on which parenesis may be given,[11] light is shed in 1 Peter's church context. Perdue says parenesis may be given either on the occasion of an aged teacher's facing death (for exam-

---

[5]*TDNT* IV, 508.

[6]J. D. McCaughey, "On Re-Reading 1 Peter," *AusBibRev* 31 (1983): 38.

[7]Contra John H. Elliott, *A Home for the Homeless: A Sociological Exegesis of 1 Peter, Its Situation and Strategy* (Philadelphia: Fortress, 1981) 43.

[8]As with E. G. Selwyn, *The First Epistle of St. Peter* (London: Macmillan, 1955) and F. W. Beare, *The First Epistle of Peter,* for example.

[9]As with F. L. Cross, *1 Peter: A Paschal Liturgy* (London: A. R. Mowbray, 1954), for example.

[10]As with Eduard Lohse, "Paränese und Kerygma im 1 Petrusbrief," *ZNW* 45 (1954): 68-89; David Hill, "On Suffering and Baptism in 1 Peter," *NovT* 18 (1976): 181-89; Balch, "Let Wives Be Submissive"; Elliott, *Home for the Homeless.*

[11]Leo G. Perdue, "Paraenesis and the Epistle of James," *ZNW* 72 (1981): 241-56.

ple, 2 Peter; Acts 20:18-35), or because of the separation of a teacher and his students (for example, James, Epistle of Barnabas), or because the recipient is entering into a social group or being elevated to a social position with new responsibilities (for example, the Pastorals),[12] or after incorporation to call the recipients to serious reflection on their initial entrance into their present group or position (for example, 1 Peter). Such parenesis as one finds in this last mentioned occasion would lead to the establishment of group identity and cohesion. (b) Context in the larger society—Are the sufferings referred to in 1 Peter (1:6-7; 3:13-17; 4:3-4; 4:12-19; 5:19) State persecution[13] or unofficial oppression?[14] The latter seems preferable to me. Suffering for the name was not limited to late Roman persecutions (Acts 5:41; cf. Mark 13:13). The sufferings, moreover, seem to be the same throughout the letter.

(4) Is it possible to describe the nature of the oppression more precisely? Pagan culture frowned upon any break with ancestral tradition in matters of religion (Cicero, *Laws*, 2:7:19-27; Plutarch, *Dialogue on Love*, 756 A-B, D). It was regarded as right to follow ancestral usages in the area of religion (Athenagoras, *A Plea for the Christians*, 1; Eusebius, *H.E.*, 8:17:6). It was believed not to be right to depart from the ways of the fathers in religion (Justin, *Hortatory Address to the Greeks*, 35; Origen, *Against Celsus*, 2:3; 5:35; 8:69; Clement of Alexandria, *Exhortation to the Heathen*, 10; Recognitions of Clement, 5:30; Eusebius, *H.E.*, 8:17:6-9; 9:1:3; 9:9a:1). This was so because it was assumed that a change of gods would lead to disruption in the fabric of society. (a) If the gods are not properly reverenced, they may pour out their wrath on the public sector at large (Horace, *Odes*, 3:6:5-8; Tertullian *Apology*, 40:2). (b) If they change their gods, citizens may not obey the Emperor (Tertullian, *Apology*, 4, 10, 42; *Scapula*, 2). (c) If they change their gods, wives, children, and slaves may not be obedient in the household to husbands, parents, and masters (Tacitus, *Histories*, 5:5; Origen, *Against Celsus*, 3:5:50; cf. Acts of Paul, where Thecla, after becoming a Christian, renounces her roles of daughter, wife, mother, and mistress). (d) Those involved in other religions will be separated from rather than integrated into the general fabric of society. They become despisers of other peoples (Tacitus, *Histories*, 5:5). Given these fears, the larger society would attempt to enforce conformity and to prevent socially divergent behavior. This would be the source of the unofficial oppression experienced by the readers of 1 Peter.[15]

---

[12]Jerome D. Quinn, "Parenesis and the Pastoral Epistles," in *De la Torah an Messie*, ed. M. Carrez, J. Dore, and P. Grelot (Paris: Desclée, 1981) 495-501.

[13]As with F. W. Beare, *The First Epistle of St. Peter*.

[14]As with E. G. Selwyn, *The First Epistle of St. Peter*.

[15]In agreement with Balch, "Let Wives Be Submissive."

(5) What are the social functions of such instruction? The exhortation and declaration given in 1 Peter have as their aim the survival of the Christian groups in a persecution context. Does 1 Peter seek to accomplish this aim by reinforcing the social cohesion of the Christian groups or by encouraging social adaptability of the Christians so as to gain a favorable response from the non-Christians? It is not, in my opinion, either-or but both-and. The pioneering study of George Homans[16] furnishes a model that allows the compatibility of these two points of view. According to Homans, human groups desire to survive. Behavior directed towards this end is determined both by what Homans calls ''an external system'' and by ''an internal system.'' Under the external system Homans treats group behavior that allows the group to survive in its environment (that is, social adaptability). Under the internal system he discusses group behavior that arises out of and contributes to social cohesion (for example, negative sentiments towards outsiders). This study works with the thesis that the parenesis in 1 Peter is what is deemed necessary for them to survive (a) as a group (b) in a hostile environment.

(a) To survive as a group demands social cohesion. This is reinforced in two ways in 1 Peter. On the one hand, the primary focus is on the Christian experience (new birth, ransoming, tasting, election) the readers share. This is the ground of their life together as Christians. On the other hand, a secondary focus is on the sufferings of the readers at the hands of outsiders. This results in the social cohesion of the Christian groups even if this was not the intention of the writer in mentioning the matter.

(b) To survive in a hostile environment demands social adaptability. Emphasis is placed in 1 Peter on political, domestic, social, and ecclesiastical behavior of the type that is regarded as the best of the cultural norms (cf. the contrast between that behavior espoused by Seneca—the best—and that reflected in Petronius's *Satyricon*—the worst). This emphasis on behavior regarded as the ideal by the hostile, larger society is intended both to disarm the critics (2:12, 15; 3:16) and to win them, if possible (3:1b-2; 3:18).

Can this perspective on 1 Peter as a whole be stated in other terms? The tensions between the Christian groups addressed in 1 Peter and the larger pagan society can be clarified if one thinks in terms of the traditional distinctions between church and sect. A church type of religious body (a) possesses a strong sense of continuity with the past, (b) is inclusive, tending to embrace the whole population of a given country or region, and (c) is likely to support the state and to assume a positive attitude toward social conventions and national culture. A sect type of religious body (a) tends to break the continuity with the past, (b) is exclusive in membership, dependent on adult decision or

---

[16]George C. Homans, *The Human Group* (New York: Harcourt, Brace & World, 1950).

religious experience, and (c) is reserved, if not critical, in relation to the state and its attitude toward social conventions and culture. Nonconformity with the world is usually accompanied by strict discipline and moral taboos.[17]

The characteristics of a church type religious body are applicable to traditional pagan religion in antiquity on all three counts. Moreover, the pagan populace that formed the environment of 1 Peter's readers perceived the Christian community as a sect type of religious body, also on all three counts. The author of 1 Peter, however, sees Christianity as a sect type of religious group on the first two counts only (as a break with the past—1:14, 18; 4:3; as an exclusive membership—1:3; 1:18; 1:23; 4:4), not on the third. In the third category he advocates behavior that is characteristic of the church type of religious group (for example, support for the state—2:13-14, 17d; a positive attitude toward participation in the social conventions and the national culture, even when this was painful—2:18ff.; 3:1ff.; 3:7ff.; 5:1-5). This did not, however, involve approval of participation in the moral excesses of the pagans (4:3-4).[18]

To summarize: The author of 1 Peter is saying first of all that the Christian is one who has had a religious experience so radical (conversion) that it involves a break with one's past and that the Christian community is com-

---

[17]T. G. Tappert, ''Sect and Cult,'' *Twentieth Century Encyclopedia of Religious Knowledge,* ed. L. A. Loetscher (Grand Rapids: Baker, 1955) II, 1008-1009.

[18]A modern analogy to 1 Peter's situation can be seen in the history of the Southern Baptist Convention. Here there are problems both of social cohesion and of social adaptability. On the one hand, Southern Baptists face the loss of social cohesion. Social cohesion was easier for Southern Baptists when there were both (a) unanimity about the necessity of a decisive religious experience (conversion/new birth), and (b) a sense of cultural difference from the rest of the country that was perceived as often abusive to us Southerners. As the South has joined the nation after the Second World War, the sense of social conflict has declined and with it the South's cohesion. As the South has become better educated (i.e., more oriented to the left side of the brain), it has tended to have problems with radical religious experience (i.e., a right side of the brain experience) with the result that it has been minimized. Taken together, these two changes have resulted in a loss of cohesion among and within Southern Baptist churches. On the other hand, Southern Baptists face cultural disdain due to the difficulty we have in social adaptability. The case of women ministers is an example. The best in the morality of our culture advocates the equality of women in every area of life including the Christian ministry. Yet, basing their arguments on a literalist reading of Scripture, the current leadership of the Convention rejects women in the ordained ministry. This failure to adapt to the best in the culture's values is seen as a moral scandal by large segments of the culture and not only brings hostility upon us but also stands in the way of our evangelistic and missionary efforts. If the Southern Baptist Convention wanted to take its directions from 1 Peter, then two things would be required. First, to preserve our social cohesion it would be necessary to emphasize the necessity of the experience of the new birth, the ransoming, the tasting, the election for all. Second, to achieve social adaptability it would be necessary to strive to embody the best of the culture's values while at the same time standing over against the worst of its moral abuses. The basic issue for Southern Baptists is the same as for the readers of 1 Peter: How can the church live in the world without losing itself?

posed exclusively of those who have had such an experience. This gives the group social cohesion, which is necessary for the group to survive as a group. He says secondly that Christians are to live in their civic, domestic, and ecclesiastical existences in terms of the highest social and cultural conventions of their time and place. They are, of course, to avoid the excesses of the worst in pagan society. The author of 1 Peter believes there are warrants to support such a life-style in the Christian tradition (OT, example of Jesus, etc.). This is necessary to enable the group to survive in its hostile environment and hopefully to flourish. It seems that the author of this letter was concerned to realize two goals: (1) the social cohesion of the Christian groups, and (2) the social adaptation of the Christian groups to their cultural setting. Without the first, Christian identity would have been lost. Without the second, Christians would have had no social acceptability, which is also necessary for survival and for outreach.

Having addressed the two issues of criteria for discerning the epistle's plan and of the understanding of the letter as a whole presupposed in this essay's plan, it is now possible to present yet another outline of 1 Peter.

Salutation—1:1-2

I. The Ground of Christian Existence and Its Ramifications (1:3-2:10)
(This section consists of five units, each with the same two components, which remind the readers of their Christian experience and call for an appropriate response. The section is held together by an inclusion: 1:2 "chosen" and 1:3 "mercy" ∥ 2:9 "chosen" and 2:10 "mercy.")
  - A. Unit One (1:3-16)
      1. The New Birth (1:3-12)
         cf. John 3:3; 1 John 3:9; 5:4
      2. (Therefore) The Call for a changed life (1:13-16)
  - B. Unit Two (1:17-21)
      1. (Since) Sonship (1:17a)
         cf. Romans 8:15; Galatians 4:6
      2. The Call for appropriate conduct (1:17b)
      3. (Because) The Ransoming (1:18-21)
         cf. Mark 10:45; Hebrews 9:12
  - C. Unit Three (1:22-25)
      1. (Since) The Purification (1:22a)
         cf. 1 Corinthians 6:11; Acts 22:16
      2. The Call to love one another (1:22b)
      3. (Because) The New Birth (1:23-25)
         cf. Titus 3:5; James 1:18
  - D. Unit Four (2:1-3)

    1. The Call to desire food necessary for growth (2:1-2)

    2. (Because) The Tasting (2:3)
       cf. Hebrews 6:4-6

  E. Unit Five (2:4-10)

    1. The Call to allow yourselves to be built into a spiritual house (2:4-8, taking *oikodomeisthe* in vs. 5 as an imperative with RSV, TEV, NEB)

    2. (Because) The Election (2:9-10)
       cf. Matthew 24:22; Colossians 3:12

II. The Norms of Christian Living and Their Warrants (2:11-5:11)
(This section falls into an ABA′B′A′′ pattern in which A designates material addressed to *all* Christians and B material addressed to *specific groups* of Christians.)

  A. To *all* the beloved (2:11-17)
    Exhortation—2:11-12a
      Motivation—2:12b
    Exhortation—2:13-14
      Motivation—2:15
    Exhortation—2:16-17

  B. To *specific groups* of Christians (2:18-3:7)

    1. Servants with non-Christian masters (2:18-25)
      Exhortation—2:18
        Motivations—(a) 2:19-20
                 (b) 2:21-25

    2. Wives with non-Christian husbands (3:1-6)
      Exhortation—3:1a
        Motivation—3:1b-2
      Exhortation—3:3-4
        Motivation—3:5-6

    3. Husbands with Christian wives (3:7)
      Exhortation—3:7a
        Motivations—(a) 3:7b
                 (b) 3:7c

  A′. To *all* the Christians (3:8-4:19)

    1. About life in the Christian community (3:8-12)
      Exhortation—3:8-9a
        Motivations—(a) 3:9b
                 (b) 3:9c-12

   2. About life in the world (3:13-4:6)

      Rhetorical question—3:13 (functions as Exhortation—Be zeal-
ous, and Motivation—No one will
harm you)

      Conditional promise—3:14a (functions as Exhortation—Do right,
and Motivation—You will be
blessed)

      a—Exhortation—3:14b-15a

      b—Exhortation—3:15b-16a

      b'—Motivation—3:16b

      a'—Motivation—3:17-22 (primary motivation—vs. 17, explan-
atory motivation—vss. 18-22

              1—Christ's example

              2—which made converts

              3—which was followed by victory)

      a—Motivation—4:1a,c

      b—Exhortation—4:1b, 2

      b'—Exhortation—4:3

      a'—Motivation—4:4-6 (Statement of fact—4:4

              Promise—4:5

              Explanatory note—4:6)

1'. About life in the Christian community (4:7-11)

      Motivation—4:7a

        Exhortation—4:7b

        Exhortation—4:8a

      Motivation—4:8b

        Exhortation—4:9-11a

      Motivation—4:11b

2'. About life in the world (4:12-19)

      Exhortation—4:12-13a

        Motivation—4:13b

      Conditional promise—4:14 (functions as Exhortation—If . . .,
make sure, and Motivation—You
are blessed)

      Exhortation—4:15-16

        Motivation—4:17-18

      Exhortation—4:19

B'. To *specific* Christian *groups* (5:1-5a)

   1. To elders (5:1-4)

      Exhortation—5:1-3

        Motivation—5:4

2. To the younger (5:5a)
  Exhortation—5:5a
A''. To *all* Christians (5:5b-11)
 1. About life in the Christian community (5:5b-6)
  Exhortation—5:5b
   Motivation—5:5c
  Exhortation—5:6a
   Motivation—5:6b
 2. About life in the world (5:7-10)
  Exhortation—5:7a
   Motivation—5:7b
  Exhortation—5:8a
   Motivation—5:8b
  Exhortation—5:9a
   Motivations—(a) 5:9b
       (b) 5:10

Letter Closing—5:12-14